HITLER'S TERROR
WEAPONS

by the same author

Hitler's Nuclear Weapons
(Leo Cooper, 1992)

Hirschfeld– The Story of a U-boat NCO 1935–1945
(Leo Cooper, 1997)

FIPS – Legendary U-Boat Commander, 1915–1918
(as translator – Leo Cooper, 1999)

HITLER'S TERROR WEAPONS

FROM V-1 TO VIMANA

by

GEOFFREY BROOKS

LEO COOPER

First published in Great Britain in 2002 by
LEO COOPER
an imprint of Pen & Sword Books
47 Church Street,
Barnsley, South Yorkshire S70 2AS

ISBN 0 85052 896 8

A CIP record for this book is
available from the British Library

Typeset in 10/12pt Times by
Phoenix Typesetting, Ilkley, West Yorkshire

Printed in England by
CPI UK

Dedication

I dedicate this book to the memory of Lt Charles Taylor USN, Senior Qualified Flight Instructor, Squadron 79M, Fort Lauderdale who, together with the thirteen men of TBM Avenger overwater navigational training flight 19, died on the evening of 5 December 1945 as the result of entering an anomalous gravity field near Great Stirrup Cay, Bahamas at about 3:15 that afternoon.

Contents

Acknowledgements

I acknowledge a debt of gratitude to nuclear physicists Pat Flannen, whose speculation about Heisenberg's experiments at Leipzig inspired this book initially, and Norberto Lahuerta, for his unstinting help with research and scientific opinion into all aspects of both V-4 projects.

I add a special note of appreciation to Brigadier Wilson, Barbara Bramall and Tom Hartman for their help and patience in coping with many late but unavoidable additions and deletions, and to Pen & Sword for having the courage to publish a book of this kind.

Introduction

Following the landings in France in 1944, the Combined Chiefs of Staff set up a number of military-civilian teams, termed the Joint Intelligence Objectives Committee, to follow the invading Allied armies into Germany with a view to seizing all Hitler's military, scientific and industrial secrets for early use against Japan. The teams worked against the clock to obtain the most vital information before it was destroyed. The result was the biggest collect of captured enemy war secrets ever assembled. One Washington official called it "the greatest single source of this type of material in the world, the first orderly exploitation of an entire country's brain-power". The Office of Technical Services, the Washington government agency originally formed to handle the collection, reported that tens of thousands of tons of material was involved. It was estimated that over a million separate items had to be handled and they most likely represented practically all the scientific, military and industrial secrets of Nazi Germany. In *A Brief History of Air Force Scientific and Technical Intelligence*, published by NAIC, the National Air Intelligence Centre, it was recorded that in 1946 at Wright Field alone, three hundred people processed over 1500 tons of documents, adding 10,000 new technical terms to the English language. The technical knowledge from these documents revolutionized American industry.

In the summer of 1944, at about the time the JIOC was set in motion, the German High Command began to contemplate the eventuality of defeat and in September that year a General Plan was elaborated to evacuate Nazis, Third Reich capital and highly advanced technical and scientific knowledge to places selected by Hitler himself, of which Argentina was the principal destination. The strategist of the General Plan was Hitler's personal ADC, Martin Bormann. The so-called "Rat

Run" to Argentina was operated through the consulates of that country in Italy and Rome and facilitated the escape of wanted war criminals. But the Rat Run, known to the Germans under the codename *Regentroepfchen* (raindrop), was a fronting operation concealing a much vaster programme aimed at retaining for Nazism in exile its financial wealth, the scientific, political and military elite of the Third Reich and certain hyper-secret specialized knowledge. This latter was of a level above and beyond the million or so secret inventions and patents to be abandoned to the Allies. Code-named *Aktion Wiking*, this section of the overall plan was begun in September 1944 by Maximilian Erth with the assistance of Philip Bouhler (head of Hitler's private office) and the Gauleiter of Lower Silesia, Karl Hanke.

The Nazis were particularly anxious to protect documents containing the highest classifications of secret knowledge designated *Geheime Reichssache* relating to the development of arms, aircraft and submarines. The most important of all these, files relating to a super aviation fuel and advanced aircraft, went by long-range Junkers Ju 390 transport aircraft directly to Argentina.

From the point of view of the US Government, the 260 tons of strategic material aboard the German U-boat *U-234* escorted into Portsmouth Navy Yard, New Hampshire, on 19 May 1945 is so absurdly secret that the fact that it is classified as top secret is a secret, as are the documents pertaining to Dr Heinz Schlicke and the nature of the assistance he afforded the Manhattan Project in the three months after his capture. The most secret item of cargo aboard *U-234* remains the eighty small cases of uranium powder which have never appeared on any USN Unloading Manifest and which will have been the fissile material for a rudimentary atomic explosive. But as far as the German High command was concerned, the voyage of this U-boat with its extraordinary cargo of war materials and passengers did not rate so highly as to fall within the ambit of the General Plan of Evacuation.

In the 1950s two crewmen of the former pocket battleship *Admiral Graf Spee* Rudolf Walter Dettelmann and Alfred Schultz, interned in Argentina, swore statements to an Argentinian commission of enquiry to the effect that on 28 and 29 July 1945 they carried out naval duties in connection with the arrival on the Patagonian coast of two U-boats of an alleged six which escaped from Europe loaded with gold bullion and passengers. Extensive sonar sweeps along the inshore coast of Patagonia in March 2002 have resulted in a contact which, pending visual confirmation, will probably be a U-boat believed scuttled in these coordinates in July 1945. As it is neither of those mentioned by the two *Graf Spee* crewmen, it is clear that the General Plan was put into effect.

A leftist correspondent of a leading Neuquen daily newspaper active in exposing Nazi war criminals in the Bariloche area of Argentina and who prefers anonymity for that reason has stated in writing that he inspected official documents confirming that the German anti-gravity experiments SS-E-IV and SS-U-13, together with the notorious Bell described elsewhere in this volume, arrived aboard a Junkers Ju 390 long-range transport aircraft which flew non-stop from Norway to Gualeguay aerodrome in Entre Rios province, Argentina, at the war's end[1]. If true, this might be seen by some as suggestive that the SS anti-gravity aircraft project was the post-war utmost priority for the National Socialist scientific elite.

Just a few days after the Nagasaki bombing in August 1945 the US authorities interrogated a German flak rocket expert whom they named only as Zinsser, a trained observer of aerial explosions. The interview document has a high reliability rating. During the interview Zinsser described certain characteristics of an A-bomb test he claimed to have observed over Germany in 1944 which he could not possibly have known about unless he had actually witnessed such an explosion. A nuclear weapons physicist whose opinion I sought thought that a small, possibly one-kiloton, device was being described, although the signs to look for were buried in the text and would elude the casual, unscientific reader of the document such as myself. That is the reason why its significance has been overlooked until now.

Unlikely as it may seem, therefore, on 11 October 1944, off Rügen Island in the western Baltic, German scientists successfully obtained a small atomic reaction from, for want of a better description, a rudimentary bomb within a lead jacket to suppress fallout. In a letter from Robert Oppenheimer to James B. Conant dated 30 November 1942 it was stated that in the opinion of General Groves, head of the Manhattan Project, a successful bomb was one "which had a 50% chance of exceeding a 1,000-ton TNT equivalent" and, as the German device seems to have fallen within this specification, Hitler's scientists won the race for the atom bomb.

The V-4 is what catches the imagination. It was described by Hitler as being a weapon "of such potent effect that all human life would be exterminated within a radius of three to four kilometres of the point of impact". This terminology could describe equally well an atomic weapon, a 250kg bomb of sarin nerve gas or even radiological material.

The looseness of Hitler's description was intended to mislead his guest at table, Marshal Antonescu of Rumania, as to the nature of this "weapon of frightfulness" and how it was to be deployed, facts which have correspondingly remained a mystery ever since.

The researcher's problem is that in the most important areas of history, particularly the Second World War, many governments intend that the truth of certain affairs is to be suppressed for ever. This may be done for a variety of reasons, both honourable and not. Thus, deep in national archives the papers which contain the true history will lie in darkness for decades and perhaps never see the light of day.

Aged servants of the former Third Reich in Germany and Austria often have useful files and documents which they are fearful to disclose lest their State pensions and those of their dependants should become forfeit on some unfortunate "technicality". A file of correspondence between an Austrian Gauleiter and Hitler pertaining to the successful development of an efficient implosion fuse capable of detonating a plutonium bomb is, to my certain knowledge, *in Sicherheit*, which means in the custody of a lawyer until the death of the rightful holder, when it is to be released to a named researcher for publication.

Even more to be deplored is the sale of microfilmed documents from allegedly classified US archives. In two references in this book the source document does not appear to have been made available to the public but was "brokered through a licensee". Exactly what the machinery is for this operation remains obscure. The author of one of the books concerned has given his word of honour that such a microfilmed document in his possession reads as he says it does, and I have no reason to doubt him. "Many researchers and physicists would give an arm for a glimpse of this document," he writes. That may be so, but what sort of history is built on such a foundation?

All this official secrecy has led to the creation of lobbies. One of them believes passionately in an SS atom bomb built in some deep catacomb in the Tyrol or Harz Mountains. Another thinks that Professor Heisenberg must have been behind everything. An opposing lobby is tied to revealed documentation which dictates that National Socialist Germany not only had no atom bomb project and no nuclear reactor, but could not possibly have had one even if they wanted because their best scientists had all emigrated.

In fact, given the right implosion fuse, a couple of rudimentary zero-energy nuclear reactors in an underground factory beside the Danube, two years and a chemical separation plant, a low-grade plutonium bomb would not have been beyond Germany's capabilities in the Second World War, and from September 1941 they knew it. Simply to dismiss as a flight of fancy the V-4 explosive mentioned by Hitler, as academics and historians have done over the last half-century, seems too easy a solution. I have yet to see anything which convinces me that Third Reich scientists developed a full-size atom bomb, as many Germans insist, but the Wagnerian monstrosity below Haigerloch church, the cave with its chain of dangling uranium cubes above a well of heavy water in the gloom, is German humour at its best. Many suspect that the standard history we have been fed is bogus and that the Third Reich must have come up with something better than this abject, dismal failure.

Re-examining with the assistance of two nuclear physicists all the wartime German nuclear documents in the hope of discovering some inconsistency, suspicion soon fell on certain experimental work at Leipzig performed by Professor Heisenberg. It was pointed out that, whether he knew it or not, what he was doing was more useful fieldwork for making a bomb than designing a nuclear reactor. If intended as the warhead in a V-2 rocket it was ingenious.

Recently released official documents allow us to deduce that in April 1945 the submarine *U-234* sailed for Tokyo direct with enough treated uranium for two of these small, laboratory-built atom bombs, a scientific passenger who specialized in fuse technology, and a large quantity of heavy water, essential ingredients in the manufacture of Heisenberg's bomb. Thus at last we may have the solution to the mystery surrounding this German submarine.

The path of the V-4 project, which was not one weapon but two, is so tortuous that it should come as no surprise to find it occupying the greater part of this book. However, the theme of the volume is the German V-weapons of the Second World War. Because they are so well known, the V-1 and V-2 are mentioned primarily with reference to their intended use in the last five months of the war. The V-3 High Pressure Pump was used operationally by the Germans to bombard Luxemburg City during the Battle of the Ardennes and merits attention for that reason.

The *Motorstoppmittel*, *Feuerkugel*, known popularly as the *Foo-Fighter*, and the other side of the same coin, the *Kugelblitz* were all exotic ideas connected with the SS electro-magnetic anti-gravity project. Some claim that the concept originated in the workshops of some other world's air force. Official documents prove the existence of all three developments, but fifty-five years afterwards, beyond a grudging admission that their airmen were not hallucinating with respect to the *foo-fighter*, the authorities have still revealed nothing about how the machines worked. Initially aircrew abstained from reporting what they had seen for fear of being grounded and hospitalized for psychiatric examination. Certainly on the evidence it is strange how the Germans, whose warships' radar needed a vast steel mattress twelve yards square at the foretop, can have made such giant strides in propulsion, aerodynamics and radar in a few months that they were able to menace enemy bomber formations at 10,000 feet with luminous aerobatic basketballs capable of making over 400 knots. It is said that these aerial vehicles, if one can call them that, had been developed by – and one hopes that they were developed by – clever SS scientists at Wiener Neustadt. They seemed to be an ingenious though harmless anti-aircraft device.

The purpose of building such vehicles so close to the cessation of hostilities, particularly in view of the unholy alliance of Allied Governments with former German military and political leaders to conceal their existence ever since, gives rise to the conviction that we should not altogether discount the possibility of a connection between the loss of the war by Hitler and the upsurge in UFO sightings from 1947 onwards, the theme of the closing chapter of this book. There is no evidence for a German flying saucer excepting claims made by German aeronautical engineers postwar that they had worked on the design or construction of the project. Nevertheless, in 1947 the USAF was absolutely certain that flying saucers existed, flew in our airspace and they suspected a German origin for them. For that reason I have considered it worthwhile to examine the evidence and to form a hypothesis for their creation in line with National Socialist ideology.

Mention must be made of the officer entrusted with running the V-weapons project from its inception. Probably the most extraordinary and enigmatic figure among the latter-day Nazi hierarchy, SS-General Dr (Ing) Hans Kammler (b. Stettin 26.8.1901) was a grey career man who had seen no fighting at the front. As engineer in charge of Building and Construction Works at WVHA, the SS-Chief Economic and Administrative Office, in 1942 Kammler had had responsibility for the planning and design of a number of death camps and had personally supervised the construction of the Auschwitz satellite camp at Birkenau.

On 7 July 1943, at FHQ Rastenburg, Hitler informed Wernher von Braun and Oberst Dr (Ing) Walter Dornberger, senior rocket scientists at the Peenemünde research establishment, that the V-2 project had been given the highest priority rating. On 22 July of that year, after the destruction by bombing of the rocket component plant at Friedrichshafen, the

SS had begun looking for an underground factory and had found a suitable location at Niedersachswerfen near Nordhausen in the Harz Mountains, the largest subterranean factory in the world.[2]

On 17 August a large force of British aircraft bombed Peenemünde. The material damage was not extensive and more than 80 per cent of the bombs fell on open land and in the nearby woods. Even the effective patterns had damaged mostly non-industrial or easily repairable facilities. Dornberger reviewed the damage at first light and concluded that the site would be operational again within six weeks, but the following day Kaltenbrunner, head of SS Security Police, arrived in order to enquire personally into an alleged security leak. The intervention provided Himmler with the opportunity to approach Hitler with a convincing argument for transferring the entire V-weapons project from the Army to the SS. The satisfactory continuation of the programme could be guaranteed only by placing it under SS supervision, he argued, ensuring secrecy by using concentration camp inmates for the work force. Hitler concurred. On 1 September 1943 Hans Kammler was promoted to SS-Gruppenführer and appointed Special Commissioner for the V-2 project. He recruited 2000 engineers and drew 15,000 concentration camp inmates from Buchenwald and Natzweiler[3] for the conversion work at the former Wifo factory now renamed *Nordhausen Central Works* and also *SS-Mittelwerk*, the latter by reason of its geographical position at the centre of Germany.

During the first week of March 1944 Kammler was given overall responsibility for Underground Constructions and now had 175,000 concentration camp inmates under his control. An SS Special Staff known as *Baubüro Dr Hans Kammler* became directly answerable to Himmler not only for the production, completion, storage and supply of V-weapon armaments but also for building a number of massive underground weapons factories the size of a small metropolis such as *Quarz* at Melk, Austria, and *Zement* I and II at Ebensee.

On 8 August 1944 Himmler appointed Kammler as General Plenipotentiary for V-2 Assembly and C-in-C V-2 Operations, which had previously been under the jurisdiction of LXV Army Corps. His *Lehr-und Versuchsbatterie 444* got off to an inauspicious start when the first two V-2 rockets of the campaign aimed at Paris on 6 September both failed through fuel blockage. After shifting location but with the same target, a successful launch was achieved on 8 September. The same day Artillery Detachment 485 obtained a hit at Chiswick, London, from the Hague. From August 1944 until the conclusion of the Ardennes

Offensive, in addition to the V-1 and V-2, Kammler oversaw the operational deployment of the V-3 High Pressure Pump and was present to observe the first rounds being fired on Luxemburg City on 30 December 1944.

On 26 January 1945 Kammler was made commanding general of the 5th Flak Division at Rotterdam, a very remarkable appointment for a man with no battle experience, and on 14 February he took over *Army Korps zbV* (zbV = for special purposes). On 31 January he came straight from the V-3 installation at Lampaden to organize the placing of two detachments of his Division's flak on the eastern banks of the Rhine. All this was satisfactorily accomplished by late February and in early March Kammler was confirmed as General Plenipotentiary to Halt the Terror Bombing. This meant that he was now responsible to the Führer directly for all anti-aircraft measures, which would have included the supremely secret versions, as well as the conventional anti-aircraft rockets produced at Peenemünde, *Wasserfall*, Hs 117 *Schmetterling*, *Enzian*, *Taifun* and the remote-controlled Hs 298 and X-4 *Ruhrstahl*. It appears that he had had powers as plenipotentiary before his appointment, since on 6 February 1945 he had signed the order to discontinue work on *Schmetterling* and *Enzian*. In either February or March 1945, or at any rate by the time Kammler had achieved the rank of SS-Obergruppenführer and General der SS, he was given complete jurisdiction for the turbo-jet fighter. Another objective which does not seem so well-documented involved transferring Dr Dornberger and his work staff in February of that year from Schwedt on the Oder to Bad Sachsa where Dornerberger was to be responsible for the development and testing of "anti-aircraft measures" and for that purpose was to set up "Development Team *Mittelbau*" under Dr Alfred Buch, a scientist. Kammler ordered a large number of firms to be co-opted to concentrate on "special equipment".

At the beginning of April 1945, for the defence of the central Harz, Kammler cobbled together an infantry corps from retreating Army units and V-1/V-2 firing commandos. He also made a determined attempt to swell SS numbers at Niedersachswerfen by recruiting Mittelwerk technicians and engineers but this does not seem to have been too successful. In any case, 500 or so of these personnel, the major part of the former Peenemünde team, had been ordered by Kammler to relocate in the Garmisch-Partenkirchen area of southern Germany, and most of them made the six-day journey by the special train sardonically known as the "Vergeltungs-Express".

Dr Wernher von Braun was told by Kammler that he, Kammler, had been made Head of the Fighter Plane Staff and "had to report to another place". On 7 April 1945 Kammler was seen leaving Mittelwerk towards the western Harz with a section of his General Staff and, apart from a cable to Himmler, sent from a village called Deggendorf, confirming his continuing loyalty to Hitler ten days later, that was the last heard of any of them.

Kammler knew virtually everything about the V-Weapons operational programme. His whereabouts after early April 1945 are unknown. There are reports of his death in action defending the Czech Front against the Soviet Army, and the latter gave short shrift to captured SS men. A recent book by Nick Cook[4] proposes that Kammler negotiated a deal for himself with the United States in exchange for Germany's anti-gravity technology. What evidence there is suggests that this was not the case. Bormann's 1944 General Plan of Evacuation was drawn up to safeguard the more advanced technological knowledge by having people like Kammler brought out of Europe before the capitulation. One must not lose sight of the fact that at the end of the war there was a huge influx of Reich money and scientific personnel into Argentina and Chile, where deep below ground perhaps some of the more important work was continued. Mr Cook's line of argument is based on the document circulated by the Polish author Igor Witkowski. This bulletin definitely states that the equipment at FHQ Waldenburg was evacuated in April and May 1945, probably to South America, by SS-Obergruppenführer Jakob Sporrenberg.

It would be in South America that the designer-builder of Auschwitz and other death camps might have felt more comfortable for his own peace of mind than in relying on a deal with the United States. One would also think it safe to assume that if the USAF had been able to make head or tail of German anti-gravity, they would not have bothered with the same old rocket propulsion methods at Cape Kennedy three decades afterwards.

An underlying thread of argument towards the end of this volume runs along the lines that far more lay behind National Socialism than a mad racialist warlord wanting to conquer the world for no good reason. Conceivably this will not find much of a welcome amongst those whose vision, being fixed on purely material causes, allows no possibility of a supra-physical impetus in history. The *determination* of the world not to understand Hitler or see the manifest signs is something which perhaps only an author who has spent countless hours poring over masses of documents can appreciate. The facts do bear investigation.

At the beginning of 1934, when Rudolf Hess swore in the entire NSDAP to Hitler in a mass spectacle bringing millions of Germans to the microphones, he said to them:

> "By this oath we again bind our lives to a man through whom – this is our belief – superior forces act in fulfilment of Destiny."[5]

Whatever Hess meant by this we have never been able to discover, but it might have been the reason why he spent all his life after 1941 imprisoned in solitary confinement. The former Gauleiter of Danzig, Hermann Rauschning recalled[6] that in the early years of the regime during the course of his discussions with Hitler (whom he described as the Master Enchanter and High Priest of the Religious Mysteries of Nazism), Hitler spoke openly about his innermost ideas – a programme to be kept secret from the masses. Rauschning continued:

> "One cannot help thinking of him as a medium. For most of the time mediums are ordinary, insignificant people. Suddenly they are endowed with what seems to be supernatural powers which set them apart from the rest of humanity. These powers are something that is outside their true personality – visitors, as it were, from another planet. The medium is possessed. Once the crisis is past, they fall back again into mediocrity. It was in this way, *beyond any doubt*, that Hitler was possessed by forces outside himself."

During Mussolini's visit to Munich in September 1937 the great psychologist C. J. Jung observed that, compared to the Duce,

> "Hitler presents the appearance of a robot. One would have said a double, in whose interior the man Hitler was hiding as an appendix, careful not to interfere with the mechanism."

Jung's final conclusion of Hitler was that:

> "He belongs in the category of authentic wizards. His body does not suggest strength. He has in his eyes the expression of a prophet. His power is not absolutely political, it is magical. Hitler listens and obeys. The true leader is always one who is

well led. The idea is confirmed by the word Mahdi, the Islamic Messiah, which translates to 'He who is well led'."

What man would have wanted such a responsibility foisted upon him? The extraordinary allegation being made here is that Adolf Hitler and the Führer were different entities inhabiting the same body.

What strikes one particularly in this context is Hitler's intuition *vis-à-vis* the motives of Stalin and the Soviet Union. It is not necessary to enlarge on this subject. What is required is for the British authorities to declassify *all the papers* relating to the interrogations of Rudolf Hess for the period 1941–1942.

It is, of course, not the intention of the foregoing to justify Nazi atrocities or the Holocaust. But we prefer to rely on the assertions of Governments and academic historians who, labouring in the realm of effects, cannot in the nature of things admit belief in cosmic intelligences, let alone their acting for change through leaders like Adolf Hitler. There is a danger in that, and the concluding chapter accentuates certain facts which should make the true situation incapable of being misunderstood.

Geoffrey Brooks
Uruguay, March, 2002

CHAPTER 1

Vergeltungswaffen:
V-1 to V-4

IN A TALK with Marshall Antonescu of Rumania at Führer HQ *Wolfsschanze* on 5 August 1944 Hitler spoke of four V-Weapons which Germany was in the process of introducing into the conflict. The source of this information is Henry Picker[7] who between 1942 and 1944 was Martin Bormann's ADC and stenographer.

The German noun *Vergeltung* has a dictionary meaning of 'retribution', 'retaliation' or 'reprisal', but its National Socialist meaning was broader, for the concept of retaliation as such merely contemplates the taking of revenge.

In the case of the United Kingdom, for example, this would simply imply taking measures to inflict more damage on British cities than the RAF and American air raids had inflicted on German cities, a militarily purposeless enterprise. It was by no means the object of the V-weapons programme to exchange 'rubble for rubble': *Vergeltung* meant the use of retaliation to terrorize the enemy's civilian population as a political tool to coerce their Government into seeking an armistice. It was not intended to punish Londoners, therefore, but to extract Britain's agreement to withdraw from the war and to expel from her soil the American presence there.

The V-1

The first of Hitler's V-Weapons was the Fieseler Fi 103 unpiloted flying bomb. It was launched either from a short ramp under its own jet power or from a low-flying Heinkel bomber. The warhead was 1 tonne of high explosive. Its maximum speed was 650 kms per hour and its range 370 kms. At the nose was a small log consisting of a propellor connected to a revolution counter preset with the number of turns of the propellor imparted at a particular speed and height in reaching a known distance. As soon as the preset revolutions were reached, the counter cut out the engine and the bomb then dropped. The weapon was grossly inaccurate and indiscriminate. London and southern England were always its intended target but in May 1943 preliminary discussions were held on the feasibility of firing the V-1 from a submarine such as the large Type XIV replenishment U-boat. After Field Marshal Milch had expressed his scepticism the idea of using the flying bomb against New York was shelved.[8]

The bombardment of London began on the morning of 13 June 1944. Ten days later Goebbels explained the intended effect of the campaign:

"Of course, a 1000-tonne raid has a different effect. But the effect of the German bombardment lies in its persistency. It's like toothache. Finally you have to do what you should have done all along. You go to the dentist. The V-weapons bombardment will be continued come what may and it will increase each month until Britain comes to her senses, that is to say, until the English inner circle sweeps aside those responsible for this insane British policy and clears the way for an understanding with us."[9]

This outlook summarizes the philosophy behind the V-weapons campaign. Rather than use the weapon against troop formations on the various fronts rapidly compressing the territory remaining in German hands, the Third Reich leadership resolved to rely entirely on the psychological effect of the terror bombardment of London and the Home Counties with the objective of forcing the British Government to the negotiating table. An unspoken hope existed that, if that were not to be the case, then perhaps the British Government might in desperation resort to some act so escalating the slaughter of German civilians that Hitler could justifiably respond with his ultimate weapons of terror.

As the bombardment entered its third week the intermittent attacks continued day and night, imposing a severe strain psychologically on the inhabitants of London. The flying bombs had already killed nearly 2,000 Londoners, although this was not a large casualty figure compared with any single great raid on a German city at that time.

By 6 July 1944 the V-1 provoked a response. In a Most Secret minute[10] to the Chiefs of Staff on that day, Churchill wrote:

> "If the bombardment of London really becomes a serious nuisance and great rockets with far-reaching and devastating effect fall on many centres of Government and labour, I should be prepared to do anything that would hit the enemy in a murderous place. . . . It may be several weeks or even months before I shall ask you to drench Germany with poison gas, and if we do it, let us do it 100 per cent . . ."

The Joint Planning Staff considered the proposal but advised that "if the Allies initiated chemical warfare, the Germans would immediately retaliate both in the field and against the United Kingdom. London would be the primary target and could expect to be attacked by flying bombs filled with gas and by up to 120 long-range bombers carrying chemical payloads." In the circumstances, the JPS was not prepared to recommend the use of chemical or biological weapons.

Germany had huge stocks of battlefield gases, together with nerve gases which were unique to the Third Reich, but a gas war with the British was not what the V-1 campaign was intended to achieve. The Luftwaffe could have launched a full-scale surprise attack at any time when it happened to suit their purposes. The Army and Luftwaffe had discussed at Münster gas depot the possibility of loading the V-1 with phosgene for use in the event of a gas war and subsequently experiments with a 1-tonne warhead of phosgene were found satisfactory. No tests were carried out with the V-2 but a payload of 2½ tonnes is mentioned in documents. The Germans had at their disposal in the west at least 12,000 tonnes of the nerve gas Tabun and vastly more of the nerve gas Sarin, which is four times more potent. Most of this material was kept in semi-readiness in 250-kg bombs. A Sarin bomb of this size was thought likely to destroy all life within several square kilometres of the exposure point.[11]

Over the period from 13 June to 5 September 1944 10,632 V-1 flying bombs were launched from Northern France of which 5,602 (52.7%) exploded in the area intended. Fighters and AA batteries accounted for 3,230 projectiles, collisions with barrage balloons brought down 231 and 1015 were failures.

From 16 September 1944 to 14 January 1945 about 1400 V-1s were fired from the North Sea coast of which 301 (21.5%) found their target area successfully.

During March 1945 a success rate of 47 hits (17%) was achieved with the 275 flying bombs despatched from western Holland.

During the defence of the Rhine in 1944/1945 11,988 V-1s were fired at Antwerp, Brussels and Liège. 2448 hits were obtained (20.4%).

In England the final death toll from the V-1 was put at 6,860 dead and 17,981 injured, Belgium suffered 4,152 dead (3,470 civilians and 682 military). In order to counter the offensive Britain committed eight fighter squadrons, 480 barrage balloons and 438 AA guns at home, while 40% of the RAF bombing effort was diverted to destroying the launching ramps.

The best system of defence involved (i) anti-V1 fighter patrols over the Channel, (ii) massed AA batteries along the coast, (iii) a second line of fighter patrols between the AA guns and London and (iv) a deep concentration of barrage balloons at the approaches to London. The defence expenditure was nearly four times greater than the operational cost of the offensive.[12]

The main problem for the attackers was to obtain precise information regarding the fall of the projectiles, and attempts were made to improve accuracy by the installation of a remote control gear.

At a meeting in November 1944 at Reichsführer-SS HQ Höhenlychen, Hauptsturmführer Otto Skorzeny argued energetically for the immediate implementation of the V-1 project against New York.[13] Himmler promised to speak on the matter to Hitler and Grossadmiral Dönitz remarked, "I see here a new and big chance of bringing about a change in the course of the war." He could hardly have been speaking of half-a-dozen conventional V-1 flying bombs and must have meant using them with a poison gas payload. According to the German historian Gellermann, in February 1945, after deciding on that course of action as a reprisal for Dresden, Hitler was talked out of the idea by Keitel and Jodl.

The Americans were well informed of these proposals through their Enigma decryption operation and spies and were concerned that even a Type VII U-boat fitted with a hangar on the foredeck could carry four V-1s and launch them with impunity within a few minutes at night or in fog. They need approach no closer than 300 kilometres from the coast.

It was not quite so simple as it seemed, however. By the end of 1944 all Type XIV boats had been sunk and the US offshore anti-submarine defences were such that the Kriegsmarine considered only the new Type XXI *Elektro-boote* capable of carrying out the operation with a prospect of surviving it. Another material drawback was the inaccuracy of the V-1. It was not remote-controlled at that stage and this factor, compounded with the pitch and roll of the boat at launch while firing on a compass bearing at a city 300 kilometres away, made the planners wonder if the target could ever be hit.

In order to overcome these problems a remote control system was tried, a version of the ZSG *Radieschen*, a passive radar which was fitted to the BV 246 glider bomb and homed in on enemy radar and Loran transmitters. This 15 kg target-seeker was found successful. A similar idea was in effect for the A9/10 rocket. The remaining technical problems to be surmounted were the relatively poor quality transmitters available and the need to have somebody put the set in place and turn it on at the right time at the target end. This meant that a number of agents would have to be landed in the United States for the task. A special version of the sea-launched V-1 was ready for use in November 1944[14], probably the Fi-103E, but the OKL development contract awarded to the *Deutsche Forschungsanstalt für Segelflug* for the V-1 *Radieschen*, which resulted in the *Ewald II* homing device and the *Sauerkirsch II* radio remote control system, did not bear fruit until April 1945, by which time hopes for the V-1 campaign were dead.

The V-2

The V-2 was the A-4 giant rocket 14 metres in length, 1.6 metres at the widest point of the fuselage and 3.5 metres across the tail assembly. Take-off weight was 12 tonnes including a 1-tonne warhead in the nose. The rocket was transported aboard a chassis known as a *Meillerwagen* which was towed by a road or rail locomotive. At the launch point it was raised upright on the detachable starting platform for firing. The fuel was a grain alcohol/liquid oxygen mixture which burned for about a minute before the rocket fell to earth in a ballistic trajectory. Maximum altitude was 80 kilometres and the range was up to 305 kilometres. During powered flight the projectile was remote-controlled from the ground or regulated by an onboard gyro-compass.

The impact of an A-4 was equivalent to fifty 100-ton steam locomotives hitting the ground simultaneously at 70 mph. Even without its warhead the rocket would excavate a crater thirty feet deep and 75 feet in diameter. The London correspondent of a Swedish national daily reported: "I have personally seen great craters made by the V-2. In urban areas a single projectile can ruin 600 houses. It is not the explosion or blast that does the damage, but the tremendous earthquake effect."

17

Accuracy was poor, however, and only 50% fell within 10 kilometres of the aiming point.

The V-2 offensive against London opened from The Hague on 8 September 1944, the first missile falling in Chiswick; the last fell on 27 March 1945. The despatch rate began at four per day and climbed to twenty-five units per day. Of 1269 launches against England, 1115 rockets (87%) arrived. The death toll from these was 2724 persons. 1739 A-4 missiles were fired at cities in France, Belgium and Holland, plus ten at Remagen, of which 1265 (73%) arrived, causing 7000 fatalities.

271 (0.8%) rockets of the total fired were designated failures.[15]

Whereas General Dwight Eisenhower was of the opinion in his memoirs that if the A-4 had been operational six months earlier it would have made the invasion "extremely difficult if not impossible", Armaments Minister Speer took the view that "the enormous scientific and technical effort, together with the bottleneck caused in raw materials and fuels, prevented a large number of jet fighters being built instead".

In the autumn of 1943 Otto Lafferenz, a director of the *Deutsche Arbeitsfront*, suggested to Peenemünde Weapons Testing Centre the building of a number of submersible containers, each holding a V-2 rocket. A U-boat would tow three of these 500-tonne barges, each 37 metres in length and 5.5 metres in diameter, underwater to the coast of the United States and, when within 300 kilometres of the target, flood the ballast tanks of the barge to bring it to an upright position projecting about 5 metres above the surface. This would allow the rocket to be fired from a gyroscopically stabilized platform.[16]

Trials were carried out with *U-1063* and apparently similar experiments were conducted later at Lake Toplitz in the Austrian Alps when manned midget submarines practised firing rockets which resembled small-scale V-2s.[17] A Kriegsmarine naval experimental station (CPVA) was located on the shore. The Lafferenz project was codenamed *Teststand XII* and *Projekt Schwimmweste*, and orders for the barges were placed with Stettiner Vulkanwerft and Schichau Werft Elbing in early December 1944.

It had been found in October 1943[18] that a U-boat towing a submerged barge had to maintain at least 4.1 knots through the water at periscope depth, for at 3.9 knots the barge lost the dynamic force necessary to hold it under. Various ideas were tried out unsuccessfully to reduce the minimum towing speed. As battery-propelled U-boats had insufficient capacity to proceed submerged at 4 knots for any length of time, and it was already dangerous enough in 1944 to voyage at normal speeds without also towing three barges, the Type XXI *Elektro-boot* was elected for the operation which involved a 30-day tow across the Atlantic at 12 knots. The time required on the surface for the operation does not seem to have been disclosed.

When the campaign began in earenest, scientists at Peenemünde had found out the hard way that a successful launch of the V-2 was virtually impossible four days or so after manufacture and a procedure known as *heisse Semmel* (hot dumplings) was in force on land whereby any V-2 to be used operationally was fired within three days of manufacture.[19] Clearly a V-2 could not be fired after thirty days in a damp transatlantic barge and so the US idea was shelved. In early December 1944 orders were placed with Stettiner Vulkanwerft and Schichau Werft Elbing. It seems self-evident that there must have been a plan to use these barges to bring Britain under V-2 fire from the North Sea.

In 1946, the Deputy Commanding General of Army Air Force Intelligence, Lt-Gen Donald Leander Putt, told the Society of Aeronautical Engineers: "The Germans were preparing rocket surprises for the whole world in general and England in particular which would have, it is believed, changed the course of the war if the invasion had been postponed for so short a time as half a year." Putt was also quoted in an aside as having stated that "the Germans had V-2s with atomic explosive warheads". A surprise is a surprise and hitherto ordinary rocket warfare had proved unproductive. The range of the V-2 was 200 miles. The crucial success of the Allied progress by December 1944 had therefore been to drive the German forces in Europe beyond this limit. The objective of the Ardennes campaign was the Belgian port of Antwerp, 200 miles from London. It was served by a short rail connection from Germany and its recapture was essential for a renewed V-2 offensive. Furthermore it was immediately available as a U-boat and Lafferenz barge base. The A-9 "winged V-2" project was resurrected in 1944/45. German testimonies allege that at least one successful test launch was made from the Harz in March 1945, and in mass production this rocket could have hit London from central Germany.

The V-3

Few commentators seem to be in any doubt but that the V-3 was the "High Pressure Pump" or "England Gun". Paul Brickhill recorded in *The Dam Busters*:

"the greatest nightmare of all was the great underworld being burrowed under a 20-foot-thick slab of ferro-concrete near Mimoyecques (between Calais and Boulogne). Here Hitler was preparing his V-3. Little has been told about the V-3, probably because we never found out much about it. The V-3 was the most secret and sinister of all – long-range guns with barrels 500 feet long!"

The V-3 was probably based on the 1885 unsuccessful ballistic principle of the Americans Lymann and Haskell and Baron von Pirquet's concept of sequential, electrically activated, angled side chambers to provide additional velocity to a shell during its passage of an immensely long tube.

In mid-1942 August Cönders, chief engineer of the Röchling Iron and Steel Works, Leipzig, rediscovered the principle while reading through technical dossiers captured by the Germans in France in 1940. He worked out an improved design and approached Armaments Minister Speer with the idea. Hitler was enthusiastic and demanded that the development should proceed immediately.

The design was for a gun consisting of numerous lengths of smoothbore metal tubing bolted together to form a barrel up to 124 metres long. Every 3.65 metres along its length was a lateral combustion chamber set at from 45° to a right angle. The shell and main propellant were loaded into an sFH18 heavy field howitzer breech. When the gun was fired, the projectile would be impelled forward by pressure from a gas cartridge, and on passing each chamber it triggered electrically another cartridge positioned there which gave the shell further velocity. This was repeated throughout its transit of the barrel. The electrical activation solved a detonation problem which had been caused by expanding gases detonating the auxiliary chambers before the arrival of the shell. The muzzle velocity was around 1500 metres/sec which was significantly greater than that of standard artillery and provided a range of about 160 kilometres. The original 10-inch calibre projectile was over nine feet in length and weighed 140 kilos with a 25-kilo warhead. Six wings opened in flight for stability. Twenty-five guns were projected which at full output would have enabled London, 150 kilometres distant, to be subjected to a persistent rain of up to 200 ten-inch calibre shells per hour. For this reason the project was nicknamed *fleissiges Lieschen*, Busy Lizzie. The *Heereswaffenamt*, or German Army Weapons Office, contracted with firms such as Skoda, Krupp, Röchling, Witkowitz Iron and Steel, Faserstoff, Fürstenberg and

Bochumer Verein for various calibres of ammunition. Towards mid-1944 20,000 shells were completed or under production.

Even before the gun trials had begun, work was started in the late summer of 1943 on a vast, well camouflaged underground gun battery to house twenty-five barrels of the HPP on the Channel coast at Mimoyecques. The barrels were to be sunk in shafts at a 50° angle 150 feet down into the ground. A slave labour force of 10,000 persons was involved in the construction and information was soon passed to London about a new mammoth "underground V-1 site".

The initial tests were carried out using barrel lengths between 50 and 130 metres, first at Hillersleben and then from a range at Misdroy near Peenemünde at the beginning of 1944. Various permutations of barrels and chambers were tried without much success. Shells were supplied by numerous manufacturers. In tests between 21 and 23 March 1944 it was found that at muzzle velocities above 1100 metres/sec the tubes lost stability and developed metal stresses. General Leeb recommended that the project be stopped for investigations. By May 1944 the gun had an acceptable range of 95 kilometres and experiments were stepped up to find ways of increasing muzzle velocity. Before any guns were delivered, the Mimoyecques emplacement was destroyed on 6 July 1944 by RAF aircraft using a 12,000-pound Tallboy bomb. This signalled the end of the project for the long-range bombardment of London and put the entire V-3 project in question.

Nevertheless further trials with the HPP with shorter barrels were undertaken at Misdroy and eventually the whole project was placed in the hands of SS-Obergruppenführer Hans Kammler, head of the V-weapons project. Under his supervision the V-3 project was accelerated for an operation in the late autumn of 1944 and, with the help of General Dr (Ing) Erich Dornberger, military commander at Peenemünde, a battery of two 50-metre long 15-cm (5.9-inch) calibre barrels with twelve right-angled side chambers was completed. An emplacement had been excavated at Bürderheidermühle on a wooded slope of the Ruwer at Lampaden, about 13 kilometres south-east of Trier, where the battery was installed under the supervision of Hauptmann Patzig and his 550-strong Army Artillery Detachment 705.

The two HPP barrels rested on thirteen steel girders anchored to buried wooden foundations and were laid to the west with a 34° elevation. 43 kilometres along the firing line was target number 305, Luxemburg City. Calculations showed that the two guns had a maximum range of 65 kilometres with a shell dispersion radius of from 2.5 to 5 kilometres.

Between the two barrels were three bunkers for the gun crews plus either side of the barrels ten smaller bunkers which served as shell and powder magazines.

The Lampaden emplacement was part of the plan for the Ardennes offensive. Ammunition supply was poor because of disruption to the railways and in view of the critical time factor it was decided to use a 95-kilo shell of 15-cm calibre with a warhead of 7 to 9 kilos. The propellant was a 5-kilo main cartridge and twenty-four additional chamber charges, a total of 73 kilos of Ammon powder per shell.

Neither gun was operational when the Ardennes offensive began on 16 December 1944. Hurried preparations were being made to support the German offensive from Lampaden. Luxemburg City, liberated by the Americans in September 1944, was finally chosen as the target for diversionary fire. Although the battery was only operational to a limited extent on 20 December, Kammler was told by High Command West to have it ready before New Year.

On Saturday 30 December 1944 No 1 Gun opened fire. The flight of shell from Lampaden to Luxemburg was 42.5 kilometres. Because of muzzle velocity variables and the variety of propellants being used it was estimated that the target zone was from 40.6 to 43.6 kilometres, giving a dispersal of salvoes of about 3 kilometres. The exact barrel elevation was set at 36° and the muzzle velocity 935 metres/second.

Two 'warmers' were fired at 2145 hrs and 2205 hrs before Oberleutnant Bortscheller ordered the gun to open fire in earnest at 2216 hrs in the presence of SS-Obergruppenführer Kammler, the battery commander and officers from a neighbouring artillery detachment. Fire ceased at 2343 hrs. Five shells exploded more or less in the city centre but what effect they had is unknown.

According to German sources, these were 95-kilo shells, probably the six-winged Röchling type numbered 32, 29, 47, 15, 28 (firing sequence). On 31 December twenty-three more were fired between 0007 hrs and 2333 hrs from No 1 Gun, while No 2 Gun was still being adjusted, this not being completed until 3 January.

Following round 17 fired at 0944 hrs the pressure tube was found to have shifted by 4 millimetres and had to be realigned. After two 'warmers' the remaining shells were fired without incident between 1943 and 1958 hrs.

    4 January 1601–2007 hrs. No 1 Gun, 16 rounds. No 2 Gun ready but did not fire.

11 January 2016–2351 hrs. Both guns fired, total 20 rounds.

12 January 1847–2224 hrs. Both guns fired, total 20 rounds.

13 January 0757–1238 hrs. Both guns fired, total 22 rounds, after which both barrels were checked and adjusted. Because of ammunition shortage, fire was not resumed until 15 January.

15 January Early afternoon, six shells exploded in Luxemburg City.

16 January Late afternoon, six rounds fired. The tower of the cathedral was hit and four persons attending mass were killed.

18 January 1421–1638 hrs. Both guns fired 19 rounds. Most of these exploded north-east of the city in the suburbs of Clausen, Neudorf and Hamm injuring 13 persons.

20 January 0808–1353 hrs. Both guns fired a total of 24 rounds.

Preparations had been taken in hand to transport and mount two more barrels with selected lines of fire into Belgium and France and existing HPP ammunition was rationed out between the four guns. By now the Americans were counter-attacking successfully in the Ardennes region and as it was obvious that Lampaden would soon be under threat, Kammler ordered the detachment to be prepared to dismantle the two pressure tubes for a withdrawal east of the Rhine in due course. The lack of ammunition remained severe.

15 February 0908–1735 hrs. No 1 Gun fired 20 rounds at Luxemburg. These all fell in unpopulated areas near Hamm and Sandweiler east of the city.

16 February 1020–1405 hrs. No 1 Gun fired four shells which fell near Fetschenhaff causing little damage. According to German sources the battery had now only six rounds left.

22 February 1745–1858 hrs. Six shells were fired, all off-target and landed in open country near Merl. This terminated the V-3 programme and the guns were dismantled for transport across the Rhine.

On 26 February US armoured units advanced to within 3 kilometres of Lampaden where they captured guns and replacement parts. A quantity of ammunition was also confiscated and tested later at the Aberdeen Proving Ground, Maryland. The V-3 HPP was considered to have limited value and needed further development. Operationally 183 rounds had been fired from Lampaden towards Luxemburg of which 143 (78%) exploded within the territory or very close to it.[20]

The V-3 suffered from lack of development due to the pressure of time. Had the Mimoyecques battery been operational against London in 1943, delivering 200 6-inch shells per hour, Paul Brickhill's fears might easily have been justified.

V-4 Uraniumbombe and the Doomsday Bomb

Hitler was pinning all his hopes on the *Uraniumbombe*. This laboratory-produced nuclear explosive was to be the warhead in the large V-2 or A9/10 rockets. The V-2 had a range of 200 miles while the A9/10 could hit New York. There was no rocket of the same species for the inter-mediate ranges and this omission was fatal. By December 1944 when the *Uraniumbombe* was ready for use in numbers for the definitive V-2 campaign, the Low Countries and France had been lost and now the range was too long. After the failure of the Ardennes campaign, in March 1945 Hitler decided on a last desperate gamble. On his last appearance at the front, he exhorted his troops to hold out until the miracle weapon should be ready, which would bring about the change in Germany's fortunes. Posterity has been left few traces of the former flak weapon based on firedamp. In principle it generated a ferocious pressure wave at ground level, killing principally by blast and suffocation, but it had a knock-on effect which threatened a structural change to the atmosphere. The mysterious loss of Luftwaffe and OKW War Diaries for the month or so in question may have been connected with the execution of Luftwaffe General Barber and several hundred pilots and airfield commanders for refusing to implement orders to use it at the end of March 1945. When captured in May that year, Hermann Goering exclaimed that he had "declined to deploy a weapon which might have destroyed all civilisation," the inference being perhaps that the use of the explosive threatened to so destabilize the climate as to bring about the cataclysm, but that Hitler had nevertheless ordered its use against the Allies on the Western Front regardless. It certainly does not look as though it happened that way round, for reasons explained later.

CHAPTER 2

The Aryan Physics Doctrine

ON 30 JANUARY 1933 the National Socialist Party under Adolf Hitler came to power in Germany. Those who saw in National Socialism nothing more than a political movement knew scarcely anything of it. It was more even than a religion; it was the will to create mankind anew.

> "One thing is certain – Hitler has the spirit of the prophet. We had come to a turning point in world history – that was his constant theme. We uninstructed persons, it was clear, had no conception of the scale of the revolution that was to take place in all life. At these times Hitler spoke as a seer, as one of the initiated. His inspired pronouncements were based on a biological mysticism . . . the pursuit of 'the random path of the intelligence' was the real defection of man from his divine mission. To have 'magic insight' was Hitler's idea of the goal of human progress. He himself felt that he already had the rudiments of this gift. He attributed to it his successes and his future eminence. He saw his own remarkable career as a confirmation of Hidden Powers."[21]

These Hidden Powers seem to have first possessed Hitler on Armistice Day 1918. He had been admitted to Pasewalk Military Hospital at the end of the war suffering from mustard gas poisoning and placed under the care of a psychiatrist, Dr Edmund Forster, who misdiagnosed his condition as psychopathic hysteria. What treatment was administered and what the correct diagnosis was remain a mystery since the Gestapo seized the records in 1933 and Dr Forster committed suicide the same year. According to Hitler while at the hospital he had experienced "a vision from another world" which told him that he needed to restore his sight so that he could lead Germany back to greatness. His anti-semitism manifested at Pasewalk. It was there that he promised solemnly to become a politician and "devote his energies to fulfilling the orders which he had received".[22]

> "Yes, Hitler continued, Nietzsche went so far as to recognize the superman as a new biological variety. But he was not too sure of it. Man is becoming God – that is the simple fact. Man is God in the making. Man has eternally to strain at his limitations. The moment he relaxes and contents himself with them, he decays and falls below the human level. He becomes a quasi-beast. Gods and beasts, that is what our world is made of".[23]

Thus was National Socialism at root an idea embracing powerful emotions harnessed towards a demiurgic transformation of the world by a new race of Aryan mankind which was, or so he imagined, at the same time the resurgence of an Himalayan race of profound antiquity. And, from the very outset, the world enemy had been identified. In a booklet published from his notes made in 1923, and published by Hohenreichen Verlag Munich in 1924 under the title *Bolshevism from Moses to Lenin: A Dialogue between Adolf Hitler and Me*[24], Hitler's tutor in magic, Dietrich Eckart, to whom he dedicated *Mein Kampf*, demonstrated that the roots of the hatred of the Jews stretched back to the pre-Exodus period in Ancient Egypt.

The oriental origins of Hitler's movement are obvious not only from its symbolism. Many National Socialist speeches, including those by Hitler, were direct translations, phrase by phrase, from the works of the Chinese philosopher Yang Shang, whose theories influenced Shih Huang-Ti (246–209 BC), builder of the Great Wall, an emperor beguiled by the esoteric language of Taoist sacred writings.[25] The German Customs list of books banned from entry into the Third Reich was fairly complete as far as the languages of Europe and America were concerned, but lacking in oriental titles – in fact entirely devoid of them. The works of the pacifist Chinese political philosophers were not on it, and even German, French and English translations of these books could come in.[26]

Rudolf Hess, interrogated in the Tower of London under the effect of a truth serum, stated that National Socialists valued the occult sciences highly and might even be, through Hitler, the puppets of a clandestine Directorate in the Orient.[27] No doubt he had other things to say. Exactly why he had to serve his sentence of life imprisonment in solitary confinement has never been made clear, but his uninvited arrival in Britain one month before *Barbarossa* suggests that he, at least, believed he had a cogent argument for the termination of Anglo-German hostilities.

The doctrine therefore had its various sources in the Orient, and although the underlying philosophy of Nazi science is undocumented, it is likely to have been the Hermetic tradition. Hitler was a disciple of the Buddhistic thinker Schopenhauer, and his success stemmed from a profound knowledge of magical causes occasioned by reading Schopenhauer's treatment of Hermeticism. By this is meant the ancient Trismegistic literature of the Hermetic tradition of which uncontested Egyptian treatises survive and thus for the second time within a few passages we found ourselves confronted by the spectre of Ancient Egypt in connection with National Socialism.

Hermetic science states that each element in matter has as its crystal a unique geometric form. Thus an assayist can recognize any mineral by microscopic examination of its crystal. The experimentalist Sir William Crooks, having spread some fine sand over the head of a drum, sounded different notes above the drumhead with a tuning fork. It was found that the sand shifted and always assumed the same unique geometric figure corresponding to the key sounded. This proved that vibration is the origin of form. All matter, mineral or organic, is merely a molecular structure held together by a keynote, from which one can infer that everything in the material universe is the result of vibration, a fortuitous concourse of atoms. The whole secret of matter is that all form is a mode of motion of the original cosmic energy, found in finer or grosser form on all planes of nature. This was the secret behind the philosophy of Schopenhauer, the guru of Hitler, that the material world is only an illusion and no physical object has any permanent reality. The only reality is the vibration.

Since Adolf Hitler had to suppress the career of a science which did not work for the benefit of humanity becoming God, but for darker, more material purposes, there dawned Aryan Physics.

Aryan Physics (the term is twinned with the expression Jewish Physics which means any scientific procedure not compatible with Aryan doctrine) was a National Socialist doctrine inspired by two German Nobel Prize winners in Physics, Professor Philipp Lenard and Dr Johannes Stark, although the impetus for it is bound to have come from

Hitler. In the four volumes of *Deutsche Physik* published in 1936, Professor Lenard had completed the unenviable task of setting out the doctrine. It was ill-defined and fraught with contradictions. The principal purpose of the two founders was to refute various 20th century developments in sub-atomic science, principally Einstein's theories of relativity, and also quantum theory, labelling them "a Jewish sedition" and "the outgrowths of an alien mentality".

In 1927 the German quantum physicist Professor Werner Heisenberg postulated his Uncertainty Principle, a proposition of far-reaching consequence for modern philosophy and science which challenged Einstein's insistence on a causal, predictable universe. Since quantum mechanics predicts that the sub-atomic world is without independent structure, this contradicts not only Einstein's theory of relativity but also the Hermetic doctrine, which states that all matter is molecular structure held together by harmonics.

Heisenberg's Uncertainty Principle and quantum mechanics assert the unpredictable and random distribution of nuclear particles. It is claimed that the theory has withstood every test devised for it, but, nevertheless, contrary to the gathering scientific evidence against Einstein's theories, both systems are even today supposed to be held in equal importance by science. Modern theoretical physicists say that in order to understand the workings of the universe from its inception, relativity theories will ultimately be reconciled with quantum mechanics in the so far elusive unified field theory, but the electron problem (in which the particle goes outside the time-space continuum or range of observation during measurement) makes this unlikely. More probably, in the opinion of many, relativity theory will ultimately have to be discarded.[28]

Einstein asserted that a three-dimensional continuum plus time is all there is. In the 1920s he pointed out that quantum physics appeared to predict that sub-atomic particles communicate with one another instantaneously and regardless of the distance separating them. This implied faster-than-light communication which was prohibited by his theory of relativity, the cardinal principle of which was the dictum that nothing can travel faster than light, since that would imply a number of unacceptable paradoxes such as time travel. In 1982 the physicists Aspect, Dalibard and Roger of the Institute of Optics at the University of Paris proved by experiment that when twin photons emitted from a calcium atom travelled a significant distance apart, and had their angles of polarization – the specific angle of orientation of the light wave – measured simultaneously, their polarizations were always found to be correlated. Einstein had stated years before that, if that were discovered to be the case, he would accept that the two protons had communicated instantaneously. Thus it would seem that the Special theory of relativity cannot stand, and time travel, UFOs from other dimensions "and a host of other paradoxes" are possible.

Much earlier than 1982 Aryan Physics suspected that when Einstein was working on the unified field theory, he realized that relativity could not be accommodated in it, but by then it was impossible for him to admit his earlier error. While dismissing relativity theory altogether, Aryan Physics also refuted quantum physics on the grounds that all unified field theories continued to view space-time in Einstein's terms. Since Hermetic science accepts other dimensions beyond our own continuum, presumably this, together with the assertion that the sub-atomic world has no independent structure, was what Aryan Physics considered was lacking in quantum theory. Since the war, through optics research and spectral analysis from the Orbiting Solar Observatory, OSO7 of NASA, we have new knowledge concerning the composition and formation of the universe. Vibratory sound fields do exist within the sub-atomic worlds which appear responsible for molecular structures maintaining their specific particle configurations. The implication is that the structure of the universe is based on harmonics.

Before the advent of quantum theory, most physicists accepted a universe that was totally causal. The success of Newton's physics was due to the apparent laws of causality seeming to exist for virtually every system. Even when prediction was impractical, classical physics still assumed that the system was causal. This mechanistic view was based on the notion that reality is composed of solid objects and empty space, and in the realm of everyday life this is still valid. The refutation of quantum and relativity theories meant the resurrection of Newtonian Physics in Nazi Germany. Inevitably this had its repercussions in the nuclear field, for as Speer explained,[29] Hitler "set his face against nuclear physics for doctrinal reasons," and evidently showed little interest in having his scientists build a nuclear reactor as a power source. The evidence also suggests that he did not want to use the atom bomb. If one can accept the idea that, far from being merely a mob-orator with a limited intellect, Hitler was literate philosophically, even if the results of his beliefs were horrendous, then the assertion of many of his contemporary scientists and military leaders may be true, that decisions in the scientific field were based on his obscure scientific doctrine or communicated to him from another level.

Professor Heisenberg Acts Unwisely

A notable personality to fall foul of Aryan Physics early on was Professor Werner Heisenberg himself. His role as the leading atom physicist in the Third Reich was an equivocal one and this book will not do much to resolve the controversy. Born in Würzburg on 5 December 1901, he was the second son of a University lecturer. During the First World War he volunteered for land service. When a soviet republic was imposed on Bavaria in April 1919 Heisenberg joined many fellow students in supporting the moderate socialists. He served with a cavalry brigade as despatch carrier and lookout.

At Munich in 1923 he obtained a doctorate *cum laude* in theoretical physics, his aversion to the experimental side of the discipline having let him down. He was still aged 22 when he qualified as a university lecturer. From May 1926 he lectured in the Danish language at Niels Bohr's Institute in Copenhagen and was called to the Chair of Theoretical Physics at the University of Leipzig in October 1927. He transformed Leipzig into a leading research centre. One of his pupils there was Carl Friedrich von Weizsäcker who would later assist him in his campaign to deflect attention away from a major atom bomb project.

When Einstein's theories were attacked in an article published by the *Völkischer Beobachter* in its edition of 26 February 1936, Heisenberg prepared a paper signed by seventy-seven professors of physics, including a number of Party members, expressing his concern to the Reichsminister for Education, Bernhard Rust, at the official policy of discrediting theoretical physics.

The nomination of Heisenberg as the leading candidate to succeed to the vacant Chair at the Faculty of the University of Munich the following year brought the matter to a head and the vehemence of the opposition to him from supporters of Aryan Physics rallying around its founders, Lenard and Stark, became almost hysterical. The swell of protest culminated in an anonymous article entitled *White Jews in Science* attributed to Johannes Stark which appeared in the SS-journal *Das Schwarze Korps* in its edition of 15 July 1937.

"Just how secure the White Jews feel themselves to be is demonstrated by the behaviour of the Professor of Theoretical Physics at Leipzig, Professor Werner Heisenberg, who in 1936 managed to smuggle an article into an official party newspaper describing Einstein's relativity theory as 'the obvious basis for further research'."

After a catalogue of complaints alleging a pro-Jewish bias in making appointments the article continued:

"In 1933 Heisenberg received the Nobel Prize at the same time as the Einstein boys, Schroedinger and Dirac – proof of the ways Jews influence the Nobel Committee against National Socialist Germany. Heisenberg paid his own tribute in August 1934 by refusing to sign the Declaration of German Nobel Prize Winners For the Führer and Reichskanzler. His answer was: 'Although I am personally in favour, political affirmations by scientists seem wrong, since it was never the practice in the past. Therefore I won't sign.' This answer identifies the Jewish spirit of its author, who considers the unity of the people and national responsibility of scientists to be improper. Heisenberg is only one example of many. They are all vessels of Jewishness in German intellectual life and must disappear as must the Jews themselves."

Johannes Stark contributed his opinion in a footnote to the article warning that:

"whilst the influence of the Jewish spirit has been removed from the German Press, literature and art as well as from German jurisprudence, it still has its defenders and protagonists among Aryan associates of Jews and those who have been pupils of Jews. In this situation, the *Schwarze Korps* renders great service if by virtue of its courageous and important utterances it directs public awareness to the amage to which German intellectual life and the education of its academic youth is being exposed by White Jews."

Realizing now that he was in serious danger, on 21 July 1937 Heisenberg responded with a letter to SS-Reichsführer Heinrich Himmler requesting a decision on the principle and offering to resign if the view of Herr Stark corresponded with that of the Government,

31

"But if that is not the case, as I have already been expressly assured by Reich Education Minister Rust, then I request you as SS-Reichsführer to defend me effectively against such attacks in this newspaper."

During the next twelve months Heisenberg was frequently summoned to hearings in Berlin. These were under the personal direction of Gestapo Chief Reinhard Heydrich. Many interrogations were conducted in the notorious Gestapo prison on the Prinz Albrecht Strasse, from where Heisenberg would return exhausted and distressed. One of the problems confronting the SS inquisition was their uncertainty of the political implications of a science they did not understand. The frightening interviews were attended by an SS physicist, Johannes Juilfs, a former student of Heisenberg, who saw to it that he was not brutally treated.

On 21 July 1938, exactly a year since his letter, Himmler exonerated Heisenberg:

"I do not approve of the attacks made against you in the *Das Schwarze Korps* article and I have therefore ensured that there will be no further outbursts against you. However, I consider it right to mention that in future before an audience, you should clearly distance yourself from the human and political identity of the researcher when recognizing scientific research results."

A scientific nonentity, Müller, acceded to the Munich Chair of Physics, while Heisenberg resumed academic life at the University of Leipzig. The degree of ferocity with which the proponents of Aryan Physics championed their view of science is difficult to comprehend. Not even Ministers were exempted from attack. Soon after taking over the Armaments Ministry in February 1942, Albert Speer found his attempts to promote atomic physics research, by which he presumably meant the development of the atom bomb, met by a "rubber wall".[30] On one such occasion he was astonished to encounter strident opposition in the Party daily *Völkischer Beobachter*, the newspaper of which Adolf Hitler himself was the owner. The editorial railed against him in an article entitled *Jewish Physics Stirs Again!* Speer also found it easy to incur the Führer's wrath in even mentioning the atom bomb, which Hitler privately described to him as "the spawn of Jewish pseudo-science".

The Discovery of Neutrons and Nuclear Fission in Uranium

Many scientists assert that the age of nuclear physics began in 1932. On 17 February that year the scientific periodical *Nature* published an article by the British researcher James Chadwick in which he announced the discovery of the neutron. It was released when alpha-radiation from a radium source penetrated a beryllium atom. The neutrons ejected from the beryllium had no electrical charge and this enabled them to penetrate close to the nucleus of the atom of many other substances tested. This was a new means of splitting the atom, but for the time being at least there was no prospect that the neutron might be used for the production of energy. Nevertheless the discovery was the foundation for the new science of nuclear chemistry and every atom from hydrogen to uranium now came in for experiment in laboratories worldwide.

Since 1934 Otto Hahn, Lise Meitner and Fritz Straßmann had been subjecting uranium to neutron bombardment in experiments at the Kaiser Wilhelm Institute for Chemistry in Berlin-Dahlem. In an article appearing in the scientific journal *Die Wissenschaften* of 6 January 1939,[31] Hahn and Straßmann announced that they had demonstrated nuclear fission in uranium. When a U^{235} isotope of uranium was struck by a neutron, $U^{235} + 1n = U^{236}$, a new unstable compound, was formed and split up almost instantaneously. As this occurred, the highly charged fragments repelled each other with a violent kinetic energy which was also very radioactive.

Of this discovery Heisenberg's former pupil Carl Friedrich Freiherr von Weizsäcker wrote:

> "I recall that for a week in February 1939 or maybe at the beginning of March I thought through the technical possibilities of atom bombs and atomic engines which all physicists had to get to know about, and discussing theoretically with a close circle of friends the major political consequences of the discovery."[32]

A chain reaction was still not absolutely certain until there appeared in the 22 April 1939 edition of the scientific periodical *Nature* the findings of three experimental physicists at the College de France, Joliot, von Halban and Kowarski, reporting that at least two neutrons eject during fission, followed in the next few minutes by a small supplementary number from the decaying fragments of the atom. As the collision between one neutron and a U^{235} nucleus brought about the creation of more than two fresh neutrons, it would probably be possible to arrange for the surplus neutrons to cause a chain reaction.

Two days after publication of this article the *Heereswaffenamt*[33] in Berlin received the first letters from scientific institutes and universities pointing out that:

> "the newest developments in nuclear physics which will probably make it possible to produce an explosive many orders of magnitude more powerful than conventional ones: that country which first makes use of [nuclear fission] has an unsurpassable advantage over the others."

Professor Heisenberg Explains his Stance

In the spring of 1939 Heisenberg made a two-month lecture tour in the United States. By now he had decided not to defect on the grounds that he would almost certainly be co-opted to build the atomic bomb which, if ready in time, was likely to be dropped on Germany. Another reason was that he thought it would be difficult to campaign to rebut Aryan Physics as an expatriate. He also felt the need to explain why he wanted to remain in Germany in the coming war, believing that friendships could outlast political differences between nations. His Italian colleague Fermi was at least able to express understanding for his decision while not agreeing with it. When Fermi suggested that Heisenberg should defect he was told:

> "History teached us that sooner or later, every century is shaken by revolutions and wars, and whole populations obviously cannot emigrate every time there is a threat of an upheaval. People must learn to prevent catastrophes, not to run away from them. I have decided to stay in Germany, even if my decision is wrong"[34]

and in an interview with Robert Jungk Heisenberg explained:

> "Under a dictatorship, active resistance can only be practised by those who pretend to collaborate with the regime. . . . I have

always been very much ashamed when I think of the people, some of them friends of my own, who sacrificed their lives on 20 July 1944 and thereby put up a really serious resistance to the regime. But even their example shows that effective resistance can only come from those who pretend to collaborate."[35]

Heisenberg was a patriot and a cultural imperialist of the old school who was rooted in Germany and had no desire to be anywhere else. In an interview immediately after the war with Professor Samuel Goudsmit, head of the *Alsos* US Scientific Mission to Europe, he stated that in his opinion physicists in the Reich had, on the whole, done only the work necessary to preserve their university positions and hold together what remained of the great German tradition in physics. His own small circle had dominated the uranium project and steered the research away from the production of nuclear weapons. To him the war was an interlude. Emphasizing that Germany had not constructed atomic weapons, he made a public ritual of contrasting the moral character of German scientists, who had deliberately obstructed the research, with that of Allied scientists and politicians who had not only built those weapons, but also used them. It is clear that Goudsmit did not accept this explanation and remained convinced that Heisenberg had been in some way involved in a German atom bomb project.

This book concludes that Professor Goudsmit was right. The fact of the matter seems to be that somebody in Germany designed an 'atomic-type' weapon, somebody then built it, a scientist described how he had seen it tested and eighty lead cases containing enough material for two more of these small atom bombs turned up on a Tokyo-bound U-boat when searched after being surrendered to the US Navy at the end of the war. Heisenberg directed the German uranium project, but as regards an atomic-type bomb he was quite certain that he had not designed it and nor could he personally have been involved in the experimental foundation work for it in any way whatsoever because there was no such thing.

As a means of correcting Press inaccuracies following the announcement of the American atomic attack on the city of Hiroshima, the contingent of German atom scientists confined at Farm Hall, Cambridgeshire, England, issued a memorandum on 7 August 1945 presenting an outline in brief of the official German Uranium Project. The document was drafted by Heisenberg, Dr Karl Wirtz, his experimental assistant, and Professor Walter Gerlach, last Plenipotentiary for

Nuclear Science, after consultation with Professors Diebner, Hahn, von Weizsäcker, von Laue, Korsching, Harteck and Bagge. Three scientists present abstained from signing.

The second paragraph alone alluded to the philosophy of developing nuclear weapons, asserting in a single sentence that "it did not appear feasible at the time to produce a bomb with the technical possibilities available in Germany". There was an explanatory footnote:

> "As to the question of the atom bomb, the undersigned confirm that they have no knowledge of any other group in Germany which had the production of the bomb *as an immediate goal*. However, if such an attempt was in fact undertaken, then it was made by dilettantes, and should not be taken seriously."

If the interned group of physicists had no knowledge of a bomb project there was no need to add the final sentence. Ultimately all that is denied is the existence of a group working towards the atom bomb *as an immediate goal*. If we suppose for a moment that there was a group which had been working on an experiment whose methodology and materials could be adapted if so desired to create a small atomic bomb, then that group would fall outside the German physicists' denial. Heisenberg was very careful with words. When he took up his pen to draft this crafty document all nine of his colleagues knew exactly which group of 'amateurs' they had in mind. As Baron Manfred von Ardenne had defected to the Russians and was building their nuclear weapons for them, they all thought it was a very good idea to point the finger in his direction early on just in case any awkward questions were asked about who built a small-scale German atom bomb during the period 1941–1944.

CHAPTER 3

Heisenberg's Pioneering Paper

A S A CONSCRIPTED reservist, Professor Heisenberg had served two months in the previous two summers with the *Gebirgsjäger*. Obeying a mobilization order late on 25 September 1939, he travelled by train from Urfeld to Berlin and reported to Hardenbergstrasse 12 at ten next morning. There he was informed that his call-up telegram had been a deception and that he should attend next door for a conference of nuclear physicists considering the possible applications of nuclear energy.

The *Heereswaffenamt* had seized the Kaiser Wilhelm Institute (KWI) for Physics at Berlin-Dahlem as the scientific centre for its uranium research project. Professor Erich Schumann was its coordinating head and he had appointed Dr Kurt Diebner, a second-rank scientist engaged on conventional explosives research, to direct it. The aim was to concentrate and coordinate at Berlin-Dahlem the secret activities of the Uranium Project. In Diebner's appointment there lay the danger that the project was vulnerable to penetration by political functionaries, as had happened elsewhere. Diebner saw the weakness of his position and agreed that the survival of the Institute depended on it having an authoritative Director. Accordingly he consented to Professor Heisenberg being invited to join the Institute as scientific adviser, travelling from Leipzig University to Berlin once a week. On these visits Heisenberg could intervene to forestall undesirable developments in research in Berlin and elsewhere[36].

Professor Schumann's address to the group emphasized the defence aspects of the enquiry. The German Reich being at war, it was of the greatest importance that Germany should be forewarned of all possible eventualities; this was the purpose of the technical appraisal they would be undertaking. Even a negative conclusion was valuable, for the military could then be reassured that no unpleasant surprises were in store.

The experimentalists were commissioned to undertake a variety of materials measurements in specified areas of research, while Heisenberg was given the written task:

> "to consider whether, under the known circumstances of the characteristics of fission processes in uranium, a chain reaction is at all possible, and if so please commit your ideas to paper."[37]

Whereas the majority of physicists were willing to affiliate with the *Heereswaffenamt* group, a large number was not prepared to relocate under one roof at Berlin-Dahlem, and thus from its inception the programme was structured with a Headquarters and three provincial satellites at Leipzig, Heidelberg and Hamburg. From about 1942 onwards there were other groups in Czechoslovakia, Germany and Austria, mainly SS who kept themselves aloof from the professors, but as early as 1941 the Reich Post Office nuclear project in Berlin had equipment for nuclear research including high voltage installations and a cyclotron.

Heisenberg completed his assignment within two months, and on 6 December 1939 he submitted his findings in the first of two pioneering papers, *G-39 The Possibility of Obtaining Energy from Fission in Uranium*[38].

Throughout the Second World War the spectre of a German atom bomb haunted many people, but from the outset Heisenberg made no attempt to disguise the possibility that one could be built.

> "If a chain reaction is possible, then the bomb is possible. Its intensity would depend on the rate of liberation of energy before the chain reaction collapsed,"

he advised the *Heereswaffenamt* in his paper. As part of the deliberate process to denigrate the German nuclear project, various historians have stated that the Germans appear not to have considered the question of the fast fission chain reaction. The official British UKAEA historian Margaret Gowing[39] added for good measure that the critical size of the U^{235} bomb appeared not to have been investigated either. Piecemeal transcripts of the German physicists' secretly tape-recorded private conversations in internment at Farm Hall, England, in 1945 were included by General Leslie Groves, head of the Manhattan Project, in his book[40] published in 1962. Following the release of the full documentation by the London Public Record Office in February 1992, it became apparent that Groves had lied when reporting what was supposed to have been said in these conversations. Groves stated that the transcripts proved how Heisenberg

> "had not thought of using the bomb designs we had used: ours took advantage of fast neutrons . . . the Germans thought they would have to drop a whole reactor."

In fact Heisenberg was recorded in conversation as saying in 1945:

> "I knew it could be done with U^{235} using fast neutrons. That's why U^{235} alone can be used as an explosive. They can never make an explosive with slow neutrons, not even with the heavy water reactor."

The purpose of Groves' lie was to pervert history by proving falsely that there never could have been a German atom bomb because the top scientist did not know the principle. This had to be done because a small atom bomb actually had been built and tested by Germany.

In his pioneering paper of December 1939 Heisenberg spoke of "enrichment". Natural uranium consists essentially of two isotopes. 99.3% of the material is U^{238}. This isotope captures free neutrons in the uranium, and this is why natural uranium cannot explode. The 'fissile' isotope U^{235} exists in natural uranium in the proportion of 0.7%. If the ratios can be changed, and the major isotope physically reduced in the material, then neutrons will be more free to act on the U^{235} atoms. If the material is sufficiently rich in U^{235} atoms, say above 50%, then it can be arranged for an explosive chain reaction to occur, although even 7% will be sufficient for an explosion of some sort.

In his report Heisenberg explained:

> "An increase in temperature results from enriching the U^{235} isotope. If the U^{235} were to be enriched sufficiently to obtain a temperature corresponding to a neutron energy of 3.5 million degrees C, . . . the mass for the release of all available fissile atoms at once, would be: $R = 10\prod 1 cms = 31.41$ cms.

"This explosive transformation of the U^{235} atoms can only occur in almost pure U^{235} , because the capture bands of the U^{238} isotopes, even when present in reduced quantities, still absorb the neutrons."

This is not a formal expression of critical size, but merely a general statement for discussion based on the idea that a fast fission atom bomb is possible provided one can obtain huge amounts of the U^{235} isotope. In Heisenberg's equation, the unknown element is l, the *diffusion length* or *mean free path*. This term is the mean distance travelled by a neutron between release from an atom at fission to absorption and fission in another U^{235} atom. It can be a variable: the American physicists, when first putting their minds to the problem, came up with estimates of critical mass ranging from Feyman's 50 kilos to Robert Oppenheimer's 100 kilos, and the Americans had far better tools at their disposal for making the measurements than Heisenberg.

The Implosion Method

In the implosion method of detonating an atom bomb, the bomb core is a subcritical mass surrounded by a uniform layer of high explosive. When the HE detonates, a massive uniform pressure of millions of pounds p.s.i. is created which compresses the core material to a supercritical density, thus causing an implosion. Obviously, since the fissile material is compressed into a much smaller volume, the *diffusion length* is much reduced. If it were to be reduced by a factor of three, i.e. uniformly compressed by the explosion to a third of its original volume, then the critical mass required for implosion is smaller by the power of nine. This might have put U^{235} within Germany's capabilities with a stupendous investment and the help of the electrical giants. The *diffusion length* is a variable depending on the quality of material and other factors. The more efficient the implosive force for the compression, the less U^{235} bomb material needed.

A crucial question is whether Germany had an effective implosion fuse in 1939. It is claimed that they were close to it, and by 1941 had made such advances in the technology of implosion fuses that they were already working on an ultra-violet type. Sources allege that an efficient implosion fuse which could set off all detonators around the bomb sphere at the speed of light was invented by Prof. (Ing) Friedrich Lachner in Vienna pre-war and a model exhibited at the Wiener Technische Hochschule (University) to a gathering of home and foreign physicists at a lecture evening. Professor Lachner was a colleague of Professor Adolf Smekal and had obtained his inspiration for the work after hearing one of Smekal's talks. Later Lachner joined Professor Stetter's team of SS physicists at Innsbruck. This group was studying the possibilities of the plutonium bomb and allegedly the implosion fuse was perfected in the course of the work.

Knowledge of the existence of this fuse in 1939, if only at the design stage, would explain Heisenberg's persisting concern about the U^{235} enrichment question, since once the fuse had been developed it cut the bomb material required to a few kilos of U^{235}. If explosives technologists could improve on a fourfold compression factor the amount of material would be reduced by substantially more.

Professor Carl-Friedrich von Weizsäcker explained:

> "Certainly we made no attempt to build a bomb. This decision was made easy because we recognized the impossibility of manufacturing a bomb in Germany under war conditions. If people now say that we set out to avoid or obstruct the building of a bomb that is a dramatization, since we knew that we were not in a position to do so."[41]

That is what we are supposed to believe. The more important aspect of Heisenberg's G-39 paper, however, concentrated on what was to occupy him for the rest of the war, the atomic pile that never was and the saga of the heavy water moderator.

Reactor Theory

It has to be stressed that uranium work did not lie at the centre of Heisenberg's interests. When confronted with the assignment, he succeeded in familiarizing himself with the semi-technological field and during the war came to be regarded as the leading expert in the German Uranium Project. If, as he seems to have claimed, he was proposing, initially at least, to be a saboteur of Nazi nuclear science, Heisenberg was in a unique position to direct the uranium work along a false path, since, as the acknowledged senior theoretical physicist, he had been entrusted with the task of formulating the theory from the outset and, having set the guidelines, continued to influence the experimental side of matters until Germany's final surrender. At the end of 1939, having been cut off from most foreign literature since the outbreak of war, he was entering new territory in attempting to establish a theory for the working uranium pile or *Uranbrenner*. His summaries in the two papers dated 6 December 1939 and 29 February 1940 respectively are still accepted today as completely correct, or at least in so far as what they actually say. But there is a material omission in these two reports. One cannot at this late stage discount the possibility of an error in his theoretical workings, but all along one has the impression that Heisenberg did not want a working nuclear reactor, and it does not seem unreasonable to suspect that he deliberately drew a false conclusion on which he was to rely later.

In the preamble to the report, Heisenberg cited as his principal source of reactor theory an article published in the 9 June 1939 edition of the scientific periodical *Die Naturwissenschaften*[42] under the title *Can Technical Use Be Made of the Energy Content of Nuclei?* written by the physicist Dr Siegfried Flügge of the KWI for Physics at Berlin-Dahlem. Under a sub-title *The Control of Chain Reactions* Flügge had stated:

> "The decisive question for the technical application of the mechanism is manifestly this: is it possible to slow the chain cascade? Adler and Halban (*Nature*, Vol 143, 1939, p.739) have entered the debate and suggested the addition of cadmium salts to the mixture beforehand. In the absence of cadmium, the reaction would soar straightaway to a stationary temperature of 100,000 degrees C."

In the mentioned article Adler and Halban had warned:

> "The danger that a system containing uranium in high concentration might explode once the chain starts is considerable."

The idea of the instantaneous explosive chain reaction in a reactor is grounded in an error of theory caused by failing to take into the mathematical reckoning the small fraction of relatively long-lived neutrons which are emitted up to a minute after fission. What should have been done in the mathematical theory was to average the slowing down and diffusion time of the lifetime of the prompt neutrons liberated within a micro-second of fission added to the mean lifetime of the 0.75% of neutrons which emerge up to 80 seconds after fission occurs. That calculation would have shown that while neutron density increases exponentially with time, the stable Period of the Reactor is not "less than 1 second" but is about 54 seconds.

The delayed neutrons play the decisive role in the safe control of modern atomic energy plants and without them nuclear power reactors would not be feasible. Heisenberg may have been genuinely under a misapprehension. On the other hand, he may have realized that this would be a useful error to have in hand if he wanted to obstruct the development of a nuclear reactor.

In later reports he was never challenged when he relied on the argument as a reason for proceeding at slow ahead with the interminable low-level experiments which filled the next five years. Knowingly or not, Professor Heisenberg accepted that the Period of the Reactor was less than one second in length, after which the reactor blew up. After the war, in his reproduction report respecting the Haigerloch B8 experiment published in *FIAT Review of German Science 1939–1945* Heisenberg acknowledged that his theory had been at fault, admitting:

"American work shows that the Period of the Reactor is substantially extended by the delayed emergence of a number of those neutrons liberated during the fission process."

And in a report about the German project prepared by A. Weinberg and L. Nordheim for A. H. Compton on 8 November 1945 the authors were of the opinion that the importance of delayed neutrons for the stability of a nuclear reactor had probably not been considered. Even if Heisenberg knew all along, however, he could hardly say so in 1947. So, throughout the Second World War, Heisenberg believed, or let it be thought that he believed, that the *Uranbrenner* – the atomic pile for power – was impossible because the reactor would explode one sixth of a second after it went critical. He did not explain this fact in writing when setting down the theory originally, although one would think he must have informed his superiors at the *Heereswaffenamt* of his fears confidentially. To make some sense out of the fact that Heisenberg and the Uranium Project spent the war years performing interesting experiments of sub-reactor geometry, and obviously had no intention of actually bringing an experiment beyond the critical point since there was sufficient heavy water available in aggregate to moderate a working reactor by 1944 but no enthusiasm for doing so, Heisenberg must have convinced Hitler of the impossibility of building a working pile. Hitler did not want a nuclear reactor in any case because it was Jewish Physics. Probably he just waved a hand in dismissal, allowing Heisenberg and the reactor project to appear to be doing something useful to keep enemy Intelligence on the hop. That really is the only logical conclusion to be drawn from the manner in which the project was conducted.

The Basis of Reactor Design

The surest method of realizing energy production from the fissioning of uranium lay in enriching the U^{235} isotope, Heisenberg explained: the more the enrichment the smaller the reactor would be. If the proportion of the U^{235} isotope in the uranium material were to be enriched by 50%, from 0.7% to 1%, success was practically certain. However, such a proceeding was prohibitively expensive.

Natural uranium could be used in the reactor vessel in conjunction with another substance, a 'moderator', which slowed down the neutrons in the reaction without absorbing them. The deceleration increased the chances of a neutron finding a U^{235} isotope to fission. Ordinary water and paraffin were not suitable as a moderator, since, being rich in hydrogen atoms, they absorbed neutrons. On the other hand heavy water and very pure carbon satisfied the requirements. Slight impurities in them could spoil the reaction, however.

Heavy water (D^2O, deuterium oxide) is four times more efficient at slowing neutrons than the purest graphite and thus a much smaller reactor is required. Surrounding the reactor vessel would be a 'reflector', a wall of material enclosing the core of a nuclear pile against which escaping neutrons are scattered back into the reaction. Heisenberg indicated that graphite blocks would be suitable for this.

· He then described a number of possible reactor arrangements. The most important was a configuration three cubic metres in size consisting of 30 tons of pure carbon in the form of graphite and 25 tons of uranium oxide which, according to his calculations, would reach the critical point and supply energy. In the supplementary paper to G-39 of 29 February 1940 Heisenberg confessed to some misgivings regarding his design for a graphite reactor and this may have been prompted by Professor Harteck's interest in it.

Professor Paul Harteck (1902–1985) had graduated in chemistry at the University of Vienna and at the age of 26 had obtained his PhD at the University of Berlin. He is credited with the discovery of parahydrogen.

In 1933 he studied nuclear physics at the Cavendish Laboratory and during this period was set the task of producing a quantity of heavy water, which he achieved by spending several weeks passing an electric current through a small electrolytic cell. The amount was minute in comparison with all the gallons of water used in the process. Later he would have charge of Germany's heavy water production process. Following his return to Germany in 1934, Professor Harteck was appointed Director of the Institute of Physical Chemistry at Hamburg. He was a Nazi Party member and his team of five co-workers were known as "the Hamburg Bomb Group".

Heisenberg had remarked that the uranium machine would shut down automatically at certain peaks of temperature, and then only resume when the temperature had fallen again. This would occur because of the expansion of metals on heating, resulting in a lowering of density and an alteration of the various cross-sections. This same increase in temperature would cause an increase in the width of the capture bands formed of U^{238} isotopes. This was due to the nuclear Doppler Effect. The widening of these U^{238} capture bands caused many more neutrons to be absorbed, resulting in a lessening of fissions until the chain reaction collapsed altogether.

In earlier conversations with Heisenberg, Professor Harteck had suggested that uranium and moderator should be segregated into a heterogeneous design more favourable for the production of an efficient reactor. When he read the mention in Heisenberg's two pioneering papers of the problems of heat, Harteck realized that there was a better way of building a nuclear reactor altogether. If a pure carbon moderator was used at extremely low temperatures, the nuclear Doppler Effect would ensure that the width of the U^{238} capture bands would shrink and the reactor would produce no heat. If it did heat up, the chain reaction would collapse. Thus all the troublesome engineering arrangements inherent in an energy-producing reactor, such as heat transfer, core and fuel cooling and temperature control, would be obviated. We may infer from his obvious disinterest that Professor Heisenberg was not honestly in favour of building a working nuclear reactor at all, for this simple experimental zero-energy design would have been a good way to look at the problem of reactor stability. But he knew the terrible danger it presented. In his initial report he had observed:

"An extraordinarily intensive neutron and gamma radiation goes hand in hand with energy producion. Even in achieving only 10kW power, 10^{15} neutrons and gamma rays are created every second. The radiation is, therefore, 100,000 times greater than that produced in a large cyclotron. Even if a substantial amount of this radiation is absorbed in the core of the pile, nevertheless the working reactor would obviously require the provision of the most comprehensive biological shielding against radiation. This applies especially at the 'switching-on' of the machine, i.e. at criticality. At the moment when the temperature reaches the stationary value of 100°C, 10^8 calories are used to produce heat leaving an excess of 5 to 10^{19} neutrons and gamma rays liberated."

The very low temperature uranium pile would produce nothing but radioisotopes and the intensely radioactive decay products of nuclear fission. Radioisotopes do have modern applications in medicine, biochemistry, biology and industry, but Professor Harteck saw another use for them.

After the war Harteck admitted[43] that his idea in proposing to build a sub-zero uranium pile was to obtain nuclear waste for use against the populations of enemy cities. This seems to have been the first time that radiological material was being seriously suggested for military purposes. Such weapons are not outlawed by international treaties, since they are not classified as chemical. The evidence suggests that Hitler was prepared to entertain radiological warfare to stave off defeat but might not have resorted to it early on in the war unless he thought it would guarantee him victory.

Professor Harteck set about building an experimental sub-critical pile immediately. His idea was simple. Dry ice sublimates slowly at a temperature of −78°C and is as pure as one part in a million. Its oxygen atoms do not absorb neutrons in significant quantities at very low temperatures. Concluding that carbon dioxide ice was an ideal moderator for his proposed experiment, Harteck asked permission of the *Heereswaffenamt* to proceed and went ahead with it at once.

He had useful contacts with the firm of I G Farben, and on 8 April 1940 he induced the firm's research director, Dr Herold, to make him a gift of a 15-tonne block of dry ice to be delivered at the end of May. The War Office agreed to supply a railway wagon to expedite the consignment from Merseburg to Hamburg, and Harteck wrote to Diebner asking for 300 kilos of uranium. This figure was on the low side, but Harteck thought that it was all that was available.

46

It must have been obvious that Harteck was expecting to perform his experiment within a week of receiving his 15-tonne block of dry ice. Diebner had only 150 kilos of uranium oxide at Berlin-Dahlem, but Heisenberg was waiting for a large delivery from the War Ministry and probably had a large hoard besides. Diebner promised Heisenberg that the large amount would arrive in June and requested him to settle privately with Harteck.

Heisenberg suggested to Harteck in a letter that he was exaggerating the urgency of his experiment, since there were a number of preparations to be made first:

"... of course if there is for any reason any urgency in your experiments, you can go first by all means. But I should like to suggest that for the time being you content yourself with just 100 kilograms."

Heisenberg concluded in a very reasonable vein that he was quite prepared to let Diebner make the final decision. Harteck replied by return, emphasizing the obvious urgency, and begged Heisenberg to loan him from 20 May, for three weeks at the most, as much of his Leipzig stock as he possibly could allow. In the expectation that Heisenberg would relent, Harteck asked Dr Herold to delay shipping the ice until the last possible moment and spoke to Diebner twice to emphasize his need for a minimum supply of 600 kilos of uranium oxide.

At the end of May Diebner loaned him 50 kilos and Dr Riehl of the Auer Company brought him 135 kilos more. Heisenberg sent nothing. When the block of ice arrived at the beginning of June the experiment was doomed and the only useful information it yielded was criteria for the distribution of neutron density in certain arrangements of uranium oxide and dry ice[44].

Heisenberg's non-cooperation prevented Harteck from obtaining a figure for neutron multiplication. This would have enabled Harteck to calculate the quantity of materials he needed for a working pile. Both Harteck[44] and Wirtz[45] made this point subsequently.

A Windfall of Uranium Oxide: Harteck Tries Again

There was no shortage of uranium oxide in German-occupied Europe. In May 1940 German forces arriving at Oolen in Belgium had discovered at the warehouses of the Union Minière Company over 1200 tons of uranium oxide and 1000 tons of other refined uranium metals. The British Government had known about this stock since early 1939 but had dropped a plan to purchase it outright and so remove it from proximity to Germany. The President of Union Minière, Edgar Sengier, appears to have made a purely business decision to leave the material for the Germans when they invaded so that his company would find favour with Hitler should he emerge victorious in the coming war in western Europe. Sengier then ordered the uranium mines at Katanga in the Belgian Congo flooded and had the mined ores shipped from Lobito to the United States. In October 1939 he transferred his offices to New York[46].

The Germans controlled the Joachimstal mines in Czechoslovakia and thus held virtually all the uranium in Europe. There was in fact so much uranium in their hands that Professor Harteck set about planning his ambitious second experiment, a heterogeneous design consisting of 20 tonnes of uranium oxide in a lattice of shafts embedded throughout a 30-tonne block of dry ice. As soon as he announced his intention, he ran up against the determined opposition of Heisenberg, who argued that the experiment was so big that all Harteck would learn from it was a great deal about 20 tonnes of dirty uranium oxide and 30 tonnes of dry ice. Why Harteck thought that was something worth knowing he could not imagine. He expected that it would not work, however, or at least not unless Harteck sent the uranium oxide to a factory for purification first.

Harteck then came under growing pressure from other quarters, probably orchestrated by Heisenberg, and these argued that it was too extravagant for a first experiment to use 50 tonnes of materials to do the whole programme at once, while Heisenberg returned to the attack by remonstrating about the unprofessional approach to the experiment.

Bitterly Harteck was forced to concede defeat, refusing to accept their opinion. He resented Heisenberg in particular, commenting that, to his knowledge, Heisenberg had never contributed a single basic idea leading to the solution of the problems of nuclear fission: he found it inexplicable that a theoretical physicist who had never been involved in a large experimental venture could be appointed as leader of a technological enterprise. It was worse than merely poor judgment. Harteck attributed Germany's failure to produce a nuclear weapon to the antagonistic attitude existing between the theoretical physicists and the experimentalists: the former considered the latter as beneath them, "a few egoists pushed the others aside".[47]

What seems to have been Heisenberg's real worry over Harteck's proposed reactor was that since it operated at sub-zero temperatures it might be easier to stabilize it with control rods when it went critical: if this sort of primitive reactor worked, it would produce the nuclear waste which Harteck wanted to use in radiological weapons. Harteck felt sure that such a programme would have brought the war to a swift end in Hitler's favour.

Was Professor Harteck serious about radioactive bombing? One must profess astonishment and credit him for having come clean on the matter after the war. Few others were honest. Considering how the dry-ice low-temperature reactor would have placed Germany's nuclear programme on an entirely different footing, he stated:

"You must be thankful this didn't occur. Not that an atomic bomb would have been made. But if you have a carbon dioxide reactor and you let it run for a certain time, the cubes or rods of uranium would have become highly radioactive. Much radioactive material could have been made which could have been thrown about. That would have been very bad[47]."

CHAPTER 4

Plutonium, Paraffin
and Moderators

IN THE AMERICAN scientific periodical *Physical Review* of 1 September 1939 Niels Bohr of Copenhagen and John Wheeler of Princeton theorized that if during fission the U^{238} nucleus captured two successive neutrons then the new compound structure should be even more fissionable than U^{235}, which of course suggested another kind of atom bomb.

Professor von Weizsäcker obtained the June 1940 issue of the same journal, the last available internationally. It contained an article offering proof of the substance ^{239}Np (neptunium) in research on the Berkeley cyclotron. This tended to validate the Bohr-Wheeler hypothesis. In his report to the *Heereswaffenamt G59-Concerning the Possibility of Extracting Energy from U^{238}* on 17 July 1940, Professor von Weizsäcker left open the question as to whether atomic decay proceeded beyond neptunium, but if it did it would probably be an explosive, he said. (In the event plutonium – element 94 – was confirmed as an explosive "with the same unimaginable effects as U^{235}" and "much easier to obtain from uranium since it can be separated chemically" in Heisenberg's paper *Die theoretische Grundlagen für die Energiegewinnung aus der Uranspaltung* presented to the Haus der Deutschen Forschung on 26 February 1942.) The Viennese experimenters Hernegger and Schintlmeister[48] had reached virtually the same conclusion about the new transuranic substance at about the same time as von Weizsäcker, although they did not lodge their paper in Berlin until December 1940.

Many millions of words have been written by learned historians in an attempt to make some sense of the German uranium project during the

Second World War. Thousands of documents have been inspected, but the story lacks coherency. The muddle over graphite is a good example. Many commentators have attempted to show that the German reactor project failed because of an error in materials measurement prejudicial to the use of graphite as a moderator. If the Germans had had graphite instead of heavy water, so their argument goes, then they would have had a critical reactor in 1941 and plutonium and a bomb, and so on. The evidence does not support this line of reasoning because in 1944 there was enough heavy water available for a working reactor but no attempt was made to reach the critical point. Moreover, to build and run such a reactor would have required a tremendous effort, and it would not have proceeded in Germany as rapidly as it did in the United States, where large manpower and enormous material resources free from constant aerial bombardment had still not produced a plutonium bomb which worked by the end of hostilities in Europe.

There is in any case rather more to the error in the graphite evaluation than meets the eye. Professor Walther Bothe (1891–1957) was an opponent of the Nazi regime and, after having been roughed up by the Nazis at Heidelberg in 1933, spent a long period in convalescence at a Badenweiler sanatorium from where he did not return to the University until 1937. Bothe had been frequently accused of scientific fraud by the Nazis before the war. There being no smoke without fire, he was probably quite prepared to repay them in his own currency if he got the chance. Professor Peter Jensen, his assistant, was a member of Heisenberg's intimate circle of three and was aware that Heisenberg wanted heavy water as the official moderator and not graphite.

In his first pioneering paper in December 1940 Heisenberg had said that graphite was suitable as a moderator and he was visualizing in his mind's eye a reactor of 25 tonnes of uranium oxide and 30 tonnes of graphite. He even had a *Most Favourable Design of Reactor* in which there would be layers of uranium oxide, heavy water and graphite. In his supplementary report of 29 February 1940 he had changed his mind and said that "the properties of graphite make it unsuitable as a neutron moderator". Nobody else thought this at the time and he submitted nothing in writing to substantiate his statement about a matter which was obviously critical to the development of the reactor project.

How convenient it was then that when Bothe and Jensen reported their results on graphite in a bulletin under the title G-71 The Absorption of Thermal Neutrons in Electro-Graphite[49] dated 20 January 1941, their

51

paper should state that experiments on the purest carbon available showed the rate of neutron capture to be so high that it was of no use as a moderator. Actually the measurements were incorrect. Professor Heisenberg explained in an interview postwar:

"Bothe's Heidelberg people got about a ton of graphite. An error slipped into his experiment. His values were too high but we assumed they were correct and so we did not think that graphite could be used. He had built a pile of graphite pieces but in between the graphite pieces there was always some air and the nitrogen of the air has high neutron absorption. Somehow he must have forgotten this. I don't know why but it is understandable."[50]

So Professor Bothe, who had been involved in neutron research since it began in 1931, had forgotten that fresh air absorbs neutrons. Without Heisenberg's knowledge, Professors Joos and Hanle at the University of Göttingen submitted research papers to the *Heereswaffenamt* even though they were not affiliated to the official programme. Their treatises *G-46/G-85 Concerning the Existence of Boron and Cadmium in Graphite*[51] dated 18 April 1941 contradicted Bothe's erroneous opinion. The *Heereswaffenamt* admitted the contradictory report and accepted that graphite was suitable as a moderator in papers G39(24) and G(40)(a) but decided against it on economic grounds.

Heavy Water

Neutrons are absorbed by the hydrogen atoms in ordinary water (H^2O). Heavy water (D^2O) is water with the hydrogen atoms removed so that the liquid which is left consists only of its deuterium atoms. Neutrons collide with deuterium molecules and lose much of their velocity but are not absorbed, which is why heavy water is an exceptionally efficient moderator when used with natural uranium in reactor processes. The production of D^2O is extremely costly: at Vemork near Rjukan in Norway, 200 kilometres west of Oslo, in 1940 the world's only large production facility, 1000 KwH of electricity was required to turn out a single gramme of heavy water. Heavy water cannot be contaminated in the normal course of events and can be used indefinitely.

A Hypothetical Meeting

There is no record of Professor Heisenberg ever having met Hitler. Nevertheless, since the latter preferred to be addressed by people who knew exactly what they were talking about instead of intermediaries, it seems logical that Hitler would have asked him to call at some stage. In broad terms Professor Heisenberg would have explained why he believed a working reactor to be impossible. As the obvious corollary, a plutonium bomb would not be possible. A U^{235} bomb would be prohibitively expensive. The Führer would then have asked, "Well what is possible?" to which Heisenberg could hardly have replied, "Nothing," for such an answer would have jeopardized the continued existence of the Uranium Project. We simply have to assume that something was put on the table. Following the logical track proposed in this book, I suggest that Heisenberg would have informed him: "I could produce a very low-yield atom bomb built in the laboratory for a rocket hitting the ground at Mach 3.5." Whereupon Hitler, rising and offering his hand in parting, would have replied, "Then we'll have to settle for that, won't we?" Actually the talk would probably have been far more circuitous than I have expressed it here, but certainly the gist must have been along those lines. Sometime in 1940 a schedule of experiments was drawn up by Heisenberg which were more useful for bomb-making than reactor-building.

Heisenberg's Mysterious Leipzig Experiments

In May 1940, at Leipzig, Professor Heisenberg took delivery of a tonne of uranium oxide sent by the *Heereswaffenamt* with which he was to start his reactor theory experiments. In *G23 Determination of the Diffusion Length of Thermal Neutrons in Heavy Water* [52], dated 7 August 1940, Heisenberg described the results of examining how the velocity of neutrons emitted by a 480 mg radium-beryllium source was reduced during their passage through 9 litres of heavy water. In *G22 Determination of the Diffusion Length of Thermal Neutrons in Preparation 38* [53], submitted in December 1940, he reported on work involving neutrons emitted into small samples of uranium oxide in a sphere of 12-cm radius. These experiments represented the preliminary work preparatory to designing a hypothetical uranium oxide reactor moderated by heavy water.

In March 1941 Heisenberg carried out experiment L-I at Leipzig University.[54] He said he wanted to establish constants using uranium oxide with paraffin. The two materials were layered alternately in a cylindrical tank. Paraffin is so rich in hydrogen atoms that it is useless as a moderator. From the experiment there was, of course, no neutron multiplication to report. Paraffin is very useful as a reflector. Used to enclose the reactor core, it prevents neutrons escaping. If the uranium fuel is arranged in alternate layers with paraffin, there could never be a chain reaction, because neutrons would be confined and absorbed within their respective layers. If one had in aggregate a critical mass of uranium, as in a bomb for example, and wanted to keep the material in sub-critical quantities with no passage of neutrons between the layers, paraffin would be a good way to do it.

There was now a long wait of five months before sufficient heavy water would be available for experiment L-II at Leipzig. During this respite there suddenly burst on the scene a scientific paper which resurrected the spectre of Harteck's radioactive weapons and worse.

CHAPTER 5

The Open Road to
the Atom Bomb

EARLY IN SEPTEMBER 1941 Professor Heisenberg received a copy
of a scientific paper of 29 pages entitled *On the Question of Initiating
Chain Reactions* [55] which explained how, from a practical standpoint, a
chain reaction could be simply and effectively brought about by the
use of methane as the moderator in a very low temperature reactor. The
author was Professor Fritz Houtermans, a Jewish scientist who was
perhaps the most brilliant physicist in the field of chain reaction theory
in the Third Reich. He was employed at the Post Office Research Institute
under Baron Manfred von Ardenne at the Lichterfelde-Ost laboratory
in Berlin. The Post Office research was funded independently. The
Postmaster-General, Dr Wilhelm Ohnesorge, was known as a pro-Bomb
Cabinet Minister close to Hitler.

The primary purpose of the report was to show the quickest and most
effective means of having a working nuclear pile. It was the obvious first
stepping stone into the atomic age. Houtermans also explained how a new
explosive U^{239} (plutonium) could be bred in his reactor. He argued that if
heat and energy were not required, then the use of heavy water or graphite
as a moderator was not necessary. If the reactor was required only for the
production of radioisotopes, then a carbon-based substance in a very low
temperature was all that was needed.

What he had observed in the course of his experiments with modera-
tors was that hydrogen molecules in carbon compounds absorbed far
fewer neutrons in extreme sub-zero temperatures. It was almost certainly
attributable to the nuclear Doppler Effect: he thought it probable that
the Doppler Effect alone would enable a liquid carbon substance to be

used as moderator. He considered the most favourable to be liquid methane, CH^4, a colourless, odourless, flammable gas which is liquid in the temperature range $-164°C$ to $-186°C$.

In common with all other Reich physicists, Houtermans was unaware of the stabilizing influence of the delayed neutrons of fission, but he had no concerns regarding the safety and stability of his design. Since the machine only operated at a very low temperature, the chain reaction would automatically collapse once the temperature began to rise substantially towards freezing point. While in theory he planned to use regulating rods to control neutron multiplication, in practice Houtermans would have found his reactor unexpectedly stable due to the unsuspected effect of the delayed neutrons.

Summarizing the paper in a section headed *The Significance of a Chain Reaction in a Low Temperature Environment as a Neutron Source and as an Apparatus for Transforming Isotopes*, Houtermans confirmed that because U^{239} (i.e. Pu^{239} plutonium) is a different element from uranium and, therefore, chemically distinct, concentrations of Pu^{239} should be obtainable relatively easily by chemical separation from the spent reactor fuel, and this would be an explosive, since it was also fissionable.

Houtermans' paper was the first properly argued scientific thesis to enter circulation in Hitler's Germany proposing a simple, low-temperature atomic pile for the production of large quantities of radioisotopes and the bomb material plutonium. It was perfectly clear to Heisenberg that Houtermans' methane pile would run. Once Ohnesorge, the Postmaster-General, saw the report he would have brought it to the attention of Hitler.

Within a tamper of U^{238}, plutonium has a critical mass of about 11 kilos, but substantially less is required depending on the force of the implosion designed to detonate the bomb. Where the compression factor is three, for example, then only a few kilos of pure plutonium are needed. Five kilos of plutonium isotopes were produced during the fission cycle of a single reactor for every 20 tonnes of U^{238}.

In a biography Heisenberg was quoted as saying that a faction comprising von Weizsäcker, Karl Wirtz, Peter Jensen and Houtermans met on several occasions to discuss the implications of the report, for:

> "We were not absolutely sure, but we now saw that it was almost certain. Von Weizsäcker in particular and I were deeply disturbed. It now looked like it was definitely possible to make a reactor. We agreed that if we could make them, then

the Americans could too. If they could make reactors, then plutonium was probably possible too, and so on. It was from September 1941 that we saw before us an open road leading to the atom bomb."[56]

In another work, Heisenberg explained how he saw things at the time:

"The situation for physicists in the United States, especially for emigrés from Germany, was totally different from our own. In America they would be convinced that they are fighting for a just cause and against an evil one. The emigrés, precisely because they had been welcomed so hospitably by the Government of the United States, would have felt obliged to contribute to the best of their ability to the American cause. But is an atom bomb, which can kill 100,000 civilians at a stroke, a weapon like all the others? Can one justify the atom bomb with the dictum 'A just end, but not an evil end, justifies the means'? Is it ethical therefore to build atom bombs for a just cause but not for an evil one? And if one accepts the principle, and it is a principle which has been imposed repeatedly throughout history, who decides what is a just cause and what an evil one? It is easy enough to establish that Hitler and National Socialism is evil. But is the American cause good? Is the principle not also valid that a society is to be condemned as evil by its choice of means? I replied, 'Why don't you speak with Niels Bohr in Copenhagen about this? If he is of the opinion that we are wrong to do this work on uranium and we should abandon it, I would find that a persuasive argument.'"[57]

The Meeting in Copenhagen with Bohr

Niels Bohr (1885–1962) had been appointed Professor of Physics at the University of Copenhagen in 1916 and was awarded the Nobel Prize in Physics in 1922. Heisenberg had been his pupil during the period 1924 to 1926. He was Jewish and emigrated from Denmark in 1943 in advance of the pogrom of Danish Jews. Bohr was understandably suspicious of Heisenberg, but, as the latter was unaware of this, it was arranged for the two of them to meet during a lecture at Bohr's Copenhagen Institute in

1941. Heisenberg's ostensible purpose seems to have been to let Bohr know in roundabout terms that senior German atom physicists would prevent an atom bomb being built in the hope that the Americans, with whom Germany was not yet at war, might abandon their own development, if they had one, thus keeping the war non-nuclear. Exactly how all this was to be arranged and agreed between the respective physicists defies the imagination. It seemed more likely to Bohr that this was either a warning to the United States that Germany was close to the atom bomb and the Americans should stay out of the war, or that Heisenberg was spying for Germany. The visit was dangerous and ill-advised[58] and Heisenberg came away empty-handed. It might be unwise to read too much into the developments in late 1941, but the feasibility of building an atomic bomb, particularly if it would be used against Germany, must have given Heisenberg food for thought. Whereas previously he might have been against the idea completely, maybe at this juncture he began to see reasons for rectifying his outlook.

The Leipzig L-II Experiment

Professor Heisenberg returned to Leipzig University where, on 28 October 1941, he carried out experiment L-II[59]. An aluminium sphere was filled with concentric alternate layers of uranium oxide and 150 litres of heavy water. In the centre was placed a nickel ball of 1.95-cm diameter containing a radium-beryllium *Präparat* which sprayed neutrons in all directions. Instruments were positioned around the sphere to measure the neutron multiplication and a neutron increment of 10% was recorded in the interior of the sphere, although this was lost to the aluminium at the periphery.

This stacked design of pile has been described as a little peculiar. Since the *Präparat* was a ball at the very centre of the sphere, the neutrons would radiate out through the alternating layers diagonally. This would not be a good way to obtain neutron multiplication, but what a central neutron source does permit, however, is for the pile to be dismantled at the end of the experiment so that isotopic transformations in each of the uranium layers can be measured along their length and with reference to their position in the sphere. Such a proceeding would be more useful for gauging where plutonium formed than for planning a heat reactor. Heisenberg's explanation was that neutrons radiating diagonally passed through alternate layers in which the heavy water layers were three to four times wider than the uranium layers. This presented a better opportunity for the neutrons to be slowed optimally for fission, since losses of medium-fast, or partially slowed, neutrons to the U^{238} capture bands were high. The measurements would also show where neutron capture was thickest in the uranium, and, if such was the information required, enable the optimum velocity of a neutron for capture by the U^{235} resonances to be established. That would also be useful information if the real purpose of the experiment was to work out the best arrangement for breeding plutonium in the uranium material.

Heisenberg admitted that the Leipzig experiments were "unusual" insofar as:

"we put the neutron source in the middle of a sphere of heavy water, then we measured the capture of the neutrons in the middle of the sphere. It was the diffusion of neutrons from the centre to the outside which we measured."[60]

The purpose of placing the neutron source at the centre of the apparatus, according to a scientific paper he wrote in 1943, was:

"to measure the volume of neutrons escaping at the surface of the sphere so as to determine whether there was a surplus over the neutrons emitted by the *Präparat*. If there was a surplus, then therein would lie the proof that a bigger construction would eventually lead to a critical uranium pile."[61]

Further Concerns about the Houtermans Paper

On 28 November 1941 Heisenberg led a stream of notable visitors to the Lichterfelde-Ost laboratory of Professor von Ardenne. According to the Swiss historian Robert Jungk[62] he had a further heart-to-heart talk with Professor Houtermans in company with Professor von Weizsäcker. This was a long, frank discussion about the work Houtermans had been doing for von Ardenne, and in conclusion it seems to have been agreed that their overwhelming priority was to conceal from the Government departments involved "*the imminent feasibility* of manufacturing atomic weapons" by which, as we have seen, he meant Pu^{239} in a low temperature reactor for a bomb.

On 10 December Otto Hahn and three colleagues from the KWI for Chemistry also called in, but what was discussed was not revealed in an official biography of Hahn[63], although it appears likely that Houtermans had already been told by Ohnesorge by that date what the Führer required from him. Early in December 1941 Houtermans had a soul-searching conversation with his protector Professor Max von Laue on the subject of a secret assignation he had been given and in connection with this task he is supposed to have sent a cryptic telegram (from a wartime Germany controlled by the Gestapo) to his former colleague Eugene P. Wigner in the United States. The message read, "Hurry! We're nearly there!" Obviously Houtermans believed in living dangerously.

Despite all the long faces, the Jewish Houtermans must have known that, at least as far as he was concerned, there was a certain inevitability about it all and so he knuckled down to the task in hand.

The Nuclear Project is Wound Down

On 3 December 1941, the Minister for Armaments, Dr Fritz Todt, notified Hitler of the faltering state of the military economy and advised him bluntly that any unplanned future expansion would have to be financed from the budgets of other departments. Consequently Professor Erich Schumann, the Director of Military Research at the *Heereswaffenamt*, ordered a reappraisal of the uranium project and warned leading scientists that the continued financial support of the War Ministry for the nuclear project was dependent on the promise of a definite military application in the short term.

On 16 December 1941, following a conference of Directors of the various Physics Institutes at the *Heereswaffenamt* HQ, an enquiry into the progress of the uranium research was started for the information of the Head of Army Ordnance, General Leeb. Whereas the report was positive in recommending that the industrial exploitation of nuclear power would benefit both the general economy and the Wehrmacht, Professor Schumann was not convinced, and all the signs were clearly visible that the military would relinquish the project even before the review had been completed.

In January 1942 it was agreed between Schumann, Leeb and Dr Vögler, President of the KW Foundation, that the latter organization would take over the research in harness with the Reich Research Council, an agency of the Ministry of Education and Science. Professor Esau, an anti-Bomb Nazi, was appointed its scientific head while the Education Minister, Bernhard Rust, would be its President.

The Army research team led by Dr Kurt Diebner was to retain a measure of independence under the restructuring and would continue to be subject to War Ministry control. As if to underline the insignificance which the *Heereswaffenamt* now attached to the uranium project, Professors von Weizsäcker and Harteck were served conscription papers that month for military service on the Russian Front and Heisenberg was obliged to exert all his influence to persuade Professor Schumann to rescind the orders and restore the two physicists to their reserved occupations.

More Odd Experiments by Heisenberg

Heisenberg himself was to continue with his intriguing experiments begun at Leipzig. At the end of 1940 the *Heereswaffenamt* had decided that uranium experiments were to use cast metal instead of uranium oxide powder. The Auer Company of Berlin had the contract for refining the uranium oxide confiscated at Oolen in Belgium, and a small plant had been set up at Oranienburg which turned out about a tonne of refined uranium oxide per month. The product was contaminated with boron, a neutron absorber, and therefore unsatisfactory. A quantity of uranium metal powder of good quality had been placed at Heisenberg's disposal and he set to work on two small experiments: L-III, to investigate the scale of neutron losses in the outer shell and separating panels of the aluminium container, and a second to see the effect of fast neutrons sprayed directly into uranium metal powder. By coincidence, Professor Stetter, an SS-physicist with a special interest in plutonium as an explosive, submitted a paper announcing his own preparations for a similar experiment, but Heisenberg decided to forge ahead because the sphere he was using was larger.

Experiment L-II had shown a slight interim neutron multiplication prior to losses in the aluminium vessel. As all previous investigations had concentrated on fissioning U^{235} using slow neutrons, he had the idea of seeing what the effect would be of using unslowed neutrons on the U^{238} capture bands. He explained:

> "The object of the experiment was to determine the neutron multiplication brought about solely by fissioning U^{235} with fast neutrons."[64]

61

Within a square tin box a simple 15-cm diameter sphere was fitted which contained the uranium powder and 500 mgs of the radium-beryllium element at its centre. The outcome showed that U^{238} could not be used as of itself to produce energy. And if he wanted to know the fact, the experiment also demonstrated that fast neutrons had to be decelerated by a moderator such as heavy water before appreciable amounts would be captured by the U^{238} resonances for plutonium breeding purposes.

On 6 January 1942 at Berlin-Dahlem, with four helpers, he embarked on experiment B-III[65]. This was a repetition of the L-I uranium oxide/paraffin test examining the advantages of having uranium metal powder instead of the oxide. It had several additional goals: to test the effectiveness of the layer thicknesses as proposed by theory, and to establish to what degree the rare U^{235} in the material should be enriched to enable a working atomic pile to be built using ordinary water or paraffin instead of the heavy water moderator[66], this being, as he knew, a very optimistic proposition.

The configuration was an aluminium sphere of 28.5-cm radius containing 551 kilos of uranium metal powder in nineteen concentric layers alternate with eighteen layers of paraffin stacked horizontally, the *Präparat* ball being placed at the centre. As with L-I there was no neutron multiplication and nor was any expected, for:

> "The experimental assemblies containing paraffin as a moderator were not suitable for neutron multiplication. They were to measure important constants for later designs."[67]

Measurement was made of the neutron distribution inside the sphere and in the ordinary water surrounding it. It was concluded that uranium metal powder was better than uranium oxide and

> "confirmed other experiments in that when evaluating the neutron figure, account should be taken of neutron capture by U^{238} isotopes".

In other words, experiments L-I and B-III with layered uranium and paraffin were concerned primarily with measuring the generation of neutrons and their capture by U^{238} isotopes, for on concluding an experiment the amount of U^{239} (which eventually decays into plutonium) forming in the uranium material was to be measured.

Speer Attempts to Resurrect the Official Project

On 7 February 1942 Dr Todt was killed when his personal Heinkel bomber crashed taking off in poor visibility at Rastenburg. Hitler decided to appoint Speer at once as successor to Todt. As has been mentioned, Speer was an enthusiast for the atom bomb, but soon found that the *Völkischer Beobachter* began to stir against him whenever he approached Hitler on the subject of atomic physics. The first convention of the Reich Research Council was held at its Berlin Steglitz HQ on 26 February 1942 under the chairmanship of Reich Minister Rust. Substantial funds became available to the project for the first time once Rust had become convinced that the heat reactor could definitely be built. In what must have been a speech glowing with optimism Heisenberg assured him not only that atomic reactors for energy production were "undoubtedly possible" but that an enormously powerful explosive could be bred in them.

In early May 1942 Speer arranged for Goering to be appointed head of a newly independent Reich Research Council. The restructuring was intended to emphasize the importance of the new committee which Speer was planning should oversee a progressive research programme for military purposes. Goering's presidential council consisted of 21 members who were either Ministers, Chiefs of Staff or high Party officials and thus the uranium project was taken over completely by the political side after all.

The Last Two Leipzig Experiments

Heisenberg's paper G-136: *The Proof by Experiment of Effective Neutron Multiplication in a Layered arrangement of Heavy Water and Uranium Metal in a Sphere*[68] was undated but delivered with a covering letter dated July 1942, the month following an accident which destroyed Heisenberg's Leipzig apparatus. The report was stamped *Geheime Kommandosache* (i.e. *very secret*), an unusual classification which may possibly be explained by the conclusion in the summary that:

"A spherical arrangement of 17-cm wide layers of heavy water and 4-cm wide layers of uranium metal density 10 separated by 2 to 5mm thick aluminium support material has a *negative* coefficient for neutron absorption. The mere enlargement of the layered arrangement described herein will lead to a uranium pile for the production of nuclear energy."

In L-II the previous year, using uranium oxide, the experiment had given a positive neutron coefficient which was very marginal: there had been a neutron multiplication but this had been lost to the aluminium material of the sphere.

L-IV consisted of two aluminium hemispheres bolted together at the equator. A chimney was fitted through which the *Präparat* would be dropped into the centre to initiate the reaction. The apparatus was bedded on a foundation of waterproofed wooden beams in a zinc tub filled with ordinary water. The internal arrangement was a 17-cm radius aluminium sphere with walls 1.2 mm thick. This contained 140 kilos of heavy water and the *Präparat*. The inner sphere rested on a lower hemispherical shell of 5-mm aluminium plate containing 90 kilos of uranium powder of density 10.8 and this in turn rested on a larger hemisphere filled with 660 kilos of uranium powder of density 9.34.

The measurements showed a neutron multiplication of 13%, and with this apparatus Heisenberg had succeeded in generating more neutrons than provided by the *Präparat* source. Simply by increasing the size of the sub-reactor one would eventually have a working uranium pile for the production of nuclear energy.

For the reactor builder the next step was an experiment in which the materials were increased and on 31 July 1942 in G-161 *Observations on the Planned Intermediate Experiment with 1.5 tonnes Heavy Water and 3 tonnes Uranium Metal* Heisenberg did precisely that. It was logical. But what was not logical was that meanwhile he had set up a duplicate of L-IV. He knew what would happen. The uranium fuel would gradually become more radioactive with the products of fission and plutonium being formed in the U^{238} resonances, but what would that have to do with reactor technology?

On 2 June 1942 the experiment began. 750 kilos of uranium metal powder in the outer shere surrounded a central sphere of heavy water. As before, the apparatus was immersed in a vat of ordinary water, the *Präparat* was dropped into the centre via the chimney, and Heisenberg, Mr and Mrs Döpel, master mechanic W. Paschen and technician G. Kunze, who monitored the gamma-radiation instrumentation, all sat back for a few months to see what would happen next.

In the U-metal/paraffin experiment B-III, measurements were made of neutron capture by the resonances along the diagonals outward from the central *Präparat*. From this information it was a straightforward matter to plot where the diminishing neutron velocities coincided with the greatest incidences of neutron capture, and this was in fact known as *Factor e/w* where w = probability of resonance capture.

The concentric inner sphere of Heisenberg's L-V experiment at Leipzig contained 220 litres of heavy water, the small nickel ball with the radium-beryllium neutron source being at its centre. This *Präparat* played a twofold role. It emitted neutrons into the heavy water where they lost a degree of momentum before proceeding into the surrounding uranium metal powder. Here they fissioned U^{235} atoms to release more neutrons into the reaction or were captured by U^{238} isotopes to decay into plutonium. Additionally, gamma radiation from the neutron source generated photoneutrons in the heavy water and these also entered the uranium. Over a period of many months this 'experiment' would be a subtle means of uranium enrichment, since a measureable proportion of the U^{238} capture band converted into the fissile isotopes of plutonium. After his return to Leipzig University on 23 June 1942, it was noticed that the sphere, which had been quietly fissioning for three weeks, was leaking bubbles. The equipment was raised from the water and an access hatch opened to inspect the interior. A hissing sound was followed by a jet of flame. The sphere was hosed down with water until the fire appeared to be extinguished. The heavy water was then drained from the inner sphere to prevent its accidental contamination, after which the main sphere was re-sealed and lowered back into the water tank for safety. A few hours later the apparatus began to give off bubbles once more and the water in the containing tank began to boil. On closer inspection it was seen that the sphere was vibrating and beginning to swell in size. The laboratory was evacuated and shortly after there was an explosion involving a hailstorm of burning uranium powder. The fire brigade succeeded in dowsing all fires except that in the sphere which was allowed to burn out over the next few days.

How did this fire start? Possibly fissioned material in the powdered uranium began to warm up. As it expanded, the pressure cracked the seal holding the two aluminium hemispheres together, allowing water to enter from the shielding tank. This would have oxidized the uranium, generating more heat. But the ignition source is a mystery. The material burnt out and the attempt to do whatever it was that was being attempted failed. So terminated this series of experiments, the purpose of the last of which seems not to have been questioned too closely previously.

Professor Goudsmit Not Deceived

The only military scientist on record as believing that Heisenberg had been involved in an attempt to build a German atom bomb is Professor Samuel Goudsmit. In his book *Alsos- The Failure in German Science* (Sigma, London, 1947) on page 183 Professor Goudsmit reproduced two sketches contained in Heisenberg's official German wartime report respecting the B-III uranium/paraffin experiment. Under a drawing of the chimneyed sphere appeared the caption "Germany's Atom Bomb" and the words "Germany's experimental uranium pile which they believed would make a bomb". Beside a slightly adulterated version of the cut-through diagram he wrote, "Diagram for the experimental 'bomb' which consisted of layers of uranium and paraffin". Professor Goudsmit was Jewish and had lost both parents at Auschwitz. His book was a non-scientific publication very popular at the time and it is possible that he was merely attempting to ridicule Heisenberg's scientific circle. But one can interpret it in another sense. Perhaps this was as far as Goudsmit, who was restrained by the various US secrecy laws, was permitted to go in print with his allegation. Joke or not, this device would have worked as the warhead of a V-2 rocket.

After five or six months in the sub-reactor sphere, the uranium powder was enriched with plutonium. In the bomb casing the material would be stacked in alternate layers with paraffin. The paraffin in the top hemisphere layers prevent premature fission by the highly radioactive Pu^{240} plutonium isotopes which would otherwise spoil the reaction when the bomb is detonated. The bottom hemisphere would be filled with iron ballast. The weight of bomb core, casing and ballast material acting as an anvil would have been limited to one tonne, the payload of a V-2, the speed of the rocket at impact rendering superfluous the four or so tonnes of HE necessary to set off the device in normal circumstances. Impact was at Mach 3.5. Because detonation would not be uniform around the bomb sphere, this method would have resulted in a 'fizzle' equivalent to several dozen tonnes of TNT, an earthquake effect and meltdown with radioactive fallout.

It was a brilliant concept, cheap to manufacture anywhere and not difficult to produce in numbers. The failure of the Leipzig experiment after only three weeks signalled the end of Professor Heisenberg's participation in the project and in midsummer 1942 the project was transferred elsewhere.

CHAPTER 6

The German Post Office Takes Over

"I, of all people, did in fact lead the way for the great advance in atomic development in the German Reich."

> Wilhelm Ohnesorge, Postmaster General, 1937-1945
> Quoted from his obituary, Soldatenzeitung, East Berlin,
> 10 March 1962.

ALBERT SPEER[69] recalled that, although Hitler did speak to him occasionally of the possibilities of the atom bomb, the strategic benefits of having it eluded the Führer. The subject was a source of irritation to Speer, for he knew that there was in existence some sort of secret arrangement involving the Post Office about which he was being left completely in the dark, and this appeared to be a matter on which, as Armaments Minister, he really ought to have been consulted.

Explaining that there were 2200 recorded points of reference in his conferences with Hitler, and that there was only a single occasion when the subject of nuclear research appeared on the agenda, being passed over "with laconic brevity", Speer noted Hitler's strengthening resolve not to pursue the matter.

Hitler's objection to the atom bomb was fundamental. He had read somewhere (almost certainly the article by Professor Jean Thibaud of the Sorbonne published on 12 March 1941) that a nuclear explosion might proceed to ignite all the hydrogen atoms in the atmosphere, transforming the world into a glowing star. German physicists could not guarantee that the theory was definitely wrong: even at Los Alamos in July 1945 the Italian-American physicist Fermi wondered aloud whether the test bomb he was about to ignite might trigger the heavens, destroying every living thing on earth. Speer thus concluded:

"Even if Hitler had not been against nuclear research on doctrinal grounds [i.e. Aryan Physics]: even if the stage we had reached in investigating the principles in June 1942 had provided the atomic physicists with an objective for the investment of thousands of millions of marks towards producing the atom bomb, it would have been impossible for our strained war economy to have brought together the technicians, materials and priorities for the project."[70]

It is an odd thing that Hitler should have appeared to shun atomic physics when speaking to Speer whilst openly affirming his enthusiasm for its future prospects to his closer companions at table. Martin Bormann's stenographer Henry Picker recorded[71] that Hitler considered the splitting of the atom to be the most important of all scientific achievements for Germany's future to the extent that it was the Führer himself who was inspirational in having the short documentary film *Gold* starring Hans Albers exhibited repeatedly in cinemas in order to popularize the subject of nuclear science. Anything short of a chain reaction was Aryan Physics.

Albert Speer wrote disapprovingly[72] about the unaccountable optimism in Hitler's demeanour whenever the subject of nuclear energy came under discussion in the early summer of 1942, and the Führer's disposition appeared to Speer to have the closest possible connection with a clique consisting of the Postmaster-General, Ohnesorge, Goebbels and Hitler's personal photographer, Heinrich Hoffmann, who were all apparently party to some big secret.

Speer concluded that, since Hitler spurned responsible sources of information and preferred to rely instead on having knowledge peddled to him by these amateurs, it all went to prove not only Hitler's partiality for dabbling, but also how little he understood of the scientific principles involved.

Hitler's Reichspost handled all telecommunications as well as the mails and had a large budget for research. Part of this was allocated to an atomic development programme for which the Postmaster-General, Wilhelm Ohnesorge, had a particular interest. The Post Office was almost completely excluded from the proceedings of the official physics community in Germany, with whom few relations were maintained beyond the odd house-call, and it was in this atmosphere of secrecy that the atomic project was enabled to flourish.

Wilhelm Ohnesorge (1872–1962) had doctorates in mathematics and physics but pursued a career in telecommunications. One of his patents, the four-wire trunking switchgear, found worldwide application. During the First World War he served at the Kaiser's General HQ as Chief of Telegraphy. At the Armistice he was 46 years of age and continued his career into diverse areas of Post Office management. An early convert to National Socialism, he was close to Hitler from the beginning of the movement and set up the first NSDAP district organization outside Bavaria, at Dortmund, in 1920. By 1929 he had become President of the Reichspost Central HQ at Berlin Tempelhof. Following the seizure of power, Ohnesorge accepted the portfolio as Secretary of State for the Post Office on 2 February 1933 and entered the Cabinet as Reichspostminister in 1937, retaining this position until the defeat.

He was a disciple of Philipp Lenard, founder of Aryan Physics, and delivered the keynote address during the physicist's 80th birthday celebrations in 1942.[73] Ohnesorge was a reserved, diligent individual much admired by Hitler[74] for his industriousness: Hitler always observed Ohnesorge's birthday with a congratulatory telegram and often an invitation to an intimate table talk at the Reich Chancellery.

Von Ardenne-The Early Career

Baron Manfred von Ardenne (1907–1997) was the eldest of five children of an Army officer. During the First World War his father served at the War Ministry evaluating secret weapons. Shortly after leaving university Manfred von Ardenne served an apprenticeship in a radio workshop laboratory. By 1924, when his first book *Rundfunk* was published, he had already acquired a small income from technical treatises, royalties and patents. While specializing in the investigation of High Frequency circuitry problems at a laboratory in his parents' house, he spent four semesters at the University of Berlin studying the principles of physics, chemistry and mathematics. Because this was the only formal training he had had in Physics, during the war the professorial team labelled him The Dilettante – 'The Amateur'. He was often invited to speak publicly about his radio experimental work and even made broadcasts on technical subjects. In 1926 he developed the simple triple-valve receiver which sold several million units and led to the purchase price of domestic wireless sets in Germany being cut by two-thirds.

By January 1928 von Ardenne was employing a number of scientific assistants and, because of the expansion of his activities, he rented a large house at Jungfernstieg 19 in the Berlin suburb of Lichterfelde Ost. The dwelling stood in 5,000 square metres of land. A Post Office contract for the production of measuring instruments enabled von Ardenne to purchase the property in 1930. He had met Ohnesorge for the first time at the Berlin Technical University in 1930. The occasion was a public meeting chaired by the Commissioner for the Reich Radio Service examining von Ardenne's far-reaching proposals to install a chain of radio relay stations across the country aimed at overcoming the problem of poor quality wireless reception in cities.

On Christmas Eve 1930 he demonstrated an elementary television to the Post Office and spent the next three years experimenting with the cathode ray tube. In 1933 at the Berlin Radio Exhibition Ohnesorge introduced him to Hitler with the most generous references to his early work for the Post Office. Early the following year Ohnesorge granted von Ardenne a private laboratory facility for radar research inside Post Office Central HQ and he patented a transducer on 25 February 1934. Despite pressure, he resisted becoming a Party member.

When Ohnesorge was appointed Reichspostminister in 1937 he signed a permanent contract between von Ardenne's Lichterfelde-Ost Institute and the Research Establishment of the German Post Office for the development of radar and television, supplemented in 1940 by nuclear physics. For the three years following 1937 von Ardenne developed electron-microscopy and his work was rewarded in July 1940 when Krupps gave him a contract for their entire research programme in that field.

Early that same year von Ardenne asked Otto Hahn and Heisenberg outright for an estimate of the critical mass of uranium for a bomb and was told "a few kilos". In these conversations, and also with Ohnesorge privately, von Ardenne had stated that he considered it technically feasible, using highly sophisticated mass separators, to obtain enough U^{235} for a bomb if one could get the cooperation of industry. He had in fact already designed a prototype separator based on the mass spectrograph, he said: a preliminary study had indicated that electro-magnetic techniques were probably the most efficient of all for separating the uranium isotopes. His paper *Respecting a New Magnetic Isotope Separator for High Mass Transport* was issued by the Reichspost Research Institute in April 1942, but ignored by the official project. When the design was examined at Oak Ridge in 1947, *Physical Review* recognized that von Ardenne's design had a better ion source than the American equivalent.

Ohnesorge was enthusiastic, but when he proposed the atom bomb to Hitler in a short interview Hitler replied, *'Das wäre ja noch schöner, daß mein Postminister die Atombombe erfunden hätte!"* (That would look good, wouldn't it, having my Minister of Posts invent the atom bomb!")[75]

Von Ardenne turned his attention to radioactive isotopes for use as tracers in the analytical fields of medicine, biochemistry and biology. He became a leading authority and his manual *The Physical Principles of the Application of Radioactive or Stable Isotopes as Tracers* published in 1944 was widely acclaimed. Representations he had made to Ohnesorge in December 1939 resulted in the Postmaster issuing instructions for the building of a one-million volt Van De Graaf generator (subsequently completed in 1941) at Lichterfelde-Ost, and he also received the component parts of a small 60-ton cyclotron for construction on site.

Professor Fritz Houtermans Joins Von Ardenne

State institutions and state-controlled or subsidized laboratories of industry in National Socialist Germany were subject to the provisions of the racial law of 7 April 1933 which proscribed Jews and various other categories of people from employment. As von Ardenne's laboratory was privately owned he was not bound by this legislation, could employ whomsoever he wanted and had made it known that he was prepared to assist in suitable cases. In May 1940 Professor Max von Laue suggested he should employ the Jewish nuclear physicist Fritz Georg Houtermans.

An Austrian national with a Jewish mother and Dutch father, Houtermans was a Communist and in National Socialist Germany his circumstances could hardly have been less favourable. He had obtained his PhD at Göttingen in 1927 and was Assistant Professor at the University of Berlin by 1933. His special field was chain reaction theory. In 1935 he accepted a position in the Soviet Union at the Ukraine Institute of Physics in Kharkov and in 1937 lectured on neutron absorption to the Soviet Academy of Science. That same year, together with other foreign communists, he was imprisoned and tortured during Stalin's great purge. In 1939 the Russians offered him rehabilitation and a full restoration of his former offices, together with Soviet citizenship, but he declined on the grounds of their maltreatment. For a Jewish Communist to prefer to take his chances with the Nazis in 1939 speaks volumes for what type of place Soviet Russia must have been at that time.

The following year he was handed over to the Gestapo at Brest-Litovsk. Paroled into the custody of Professor von Laue on the condition that he remained under Gestapo observation and did not engage in any State or University research project, Houtermans was thus placed with von Ardenne. In August 1944 Houtermans issued a report from the Reich Bureau of Standards, a State office, which indicates that for the purposes of the Civil Service law he had been reclassified as a non-Jew.[76] What he must have done in the meantime to achieve this turnaround is suggested further on in this chapter.

Houtermans started work with von Ardenne on 1 January 1941. His most significant work at Lichterfelde-Ost was the report published in August 1941 describing the building of a zero-energy breeder reactor for plutonium which caused the furore with Heisenberg.

The Underground Developments at Lichterfelde-Ost

In his autobiography[77] von Ardenne stated that, because of his arrangement with Ohnesorge to install the cyclotron, an apparatus which required the personnel using it to be shielded against radiation, he now had a reason for requesting the construction of several large underground concrete bunkers at his Lichterfelde-Ost institute.

The main bunker was ten metres down and had a floor area of 100 square metres. The steel-reinforced concrete walls and ceiling were 1½ metres thick and, needless to say, this would have given enough radiation protection to the occupants of the house and the neighbours against whatever might have been going on in the bunker. Adjacent to it was a smaller bunker housing the 250 kW transformer station and next to that, but without a connecting door, an air-raid bunker measuring six metres square.

This underground complex was ready by the late autumn of 1942 which was, as von Ardenne confirms, just before the step-up in bombing activity over German cities in which Berlin was to become the major target. He added that he had made up his mind to put all the most valuable instrumentation and the important installations into a small area of the bunker in a working condition, but according to his diary of events added as an Appendix, the main evacuation of the laboratory did not take place until 1 August 1943. There is, therefore, a period of about nine months between the autumn of 1942 and the end of July 1943 when the use of the greater part of the main bunker has not been accounted for, and at a time

72

when Berlin was being subjected to extremely severe air raids. Moreover, von Ardenne mentioned that Professor Houtermans had been overjoyed at the chance to use a cyclotron, of which the only other such model available in all of Germany was at Miersdorf. Use of the machine had also been promised to Professor Hahn as a means of forging a closer relationship with Hahn's Berlin-Dahlem circle, but von Ardenne's cyclotron was never operational "because of the air war". So it came about that the cyclotron, the purpose for which the bunker complex had been built, an invaluable apparatus of which only one other model existed in the Reich in 1942, and a source of envy to all, was never completed.

The Lichterfelde-Ost cyclotron was an excuse: the bunkers were obviously constructed for war work with radioactive materials. They were, in fact, the laboratory where the prototype V-4 was to be built. Heisenberg's Leipzig experiment was to be continued by Houtermans.

Contaminated Uranium Delays Project

When the *Heereswaffenamt* ordered the changeover from uranium oxide yellow-cake to uranium metal powder in December 1940, the manufacturer *Degussa* turned out a metal which was contaminated by calcium from the thermic reduction process. The plant was small and had a production capacity of one tonne of metal per month. There were only six workers, but output never reached capacity. Throughout his 1941 report, Professor Houtermans had stressed the importance of using the purest metallic uranium to reduce the capture of neutrons by impurities. The *Degussa* product was not good in this respect.

According to the returns, all the uranium metal produced in Germany during the war was allegedly cast at one of the two *Degussa* plants and totalled about 14 tonnes. Nine tonnes was powder and five tonnes plates or cubes. It was reported that the reduction of the oxide to metal powder in quantity and to a high specification was not an economical enterprise in Germany. This is not a very convincing statement, but, if true, one assumes that the material would have been imported. Uranium metal powder is fine, grey and highly pyrophorous and tends to ignite spontaneously on contact with air. If shipped aboard a merchant vessel it would have to be stowed on deck as hazardous cargo and located where it could be jettisoned easily if necessary, since once afire it is extremely difficult to extinguish.

It may, of course, have been something else entirely, but a shipment of seventy to eighty sacks of a very fine grey powder, each sack being about 10 inches high with a diameter of about 12 inches and estimated to weigh 200 cwts (100 kilos) was reported to have been stowed aboard a German blockade runner at Yokohama in 1942. A mate with many years' experience of cargo handling, Fritz Kurt[78], stated that he had never seen a similar substance before and, despite his tactful enquiries, failed to establish the nature of the "mysterious heavy contents". The author Charles Gibson[78] observed that Goering, who was head of the Reich Research Council in charge of nuclear supplies in addition to his other roles, had an unexplained special interest in the material.

It seems at least an interesting possibility that, for reasons of product quality, a technical cooperation existed between Japan and Germany for the manufacture or purification of uranium metal powder, and by 1944 at the latest nuclear materials such as beryllium were being exported in the other direction.

The Uranium Bomb

The only publication from an authoritative source where the actual building of a German uranium bomb is mentioned specifically is Henry Picker's *Hitlers Tischgespräche*, which is based on stenographic notes taken down at mealtimes at the Führer's HQ between 1941 and 1944.

The daily routine at Führer HQ *Wolfsschanze* was described by Hitler's Luftwaffe ADC Nicolaus von Below in his memoir *Als Hitlers Adjutant 1937-1945*.[79] Hitler ate punctually at two in the afternoon and at seven thirty. If no special visitors were expected, he would take his time at table, often up to two hours. In these several years at mealtimes he would speak freely on many subjects, maybe just seizing on a random theme. The atmosphere at table was free and unforced. Conversation was spontaneous and there was no kind of compulsion about what could be discussed. On subjects of general interest, when Hitler contributed his opinion, silence would be maintained. It might occur occasionally that he held the floor for up to an hour, but this was the exception rather than the rule.

The major part of these monologues was taken down in shorthand by a National Socialist lawyer, Heinrich Heim. When Heim decided to return to Munich in the spring of 1942, the Gauleiters were canvassed to suggest a candidate to fill the vacancy. Among the names supplied was that of a senior privy councillor, Dr Henry Picker. The Party Chancellors drew up a short list of names and left it to Hitler to make the decision. Senator Henry Picker had been active for the NSDAP in Wilhelmshaven and in 1929 had arranged for Hitler to meet representatives of the Navy and naval dockyard. On his visits to the port Hitler was made welcome on numerous occasions as a guest in the Picker household and his selection of Picker was therefore much of a formality.

Picker's position at Führer HQ was dissimilar to that of Heim in that he had no standing as a Party official or lawyer but was only Martin Bormann's adjutant. One of his standing duties was to take a note of Hitler's conversations during the official meals, a task performed for the information of Bormann who was thereby enabled to keep abreast of developments in Hitler's thinking more or less as it cropped up.

The notebooks were released in 1951 by German Bundespresident Theodor Heuss and the shorthand jottings used as the basis for the volumes of *Hitlers Tischgespräche im Führerhauptquartier* which have been published in many editions subsequently. All three of Hitler's military adjutants of the time authenticated the texts, affirming that they truly and accurately reflect the substance of Hitler's conversations at table.

Picker was in almost permanent contact with Hitler's Chief ADC, SS-Obergruppenführer Julius Schaub (1898–1968), who had been a Party member from its beginnings. A willing and devoted manservant, Schaub was also Hitler's chauffeur and the only member of the Führer's entourage who belonged to the *Alte Kämpfer*. He was the guardian of nearly all Hitler's secrets.

There are numerous references to *Uraniumbomben* in Dr Picker's testimony, but these were not atom bombs as such, which physicists and politicians knew by the term *Uranbomben*. Hitler had no wish for a full-blown nuclear explosion and so we must be clear that *Uraniumbomben* were not atom bombs but something else.

Picker reported Schaub as saying that the *Uraniumbomben* were the fearsome weapons (*die fürchterlichen Waffen*) on which Hitler was actually basing his strategy and his hopes. Picker described where the *Uraniumbomben* were developed and mentioned the unprecedented security measures in force there:

"Dr Ohnesorge's *Reichspost-Forschungsanstalt* in Berlin Lichterfelde where – in parallel with an unsuccessful professorial team – a prototype of the German *Uraniumbombe* was in fact developed up to the stage of construction, received visits from Hitler during his periods of residence in Berlin, during which Dr Ohnesorge never once permitted Hitler's military entourage to view the research establishment. Ohnesorge, born in 1872, insisted on the greatest secrecy. Amongst co-workers in the Reich Research Institute were such authorities as the atom physicist Baron Manfred von Ardenne."

The phrase *in parallel with an unsuccessful professorial team* hints at a connection between Professor Heisenberg's failed Leipzig experiment in 1942 and what Houtermans was now attempting at Lichterfelde. Precisely as at Leipzig, or so we may be permitted to assume, the underground bunker below Manfred von Ardenne's property was a laboratory for the production of plutonium-enriched irradiated uranium powder. A number of aluminium spheres containing the powder, heavy water and a *Präparat*, surrounded by an array of measuring instruments, sat immersed in their respective tubs of ordinary water for a period of months breeding plutonium and the radioactive products of fission. So secret was the laboratory work at Jungfernstieg 19, Lichterfelde-Ost, that even Hitler's personal SS-bodyguard could not be permitted to see anything of what went on there. Presumably when Hitler arrived he would be escorted inside by Ohnesorge and von Ardenne leaving the 3-axled Mercedes charabanc with Schaub and the SS-*Führerbegleit* in the driveway. After a conversation in the Baron's pleasant reception room with its heavy curtains and suits of armour, Hitler would descend into the bunker to inform himself of how it was all coming along. Here he would be welcomed by Professor Houtermans and probably Dr Siegfried Flügge, who was with von Ardenne at material times and who refused to sign the Farm Hall declaration.

Henry Picker copied into his notebook the very words spoken by Hitler. The target of the *Uraniumbomben* was to be the civilian population of the United States. The means of delivery was to be the A9/10 intercontinental rocket. According to Hitler's personal ADC Julius Schaub, who had been told about the *Uraniumbombe* by SS-colleagues at the place where it was assembled, it was *in der Grösse eines kleinen Kürbis*, "the size of a small gourd". Hitler was confident that the arrival of the first few *Uraniumbomben* on New York would swiftly render the American President "ready for peace" – (*friedensbereit zu schiessen*).

Rumours of a Miracle Weapon Begin to Circulate

The hope inspired by the development of Heisenberg's V-2 bomb can be seen from the growth of rumours about a miracle weapon beginning in the late summer of 1943. Coinciding with the termination of von Ardenne's involvement in the project, the breeding of the radioactive material, the month of July 1943 was marked by the first verbal salvoes opening the V-weapons campaign, and SS-originated rumours soon began to circulate about new bombs "built on the atomic principle" of which twelve would suffice to destroy one million inhabitants of a city. In visits to the Ruhr and Rhineland, Goebbels is alleged to have said a good deal more on the subject of 'atomic type' weapons than he ever allowed to appear in print. On 23 February 1944, at a confidential meeting of all Gauleiters, Reichsminister Goebbels promised,

> "Retribution is at hand. It will take a form hitherto unknown
> in warfare, a form the enemy, we hope, will find impossible
> to bear."

The use of monstrous explosives spraying radioactivity far and wide was previously unknown in warfare, whereas the use of rockets and bombs was not. Goebbels' dark references were echoed by Hitler himself in a speech to troops reported in the RMfVP (Reich Propaganda Ministry) circular *Tätigkeitsbericht* of 25 September 1944 when he said,

> "God forgive me if I have to turn to that terrible weapon to
> end the conflict."

He could not have meant the V-1 and V-2, since by then both had been used against Britain, and the V-3 High Pressure Pump was not only still undergoing research but was also out of range. Therefore he must have meant the V-4.

From Lichterfelde-Ost the material for V-4 was passed to the SS scientists with instructions for manufacture. Schaub told Picker that the *Uraniumbomben* were being produced in a "subterranean SS factory in the South Harz mountains with a force of 30,000 workers" (*werden in einem unterirdischen SS-Werk im Südharz mit einer Produktionskapazität von 30,000 Arbeitskräften hergestellt.*) Professor Seuffert's SS laboratory was located in an underground section of the Ohrdruf complex in the southern Harz and one presumes this was where Schaub must have meant.

Although the V-2 was conceived as a long-range weapon for use from mobile launch sites, in the summer of 1943 a huge assembly and storage bunker with a concrete roof seven metres thick was begun at Watten south-west of Dunkirk. On 27 August and 8 September 1943 it was hit by 484 heavy bombs and destroyed. A massive new bunker complex extending over five hectares at Wizernes near St Omer survived all efforts to destroy it and was operational until Allied forces overran the area in 1944.

The British rocket scientist Philip Henshall stated that these monumental bunkers were capable of launching not only the V-2 but all projected developments including the gigantic A9/10 two-stage intercontinental rocket which was 26 metres in length and nine metres wide across the tail assembly.

Measurements proved that the working heights inside each silo could accommodate the projected A9/10 rocket minus its warhead. He considered that Watten was completely self-contained and impregnable from the exterior by virtue of its massive armoured doors, while at both locations the 23-feet-thick lid forming the dome to the structures could not be penetrated by any known bomb even hitting directly. Since the greater part of the concrete constructions were bunkers and silos, none of which were necessary for launching V-2 rockets, the actual purpose must have been to store nuclear materials and house the A9/10 "New Yorker".

In November 1944, according to Otto Skorzeny, all the talk was of

"a dreadful weapon based on artificially bred radioactivity".[80]

Such talk stemmed from among his own SS colleagues. But it was just talk. The budgetary restrictions, the diversification and experimentation into other interesting rockets and guided missiles, the invasion of Normandy and the time required to mass-produce a huge stock of the V-4 atomic explosives ensured that nothing would come of the weapon for America on which Hitler was pinning all his hopes. By the time they were finally ready even London was out of range.

Covering Over the Traces

On 1 August 1943, according to his autobiography, von Ardenne at last obtained vacant possession of the underground bunker complex and proceeded to remove most of his laboratory into it, thus terminating his association with the 'atomic' project.

Von Ardenne does not state how Professor Houtermans occupied his time at the laboratory between August 1941 and August 1944. Whilst von Ardenne and his co-workers produced a total of forty scientific papers in that period, Houtermans published only his August 1941 report, amended in 1944, and a brief work on separation in ultracentrifuges in February 1942.

Houtermans told the Swiss scientific author Robert Jungk[81] that he was in no position to refuse a task set him by Professor von Ardenne. He stated that, although he knew that plutonium could be bred in a nuclear reactor, he "did not report on that aspect of his work" since he had not wished to alert the authorities to the possibility of making atom bombs. He also stated that his 1941 thesis had been placed in a safe at Post Office Headquarters by Dr Otterbein so that there should be no publication of his studies in the *Heereswaffenamt* secret dossiers, and in that safe it had safely remained until 1944.

This was not true. He had reported on U^{239}, known today as plutonium, in one and a half closely typed pages, and, as his 1944 amendment to the report clarifies, he had intended for the report to remain secret, but, as it had been circulated, he now wanted to add some notes to it.

Hitler once said that he would tell any lie for Germany, but never for himself. Perhaps that is the criterion we should use to judge kindly the scientists and military men who manufactured the bogus history of the failed German atomic project. Groves and Houtermans definitely did lie about it after the war: Goudsmit insinuated that Heisenberg was lying: despite what British Intelligence and Senator Picker might say, nothing ever went on at Baron von Ardenne's Institute, or so he maintained, unless you meant honest-to-goodness work on identifying potato bacilli and microscopic radioactive tracers; nor, for that matter, did Hitler ever visit, according to von Ardenne's published diaries, from which may be inferred either that von Ardenne was lying or Hitler's SS-valet Julius Schaub was lying. And von Below, who was not only Hitler's Luftwaffe ADC but also Speer's ADC to Hitler at FHQ, who swore a certificate that Henry Picker's shorthand diaries were, as far as he knew, verbatim and true, ultimately knew nothing whatever about anything which one might call an *Uraniumbombe*, although as Hitler's Luftwaffe ADC he, of all people, would have known about it. All this dishonesty was and is directed at misleading the public, and even in Houtermans' case one feels aggrieved that ultimately he wasn't forthright.

In May 1940, as a Jewish communist, Houtermans was proscribed, under the Nazi racial and political laws, from working in any State enterprise and was subject to Gestapo supervision, often a slippery path to extinction. His scientific prowess saved him. By 1944, however, Professor Houtermans was employed at the Reich Bureau of Standards, a civil service institution, which meant that he had ceased to be classified as Jewish. Later he was entrusted with an intelligence gathering mission to the Soviet Union which meant effectively that he had done a complete *volte-face* as regards Communism. In fact, not only was he no longer a Jewish Communist, he was attached to the SS Sicherheitsdienst, for after 1942 all German agents were operated by Amt VI at the SS-RSHA[82] under Walter Schellenberg.

Our gripe with Houtermans is not for all his manouevring (since, for all we know, he may actually have become, if not a National Socialist then at least a convinced anti-Communist, and that is entirely his affair) but that ultimately, in common with people like Groves, he became part of the Allied-German conspiracy against true history. He was the only scientist of any consequence attached to the Reichspost project to be interviewed by the American Intelligence Mission *Alsos*. When seen by them at Göttingen on 17 April 1945, he gave them the impression that he had only been on the fringe of German nuclear research and satisfied them that he was unable to contribute any intelligence of particular importance. His Government had sent him to the Soviet Union to learn what nuclear research was being undertaken there, but he had discovered nothing much of note, although he thought that the Russians were very interested in the subject and he had heard a rumour that Professor Kapitza was working on it, obtaining uranium ore from the Ferghana district of Turkestan.

It was all pretty vague and *Alsos* let him go. They reasoned that he was obviously not the kind of man from whom anything useful might be obtained: he had merely worked on the independent Reichspost project under the ridiculous figure of Postmaster Ohnesorge, and, as Professor Goudsmit, head of the *Alsos* scientific intelligence mission stated in his book[83], the Reichspost nuclear programme was something of a joke for the Americans. Whether they actually thought that, or whether Goudsmit said so to disguise its importance, is another matter entirely but certainly London had been under no illusions. On 28 November 1944 the British Nuclear Physics Directorate known under the cover name as Tube Alloys (TA) sent an intelligence report to General Leslie Groves, head of the Manhattan Project, advising him:

"The activities of the Reichspost research department may of course imply that this Government department has a connection with the official nuclear physics work. In the first instance, detailed investigations of the TA project in Germany [should] be concentrated in two areas, Berlin and Bisingen and the surrounding country. In Berlin it should be possible to examine the various laboratories of the Reichspost and the private laboratory of von Ardenne. These two preliminary investigations are likely, if conditions are favourable, to provide an accurate picture of TA work in Germany."

At the end of hostilities in Europe, the Lichterfeld-Ost villa, together with all its valuable equipment, including the ruins of the 1-million volt Van de Graaf generator, the unused cyclotron and the prototype electro-magnetic isotope separator all went to the Russians, as did von Ardenne himself, as he had planned. For the next six years he worked on the USSR atomic weapons project on the Black Sea. Ohnesorge, too, preferred the Soviet zone. In March 1962, in the West the death passed unnoticed of the man who "led the way for the great advance of atomic development in the Third Reich".

CHAPTER 7

The Doomsday Bomb

In captivity at Farm Hall, Cambridgeshire after the capitulation, the atom scientists Werner Heisenberg and Otto Hahn were secretly tape-recorded in conversation immediately following the announcement of the dropping of the atomic bomb on Hiroshima.

Heisenberg: "Did they use the word "uranium" in connection with this atomic bomb?"

Hahn: "No."

Heisenberg: "Then it's got nothing to do with atoms, but the equivalent of 20,000 tons of HE. I am willing to believe that it is a high pressure bomb and I don't believe that it has anything to do with uranium, but that it is a chemical thing where they have enormously increased the whole explosion."

(PRO, Kew WO 208/5019)

BRITISH INTELLIGENCE KNEW about the dual project of atom bomb and heavy-air bomb. In *BIOS Final Report No 142(g)* it was said that:

"as the research on the atomic bomb under Graf von Ardenne and others was not proceeding as rapidly as had been hoped in 1944, it was decided to proceed with the development of a liquid air bomb."

This was very probably the pressure bomb spoken of by Heisenberg in captivity at Farm Hall. The Fuel-Air Explosive (FAE) belongs today in the arsenal of all the major powers. It is made up of liquid ethyl oxide and certain secret aluminium compounds. The substance is released as a cloud of gas and ignited, resulting in a fearful explosion with an enormously strong pressure wave. The weapon was developed by Dr (Ing) Mario

Zippermayer, an Austrian born in Milan in 1899 who had been an Assistant Professor at the Karlsruhe Technical University.

Taking up his work, the Ballistics Institute of the TAL (*Technische Akademie der Luftwaffe*) began to research the physics of rarified media explosions. When in mid-1944 a series of devastating explosions caused by the accidental escape of ethylene gas flattened the synthetic gasoline refineries at Ludwigshafen, a small special TAL team sat on the commission of enquiry. TAL's huge factory in the Bavarian Alps co-operated with the nearby *Heereswaffenamt* experimental centre at Garmisch-Partenkirchen and developed small cylinders charged with both gaseous and liquid ethylene. This was the forerunner of the modern FAE bomb.

Dr Zippermayer's original intention had been for an anti-aircraft explosive having coal-dust as its principal ingredient. When ignited it exploded, creating, as was hoped, a huge shock wave which could destroy a group of enemy bombers. Zippermayer's laboratory was at Lofer in the Austrian Tyrol. His preliminary experiments there confirmed that an aircraft in flight could be brought down by having a violent, fiery gust fracture its wings or rudder, but difficulties in determining the correct charge, and problems timing the ignition phase, led his technical staff to consider changing the combustible from solid to gas.

The Tornado Bomb

A special catalyst had been developed by the SS in 1943 and the following year Zippermayer turned his energies to a heavy air (*Schwere Luft*) bomb. Encouraging results were obtained from a mixture consisting of 60% finely powdered dry brown coal and 40% liquid air. The first trials were carried out on the Döberitz grounds near Berlin using a charge of about 8 kg powder in a tin of thin plate. The liquid air was poured on to the powder and the two were mixed together with a long wooden stirrer. The team then retired and after ignition everything living and trees within a radius of 500 to 600 metres were destroyed. Beyond that radius the explosion started to rise and only the tops of trees were affected, although the explosion was intense over a radius of 2 kilometres.

Zippermayer then conceived the idea that the effect might be improved if the powder was spread out in the form of a cloud before ignition, and trials were run using an impregated paper container. This involved the use of a waxy substance. A metal cylinder was attached to the lower end of the paper container and hit the ground first, dispersing the powder. After 0.25 seconds a small charge in the metal cylinder exploded, igniting the funnel-shaped cloud of coal dust and liquid air.

The ordnance had to be filled immediately prior to the delivery aircraft taking off. Bombs of 25 kgs and 50 kgs were dropped on the Starbergersee and photographs taken. SS-Standartenführer Klumm showed these to Brandt, Himmler's personal adviser. The intensive explosion covered a radius of 4 kilometres and the explosion was felt at a radius of 12.5 kilometres. When the bomb was dropped on an airfield, destruction was caused as far as 12 kilometres away, although only the tops of trees were destroyed at that distance, but the blast flattened trees on a hillside 5 kilometres away.

These findings appear in the British Intelligence Objectives Sub-Committee Final Report No 142 *Information Obtained From Targets of Opportunity in the Sonthofen Area*. Although one suspects initially that the radius of the area allegedly affected as described in this report had been worked upon by the Propaganda Ministry, the fact is that this bomb is never heard of today. Furthermore British Intelligence published the report without comment and what tends to give the description weight is the fact that the Luftwaffe wanted aircrews flying operationally with the bomb to have knowingly volunteered for suicide missions. The idea that the bomb had unusual effects was hinted at not only by the head of the SS-weapons test establishment but also possibly by Goering[84] and Renato Vesco[85]. On 7 May 1945 in American custody, Goering told his captors, "I declined to use a weapon which might have destroyed all civilization". Since nobody knew what he meant, it was reported quite openly at the time. The atom bomb was not under his control, although the Zippermayer bomb was. Vesco reported that the supreme explosive was "a blue cloud based on firedamp" which had initially been thought of "in the anti-aircraft role". On the Allied side, Sir William Stephenson, the head of the British Security Coordination intelligence mission stated:

"One of our agents brought out for BSC a report, sealed and stamped *This is of Particular Secrecy* telling of liquid air bombs being developed in Germany of terrific destructive power."[86]

A 50 kg bomb was said to create a massive pressure wave and tornado effect over a radius of 4 kms from the impact point, a 250 kg bomb for up to ten kms. A sequential disturbance in climate for a period after the explosion was reported. Radioactive material added to the explosive mixture was possibly to give it even better penetration and distribution. Zippermayer's device fits the idea of a high pressure bomb which Professor Heisenberg seemed to know about and to which he alluded in his eavesdropped conversation at Farm Hall. The bomb would have been the equivalent of a tornado but covering a far wider diameter, sucking up in its path everything but the most solid structures and scattering radio-active particles over the wide area devastated by the initial explosion. The survivors of the explosion would be suffocated by the lightning effect at ground level burning up the surrounding air.

The head of the SS-Weapons Testing Establishment attached to the Skoda Works was involved in the destruction of the catalyst at the war's end.[87] He had personally witnessed it being tested at Kiesgrube near Stechowitz on the Czech–Austrian border. These must have been the first tests, since he describes the astonishment of the observers at the force of the blast and tornado effect. Various other smaller tests were carried out at Fellhorn, Eggenalm and Ausslandsalm in the Alps. After these a larger experiment was made at Grafenwöhr in Bavaria described by the SS-General in the following terms: "We were in well-constructed shelters two kilometres from the test material. Not a large amount, but what power – equal to 560 tonnes of dynamite. Within a radius of 1200 metres dogs, cats and goats had been put in the open or below the ground in dug-outs. I have seen many explosions, the biggest in 1917 when we blew up a French trench complex with 300,000 tonnes of dynamite, but what I experienced from this small quantity was fearsome. It was a roaring, thundering, screaming monster with lightning flashes in waves. Borne on something like a hurricane there came heat so fierce that it threatened to suffocate us. All the animals both above and below ground were dead. The ground trembled, a tremendous wind swept through our shelter, there was a great rumbling, everywhere a screeching chaos. The ground was black and charred. Once the explosive effects were gone I felt the heat within my body and a strange numbness overcame me. My throat seemed sealed off and I thought I was going to suffocate. My eyes were flickering, there was a thundering and a roaring in my ears, I tried to open my eyes but the lids were too heavy. I wanted to get up but languor prevented me." An area of 2 kilometres was utterly devastated. Several observers on the perimeter were seriously affected by the shock wave and appeared to suffer from a kind of intoxication effect which lasted for about four weeks. That the weapon failed to make its debut on the battlefield in 1943 arouses the suspicion that very real fears existed regarding its knock-on effect on the climate. Within sight of Gernany's defeat, it was tested again at Ohrdruf in the Harz in early March 1945 (see Chap 10).

CHAPTER 8

The Decision not to Drop the German Bomb

H ITLER HAD SET himself, or been set, specific guidelines for the introduction and use of new weapons. In 1940 he had given Ohnesorge the impression that he was not interested in having an atom bomb. Two years later, within a few weeks of taking office, Armaments Minister Speer accepted that Hitler "did not want the bomb for doctrinal reasons".

During a conversation with Field Marshall Keitel, Foreign Minister Ribbentrop and the Rumanian Head of State Marshal Antonescu on 5 August 1944[88] only a fortnight after the 20 July attempt on his life, Hitler spoke of the latest German work on new explosives "whose development to the experimental stage has been completed". He added that, to his own way of thinking, "the leap from the explosives in common use to these new types of explosive material is greater than that from gunpowder to the explosives in use at the outbreak of war". When Marshal Antonescu replied that he hoped personally not to be alive when this new substance came into use, which might perhaps bring about the end of the world, Hitler recalled reading a German writer who had predicted just that: ultimately it would lead to a point where matter as such would disintegrate, bringing about the final catastrophe. Hitler expressed the hope that the scientists and weapons designers working on this new explosive would not attempt to use it until they were quite sure that they understood what they were dealing with.

There can be little doubt that the subject under discussion was fissionable weapons material and, if that is so, then Hitler confirmed that the

Germans had the weapon and that it was ready for testing in August 1944. The actual test took place two months later.

The difficulty with all these new weapons was the same, Hitler said. In general, he had ruled that a weapon should be brought into use immediately if it was guaranteed to bring the war to a victorious conclusion forthwith. This rule held good even if no counter-measure had yet been devised. In the majority of cases, however, the probability existed that the enemy would eventually obtain the same substance for himself, so the counter-measure was essential. Accordingly he had ordered that no weapon should be deployed by Germany first until Germany had developed the counter-measure to it.

SS-Obersturmbannführer Otto Skorzeny stated that when he saw Hitler in November 1944 their conversation came round to the atom bomb. Hitler said,

> "Of course! But even if the radioactivity could be controlled, and you used fission as a weapon, then the effects would be terrible . . . it would be the Apocalypse. And how would one keep such a thing a secret? Impossible! No! No nation, no group of civilised people could take on such a responsibility. The first bomb would be answered by a second and then humanity would be forced down the road to extinction. Only tribes in the Amazon and the primeval forests of Sumatra would have a chance of survival."[89]

We must now place ourselves in the shoes of the 20 July plotters determined at some stage to overthrow Hitler. The U-boat offensive in the Atlantic had been defeated. German cities and industry were being pounded day and night by bomber fleets which roamed across Reich airspace with impunity. The Army and Waffen-SS were close to exhaustion, defending the ever-shrinking perimeter of Greater Germany. The situation was not completely hopeless, but it would not be long before it was.

Ernst von Weizsäcker, the father of Heisenberg's close colleague, was Under-Secretary of State at the German Foreign Office, where he was one of the opponents of the Nazi regime. In 1938 he had informed the British Foreign Office of the existence of a group of civilian and military leaders ready to overthrow the Nazi Government if Hitler should go to war over Czechoslovakia, and was himself a major conspirator in what appears to have been the best-prepared coup ever planned against Hitler.

But Chamberlain and Lord Halifax, who had been asked to provide a strong demonstration of their determination not to tolerate the assimilation of the Czech state, disregarded the request, believing that an accord with Hitler was still possible. The German plotters were dismissed as Jacobites. The elder von Weizsäcker remained a focus of resistance in the Nazi State at war but was ultimately convicted at Nuremberg for alleged war crimes on the basis of his signature to certain documents.

According to Hitler's Luftwaffe ADC Nicolaus von Below[90], the SS interrogations of the July 1944 plotters reported widescale treason by military leaders throughout the preceding four years: the preparations for the French campaign, the dates of the attack and the objectives of the first operations: even the beginning of the Russian campaign had been betrayed.

Long before the attempt on Hitler's life the plotters had approached the Allied camp to establish terms for peace. Unconditional surrender was obviously not acceptable, yet, beyond that, all they got was encouragement to carry through their plans to overthrow Hitler. The Soviet author and former ambassador to Bonn, Valentin Falin[91], demonstrated by reference to Russian secret archives that the resistance movement penetrated to the highest military level in Germany and had contributed substantially to the success of the Allied invasion of occupied France in June 1944.

Professor Heisenberg, who in June 1944 had turned down an invitation by a Professor of History of his acquaintance, Adolf Reichwein, to participate in a plot against Hitler, frequented a social group known as the *Mittwochgesellschaft* (Wednesday Club). This was an intellectual forum of conservative opposition to Hitler composed of academics, civil servants and industrialists. Its members included the diplomat Ulrich von Hassell: General Ludwig Beck, the nominal head of the military conspiracy against Hitler; the philosopher Spranger; the Prussian Finance Minister Popitz; Ferdinand Sauerbruch, the Chief Surgeon of the German Army, and Rudolf Diels, the founder of the Gestapo. Reunions were held at the Harnack House in Berlin-Dahlem, the headquarters of the Kaiser Wilhelm Institute.

At the meeting of 12 July 1944[92] Heisenberg addressed the forum with a talk entitled "What are the Stars?" which appears to have been a cover for a discussion about nuclear fission. Spranger observed that these scientific developments promised to change the way men thought about the world, General Beck was more explicit and said that if atomic energy could be used for bombs then "all the old military ideas would have to be changed". This implies that the question of the atom bomb must have been discussed. Just before leaving Berlin for his home at Urfeld on 19 July, Heisenberg delivered minutes of the meeting to Popitz. The attempt on Hitler's life was made the next day.

Dr Kurt Diebner and ten assistants had set up an atomic laboratory in the cellar of a school at Stadtilm in the Harz, about thirteen kilometres from Ohrdruf, where Oberst Graf von Stauffenberg, the ringleader of the conspiracy, stayed regularly on the Wachsenberg, which was a favourite meeting place for officers and scientists working in the Ohrdruf area. Frau Cläre Werner, a watchtower lookout who resided on the mountain, recalled Stauffenberg visiting on a number of occasions and she still had possession of items of property he had left with her on his final visit.[93] Why should Stauffenberg have come so often to Ohrdruf when he worked in Berlin? Did the German resistance movement have more than a passing interest in what was going on at Stadtilm and its subterranean environs?

The German author Harald Fäth[94] reported that in the 1960s Gerhard Rundnagel, a master plumber who worked in the Stadtilm atomic research laboratory, gave evidence to a DDR judicial enquiry about the wartime activities there. In the depositions Rundnagel made a statement that the Stadtilm Research Institute had not been properly plumbed in and so was not really up and running. As far as he could see the scientists there were not actually working on anything. This left a lot of time for talk and Rundnagel described conversations he had had at the beginning of July 1944 with Dr Rehbein, a scientist at Stadtilm. Rehbein is alleged to have told Rundnagel that what was under development there was a type of bomb which had a greater explosive power than anything that an old weapons engineer such as himself could possibly envisage. Rehbein then went on to say, "Within a few days you will hear a decisive announcement on which will depend the outcome of the war." On 20 July 1944 the unsuccessful attempt was made on Hitler's life. When Rundnagel asked Dr Rehbein later if that was what he had meant, the scientist laughed and replied, "Now it will never be used. The war is lost." There are two ways of looking at this statement. Rehbein may have been suggesting that once Germany could make the official announcement that an atom bomb had been successfully tested, Hitler would be in a strong position to negotiate with at least one of his enemies. Because of the conspiracy against him, however, the evidence of disunity and betrayal perceived by foreign governments abroad would reduce figuratively the bomb's impact.

But there is an alternative interpretation. Along with other scientists in

Dr Diebner's entourage, Dr Rehbein may have been an associate of the anti-Hitler faction who wanted the Führer out of the way so that the German military could use the bombs physically to negotiate peace on terms more favourable than unconditional surrender. If it had become known to the resistance that, once tested, Hitler was resolved not to deploy the small atom bombs operationally, this would explain not only why the plotters struck when they did, but would justify Rehbein's remark that the war was lost, for with Hitler remaining as leader the atom bombs would never be used, or at least would be used only in response to the enemy's first use; yet the atom bomb, used in quantities, was, in the view of the plotters, Germany's last hope.[95] The sense of the words attributed to Dr Rehbein seem to favour the latter interpretation.

The fantastic idea current in 1944 of the effect of even a small atomic explosion is conveyed by an article in the Swedish newspaper *Stockholms Tidningen* in August 1944, and reported in Germany by the *TranSozean Innendienst* news agency:

> "In the United States scientific experiments are being carried out with a new bomb. Its explosive substance is uranium, and when the elements within its structure are liberated, a force of hitherto undreamed-of violence is generated. A 5-kilo bomb could create a crater one kilometre deep and of forty kilometres radius."

In all the foregoing we have a possible explanation for Professor Heisenberg's activities. Throughout the Hitler period he was opposed to the regime. He had remained in Germany in 1939 in order to sabotage the atom bomb and radiological warfare projects. In September 1941 he had taken a philosophical standpoint that a regime is to be considered evil by reference to the means it uses to impose its policies, and the atomic bomb was evil. In 1943 the United States had begun work on its atomic arsenal, a fact of which he would probably have been aware. In Germany a strong military resistance was developing of which Heisenberg had knowledge. He knew from von Weizsäcker that terms for an honourable conclusion to hostilities other than unconditional surrender were not available to Germany if that resistance succeeded in overthrowing Hitler. Heisenberg was a patriot. War was war, and, with Hitler removed, what German wanted Stalin or Roosevelt running the country? Therefore the idea of building a bomb of some description had been forced on him, for there had to be some sort of bomb, a bomb inevitably designed and built during the chancellorship of Hitler as Führer, but intended for use in diplomacy by those who would succeed him.

This pre-supposed, of course, that Hitler actually could be got rid of. The suggestion has been made in various quarters that he was in some way under the protection of higher powers determined that he should see his mission through.[96] No assassination attempt could ever succeed because there would always be the hand to re-position the offending attaché case with its bomb, or Hitler would change his schedule unexpectedly and leave the building minutes before a bomb went off. As was referred to in the Introduction, two well-placed authorities who observed Hitler pre-war had the impression that he was a medium, and mediums do claim that nothing can harm them seriously during the times when they are possessed by gods or spirits.[97]

If the plotters had succeeded on 20 July 1944, and the SS had not taken over the running of the country in the aftermath, the death camps would presumably have been abolished, but one sees no easy way how a continuation of the war against the Western Powers could have been avoided. Probably Germany would have found Stalin willing to re-align the Soviet Union in some manner with the new Reich and possibly Japan, particularly if a demonstration of the new explosives or the nerve gases could have been arranged. Whether that was something which the supporters of the plot against Hitler would have found acceptable as the price of removing him we have no means of knowing.

CHAPTER 9

Brighter than a Thousand Suns – for Two Seconds

THE 114-STRONG Allied Intelligence Mission codenamed *Alsos* was under the overall control of the head of the Manhattan Project, General Leslie Groves. It had arrived in France in August 1944. Its scientific head was a physicist, Professor Samuel Goudsmit, a Dutch émigré. His selection had been approved by the Office of Scientific Research and Development and by General Groves personally. Although a physicist, he was not connected with the US nuclear weapons project in any way, having spent most of the war working on radar. He may have had limited access to technical information, but probably not enough really to get him to grips with the task he had been given.

Whereas the scope of the intelligence activity extended beyond the German uranium project, Goudsmit's group of scientists were concentrating their investigation into all aspects of uranium research. From the outset Goudsmit was dogmatic: "No one but Professor Heisenberg could be the brains of a German uranium project and every physicist throughout the world knew that."[98] When American military realists suggested dryly that possibly other scientists of whom Goudsmit had never heard might be secretly working on some form of uranium weapon, Goudsmit derided the idea as an impossibility: it had to be Heisenberg. And, in the end, he was probably right.

The Logic of Professor Goudsmit

In common with many modern academic writers, Professor Goudsmit had difficulty in establishing exactly what Heisenberg *had* been working on and there was nothing unusual in that; but then he went one step farther and got confused, or so he would have us believe. In July 1942 Heisenberg had realized that his next reactor experiment was likely to approach uncomfortably close to the critical point. As has been mentioned before, he was apparently labouring under the mistaken belief that a power reactor could not be controlled and would explode at criticality. This false belief was founded in an error in mathematical theory regarding the Period of the Reactor. In his paper *G-161 Observations on the Planned Intermediate Experiment with 1½ tons of Heavy Water and 3 tons of Uranium Metal* he wrote:

> "We need to understand about reactor stability. Our foremost fear is that the entire fission process at criticality will occur explosively in a fraction of a second while the heavy water is still practically cold. Whether the reactor stabilizes or explodes rests solely on the behaviour of the energy bands. If the width of the energy bands is insufficient for stability, then it would seem that there is no other factor which can prevent the chain reaction cascade. This event would take place in a large reactor in -400 secs-1 and the neutron count would suddenly reach 10^{28}, enough for instantaneous energization of the fuel."

Because he was working on the stable Period of the Reactor being less than a second, Heisenberg contended that it was impossible to harness energy in any reactor producing heat, or too dangerous to find out, which amounted to the same thing. Until the end of the war Heisenberg and Diebner practised interesting sub-critical reactor geometry, but no attempt was made to get a reactor going. This explains the perplexity of Karl Wirtz, his experimentalist, who confirmed that "enough heavy water was available, in principle, to achieve a critical reactor"[99], and that if in 1944 Heisenberg's group and Diebner's group had combined their heavy water resources in a single experiment, there would have been sufficient to moderate a working pile. Rift there might have been, but if either had really wanted to go ahead with the definitive experiment, a word in the right quarters would surely have been sufficient.

If Goudsmit did not understand the mathematics of reactor stability, his ignorance of what was being said by Heisenberg in the report could have led him to draw an unwarranted conclusion. After the liberation of Strasbourg on 29 November 1944, while evaluating dossiers found in a filing store at the University, Professor Goudsmit said he found a scientific paper by an unnamed author which described a German "reactor bomb". This report, if it ever existed, has not yet been declassified by the US authorities and all there is to go on is Goudsmit's vague sketch of the so-called reactor-bomb (see Appendix), which is actually nothing more than a copy of Heisenberg's B-III experiment. It seemed pretty obvious to Goudsmit that, if Heisenberg believed his nuclear reactor would blow up, then surely that would amount to a sort of reactor bomb. This would be, in fact, the German atom bomb!

He is supposed to have informed Groves at once that the Germans had not been working on the fast fission uranium bomb and were thinking they could drop a nuclear reactor instead. Unlikely as it may seem, Groves accepted all this and included it in his own book.[100] The whole thing is set out in black and white, but of course makes no sense if Heisenberg knew the principle of the fast fission atom bomb, which he obviously did. That was why Groves lied about that aspect of Heisenberg's knowledge. Groves knew they would both be dead by the time the transcripts were declassified. But what was the point of the subterfuge?

The answer must be that American Intelligence knew Heisenberg had designed, or at least had a hand in planning, a viable rudimentary German atomic bomb, and it was not convenient politically, then or now, to admit that embarrassing fact. This meant that atomic history had to be re-designed in some manner. Justifiably it leads us to theorize that the Heisenberg bomb actually did look like experiment B-III, and by labelling it the "reactor bomb" for the contingency that someone might blab, Groves and Goudsmit conjured up a falsified theory to explain it away.

The German Atom Bomb

The probable amount of plutonium-enriched uranium powder used in the bomb would have been in the region of 750 kilos. The sphere, resembling Heisenberg's B-III sub-critical reactor, had a diameter of no more than a couple of feet. Paraffin and uranium would have been arranged in alternate layers no wider than an inch each. Paraffin is an excellent absorber of radiation, but its primary purpose here was to stop the Pu^{240} emissions causing premature fission. It is on account of Pu^{240} being so radioactive that there is a risk of predetonation. This is the reason why an implosion fuse working at the speed of light is required in order to set off a plutonium bomb. Did Germany have such a fuse? According to the CIOS-BIOS/FIAT 20 report, in May 1945 Germany had every kind of fuse known to the United States in October 1946 – radio, radar, wire, continuous wave, acoustic, infra-red, light beams and magnetics "to name just some". Nuclear physicist Pat Flannen commented:

> "The plutonium-enriched uranium would have to be kept atomically isolated until the moment of detonation. Shielding, capable of stopping the Pu^{240} from undergoing premature fission, would have to be provided, that would have to remove itself at the moment of nuclear assembly so quickly that the Pu^{240} would have no time to react before the Pu^{239} did. For this bomb to work, three things would be required:
>
> A. – An excellent radiation-absorbing substance such as paraffin to block the emissions of the Pu^{240} but which would nevertheless disperse quickly on umpact, being a liquid.
> B. – The closest proximity of the plutonium-enriched uranium sub-critical masses, so that fast assembly could be assured. No more than a couple of inches.
> C. – The highest assembly speed possible, more than Mach 3.5.
> If imploded at the speed of light, the cutaway sketch meets all of these criteria."

An English scientist who delivered a written opinion about the feasibility of the German test stated that the fallout would still be detectable today if the device had been tested "and large parts of Europe would still be uninhabitable". This question of fallout is commonly misunderstood by non-nuclear scientists. When an atom bomb is detonated, neutrons react against a surrounding jacket of material such as U^{238} or beryllium to enhance the blast, which has the secondary effect of increasing fallout. If the purpose of the German test was only to prove the reaction and the correctness of the theory, and the blast effect was not required, the structural parts of the bomb would have been layered with zirconium or bismuth within a tamper of lead. Fallout in this case would have been negligible.

The Atomic Bomb Testing Station

In June 1945, before the first American atomic test in New Mexico, former inmates of Buchenwald concentration camp, which supplied labour for Ohrdruf, reported that the Russians had discovered two German 'atom bombs' on a Baltic island.[101] This would probably have been Bornholm, which was occupied in a surprise move by Russian forces at the end of the war. The London *Evening Standard* and the Danish *Politiken* published communiques from Washington that there had been a secret atomic laboratory on the island and this had been the reason for its sudden 'liberation' by the Soviets. The team of German scientists on Bornholm, which included a Yugoslav, were all said to have been taken off to Moscow with their equipment and documentation.

Peenemünde, on the Usedom Peninsula, was a development and test centre for various V-weapons. Allen W. Dulles, who eventually became head of the US Secret Service, was attached to OSS Zürich during the war and on 19 June 1943 sent a cable to his superior in Washington, William Donovan, stating that heavy water was being shipped from Norway to Peenemünde where a German atomic laboratory had been identified.[102] The report was passed to David Bruce, head of British Military Intelligence, in London and resulted in the devastating air raid on Peenemünde on 17 August 1943. Thus the most serious reports indicated activities in the Baltic, and in particular Bornholm and Peenemünde. Following Hiroshima and Nagasaki, two English newspapers, the *Daily Telegraph* and *Daily Express* reported on 9 August 1945 that a senior "Nazi atom scientist" had been killed at Peenemünde during the raid although his identity was not revealed. What use such a report has for the newspaper-reader is difficult to fathom. Two days later, on 11 August, the *Daily Telegraph* at page five under a heading *Nazis' Atom Bomb Plans* referred to defensive measures being taken in Britain in August the previous year on the basis of a "highly secret memorandum which was sent that summer to the chiefs of Scotland Yard". The article went on:

"Reports received from our agents on the Continent early last year indicated that German scientists were experimenting with an atomic bomb in Norway. According to these reports, the bomb had an explosive radius of more than two miles and was launched by catapult."

Disappointingly the *Daily Telegraph* supplied no further details either of bomb or its unique means of delivery and later:

"reliable agents in Germany reported that the bomb had been tested and proved a failure."

A one kiloton device within a lead tamper sprays lethal neutrons over an area two kilometres in diameter. When testing such a device, it might have been interpreted by agents as a failure if a mammoth explosion had been expected. The German observer Zinsser (whose report is reproduced in full below) mentioned having observed several 'atom bomb' tests, and this may have been one of them.

In the train of the two nuclear attacks on Japan on 6 and 9 August 1945, the US Intelligence services began questioning all Germans in captivity who might possess information respecting possible German nuclear tests. An official paper was forwarded by COMNAVEU London on 24 January 1946 respecting the interrogation of a German prisoner on 19 August 1945.[103] The layout of the first page is as follows:

INTELLIGENCE REPORT
Subject: Germany Aviation.
Evaluation, Scale A1 to E0: B1.
Subject: Investigations, Research, Developments and Practical Use of German Atomic Bomb.
(1) Enclosure will be of interest to BuAer (E-32) and BuOrd (Re8).
(2) Enclosure is a discussion of the developments of the German atomic bomb. (Only one page declassifed)
Prepared by:
R.F.Hickey, Captain, US Navy.
Tulley Shelley, Commodore, US Navy, Intelligence Officer.

The accompanying page reads as follows:

"47. A man named ZINSSER, a Flak rocket expert, mentioned what he noticed one day: In the beginning of October 1944 I flew from Ludwigslust (south of Lübeck), about 12 to 15 km from an atomic bomb test station, when I noticed a strong, bright illumination of the whole atmosphere, lasting about 2 seconds.

48. The clearly visible pressure wave escaped the approaching and following cloud formed by the explosion. This wave had a diameter of about 1 km when it became visible and the colour of the cloud changed frequently. It became dotted after a short period of darkness with all sorts of light spots, which were, in contrast to normal explosions, of a pale blue colour.

49. After about 10 seconds the sharp outlines of the explosion cloud disappeared, then the cloud began to take on a lighter colour against the sky covered with a grey overcast. The diameter of the still visible pressure wave was at least 9000 meters while remaining visible for at least 15 seconds.

50. Personal observations of the colours of the explosion cloud found an almost blue-violet shade. During this manifestation reddish-coloured rims were to be seen, changing to a dirty-like shade in very rapid succession.

51. The combustion was lightly felt from my observation plane in the form of pulling and pushing. The appearance of atmospheric disturbance lasted about 10 seconds without noticeable climax.

52. About one hour later I started with an He 111 from the aerodrome at Ludwigslust and flew in an easterly direction. Shortly after the start I passed through the almost complete overcast (between 3000 and 4000 metre altitude). A cloud shaped like a mushroom with turbulent, billowing sections (at about 7000 metres altitude) stood, without any seeming connections, over the spot where the explosion took place. Strong electrical disturbances and the impossibility to continue radio communication as by lightning, turned up.

53. Because of the P-38s operating in the area Wittenberg-Merseburg I had to turn to the north but observed a better visibility at the bottom of the cloud where the explosion occurred.

Note: It does not seem very clear to me why these experiments took place in such crowded areas.

For the Commanding Officer
Helenes T. Freiberger, AC. Captain
Distribution List: 248 copies in all.

Making Sense of the Zinsser Report

The Zinsser Report has a distribution list of 248 copies to eighteen different departments. This means that for security reasons the document will not be worded so lucidly as if it were a secret report from one person to another. The report is written by a US Navy Intelligence officer and couched in the usual intelligence style which is intended to make it difficult to read.

First, this is a report about observations made by a German prisoner while in captivity in the United States on 19 August 1945. All his captors are prepared to state is that his name is Zinsser and that he is a flak rocket expert. We are not enlightened as to whether he is Luftwaffe or a civilian scientist, but, as he is not described in the report as a "P/W", it is a fair assumption that he is a scientist from Peenemünde where the new generation of flak rockets were assembled and tested. Numerous converted He 111-H bombers were attached to the Karlshagen experimental station near Peenemünde for the testing of new types of aerial weapons. These reliable machines served for rocket launching, flight measurement and aerial photographic roles.

Because of an obviously trained eye for detail, Zinsser is accustomed to observing explosions, but this explosion is different and is "in contrast to normal explosions". Since all Luftwaffe aircraft would have been warned to avoid transit near a proposed explosive test area that day and in the report he states that the combustion was lightly felt from his "observation plane", it is obvious that Zinsser was an appointed test observer. A flier off his course and passing by accident through a test area would not describe his aircraft as an "observation plane", nor would he have stayed around to make copious detailed notes about what he saw.

Where did this test take place? What is definite is that it did not occur fifteen kilometres from Ludwigslust. If we insert one word we can make sense of it. Zinsser flew "from Ludwigslust (south of Lübeck) *TO* about 12 to 15 kms from an atomic bomb test station". This could be anywhere but would be about the right distance to observe a 1-kiloton neutron bomb test. An Italian emissary representing the exiled former Italian dictator Mussolini stated that on 11 October 1944 he attended the test of a "small-scale atom bomb" at the Baltic island of Rügen, not far from Peenemünde. A two-second illumination of the entire atmosphere during a nuclear explosion indicates a device equivalent to 1000-tons TNT.[104]

The well-known *New York Times* correspondent W. L. Laurence, a

Pulitzer Prize-winner in 1937 and 1946, who had associated with physicists long before the Manhattan Project, was allowed to fly in one of the three B-29 aircraft which took part in the atomic bombing of Nagasaki. His eyewitness report was published on the same day, 9 August 1945. His article was an absolute sensation, but Zinsser's account is more complete, particularly in two material respects.

> **Zinsser**: ". . . when I noticed a strong bright illumination of the whole atmosphere lasting for about two seconds."
> **Laurence**: ". . . all of us became aware of a giant flash that broke through the dark barrier of our arc-welder's lenses and flooded our cabin with an intense light."

> **Zinsser**: ". . . and the colour of the cloud changed frequently . . . it became dotted after a short period of darkness with all sorts of light spots, which were, in contrast to normal explosions, of pale blue colour."
> **Laurence**: ". . . we removed our glasses after the first flash but the light still lingered on, a bluish-green light that illuminated the entire sky all around."

> **Zinnser**: "The combustion was lightly felt from my observation plane in the form of pulling and pushing."
> **Laurence**: "A tremendous blast wave struck our ship and made it tremble from nose to tail."

> **Zinsser**: "The clearly visible pressure wave escaped the approaching and following cloud formed by the explosion."
> **Laurence**: "Observers in the tail of our ship saw a giant ball of fire rise."

> **Zinsser**: "Personal observations of the colours of the explosion cloud found an almost blue-violet shade."
> **Laurence**: "By the time our ship had made another turn in the direction of the atomic explosion, the pillar of purple fire had reached the level of our altitude."

> **Zinsser**: "During this manifestation reddish-coloured rims were to be seen, changing to a dirty-like shade in very rapid succession."

Laurence: *Failed to mention this red coloration which is caused by nitric oxide.*

Zinsser: "A cloud shaped like a mushroom with turbulent, billowing sections stood (at about 7000 metres altitude) over the spot where the explosion took place."
Laurence: "It [the mushroom cloud] retained that shape when we last gazed at it from a distance of about 200 miles."

Zinsser: "About an hour later, I started with an He 111: shortly after the start I passed through the almost complete overcast . . . strong electrical disturbances and the impossibility to continue radio communications as by lightning turned up . . ."
Laurence: *Did not mention this typical phenomenon of an atomic test.*

Radio and Radar Interference is an unwanted side-effect of atomic explosions and never occurs during normal explosions. Very few specialists were aware of this phenomenon in August 1945; only radio operators and pilots of aircraft near an atomic test would have observed it. It is the result of the radioactivity of the fission fragments, and the cloud containing the weapon debris will be in an ionized state for a considerable period. An explosion can also cause temporary regional changes in the ionosphere. The operation of long-range radio communication or radar observation in channels affected by such perturbations could be degraded or blocked.[105]

The only possible explanation for the foregoing is that Zinsser, whoever he was, saw the test of a 1-kiloton lead-jacketed German atom bomb and so, if there ever was such a thing, Hitler's scientists won the race to the atom bomb.

CHAPTER 10

The Sands of Time Run Out

"The Germans were preparing rocket surprises for England in particular, which would have, it is believed, changed the course of the war
if the invasion had been postponed for so short a time as half a year," Lt-
Gen Donald Leander Putt, Deputy Commanding General, US Army Air
Force Intelligence, told the Society of Aeronautical Engineers in a speech
in 1946. Since he was speaking here of rockets, Lt-Gen Putt was implying
that forcing the Germans back to their own frontier by December 1944
was critical to the Allies not losing the war. In December 1944 the
Germans launched a military operation, the purpose of which no historian has explained satisfactorily: the Ardennes offensive, which began on
the 16th of that month. Hitler's motorized forces were to bear down on
Antwerp with the intention of recapturing the port. For the purpose he
had released huge quantities of fuel and ammunition and transferred the
bulk of his panzers from the East. Two full divisions – one SS and one
Wehrmacht – were deployed. Secrecy was absolute. Hitler's Luftwaffe
ADC von Below remarked in his 1982 memoirs that even he could not
understand why Hitler wanted to go to Antwerp – "a place that led
nowhere". And at the same time orders were placed with naval shipyards
at Stettin and Elbing in the Baltic for twenty-four 500-ton submersible
barges able to transport and launch V-2 rockets. Antwerp was a sea port.
Antwerp was 200 miles from London. The maximum range of a V-2 was
200 miles. Launched from a submersible barge, a V-2 could hit London
from the River Scheldt on which Antwerp stood. Here we begin to see the
logic. But the V-2 campaign had been a failure. Hitler knew that. There
had to be something extra to make all this worthwhile.

In an aside to accredited journalists Kurowski and Romersa it is alleged that Lt-Gen Putt had added, "The Germans had V-2s with atomic explosive warheads". Hitler told Otto Skorzeny[106] that the whole point was to introduce "a new and really revolutionary weapon which would take them utterly by surprise" – the same expression as used by US Lt-Gen Putt in his speech. If the *Uraniumbombe* was ready, and he now had the deadly warhead mass-produced to fit into his V-2s, then the picture makes some kind of sense at last. In this new campaign every V-2 arriving from the heavens on London at Mach 3.5 would crush into a critical mass on impact a sphere in its nose or waist filled with half a tonne or so of plutonium-enriched uranium powder. The assembling of the material, though instantaneous, lacked symmetry, and so a full chain reaction would not develop, but there would certainly be a "fizzle" equivalent to up to 50 tons of TNT, meltdown and fallout. And every V-2 would bring the same punishment until Britain pulled out of the war and all troops of the western Alliance departed from the European mainland. It was a bold plan.

Once it was obvious that the Ardennes offensive had failed, Hitler admitted defeat to his Luftwaffe ADC[107] in terms similar to, "I know the war is lost. The enemy superiority is too great."

Horten Ho XVIII bomber

Before the war the first Chief of the Luftwaffe General Staff, Wever, had demanded a fast, four-engined bomber. The initial designs, the Ju 89 and Do 19, had flown but were either scrapped or relegated to other duties, and Goering had abandoned the four-engined series subsequently in favour of the Ju 88. This was due partly to the raw materials situation but also to the fact that double the number of two-engined machines could be manufactured, which looked good in the production figures. Goering was therefore the party responsible for the decision not to have a long-range bomber fleet, and in the upshot it was probably fatal for Hitler.

At the end of 1944 the development of new types of bomb for use against the United States from Germany and possibly from bases in Japan kick-started a bomber-building programme into life.

An aircraft specifically built as an atomic-type bomb carrier[108] was the Horten XVIII, although its designers were not made aware of that fact until after the war, its purpose being camouflaged by the Luftwaffe as the maritime anti-convoy role. The RLM requirement drawn up in mid-1944 stipulated a radius of action of 9000 kms, enabling the aircraft to make the round trip from Germany to New York without refuelling, carrying an outward bomb load of 4 tonnes. This payload would be about right for a German 'atomic-type' bomb with a 500-kilo core, most of the rest being casing and the conventional explosive needed to implode the device. At a conference of top aircraft manufacturers in the autumn of 1944, Messerschmitt, Focke-Wulf, Blohm & Voss, Junkers, Arado and Heinkel were invited to tender designs, but when submitted none were able to meet the radius of action, particularly after the figure of 9000 kms had been increased to 11000 kms.

Reimar and Walter Horten were not in the mainstream of aircraft manufacture. Before the war their specialist field had been unpowered gliders of very high aspect wing ratio. Their design with a glide ratio of 45:1 was greater than an albatross, and this best performance by a flying wing stood until at least the early 1970s. When war came the brothers' interest widened and designs for powered versions of the flying wing began to flow from the drawing board. The Hortens were told of the disappointing progress made by the major manufacturers and in November 1944 the Luftwaffe asked them to submit a design for a long-range bomber. They worked on the project full-out through the Christmas period and came up with ten variations for a 'flying wing' bomber, basically a wooden boomerang driven by a permutation of from four to eight turbo-jets.

The final version tagged Ho XVIIIA had six Junkers Jumo 004B turbo-jets at the rear of the fuselage fed by air intakes in the wing's leading edge. A rocket-boosted skate would be jettisoned at take-off and landing effected on a skid. Construction was predominantly wood held together with a carbon-based glue. This gave the aircraft a low radar profile.

According to Speer, Hitler was very taken with the whole project, but when between 20 and 23 February 1945 Goering chaired a further design conference at Dessau, the lobbyists got their way and a few days later Goering told the Horten brothers to work in collaboration with Junkers engineers. As these had quietly co-opted some Messerschmitt people to their team, the project was now run by committee.

The Messerschmitt-Junkers idea was to fit a huge vertical fin and rudder aft and relocate the engines below the wing. These changes increased drag and thus reduced the range but again they got their way, and the final design had two large vertical fins with a cockpit at the leading edge. The six Jumo jets were to be slung in two nacelles one to each side of the central fuselage. Between these was the bomb bay which also housed a tricycle landing gear.

This variation did not find favour with the Horten brothers and they designed their own improvement, Ho XVIIIB, a flying wing with a crew of three seated in a plexiglass blister in the nose, propulsion being provided by four Heinkel Hirth SO11 turbo-jets each developing 1200 kgs thrust and housed below the wing in gondolas insisted upon by the development authority for safety reasons. This arrangement resulted in a weight saving of about a tonne enabling the replacement of the skid by a fixed 8-wheel undercarriage streamlined in flight by doors to reduce drag. The aircraft would have a speed of about 850 kms/hr, an operational ceiling of 16 kms and could remain aloft for 27 hours. Although armament was considered unnecessary by the Luftwaffe, the Hortens suggested two Mk 108 3-cm cannon directly below the cockpit. A special carbon-based paint and a honeycomb dielectric material pasted over the outer skin were used to suppress the reflection of radar beams.

On 23 March 1945 the design was approved by Goering and the Hortens were told to approach Saur, Speer's deputy, to find a suitably protected production facility. Kahla in the Harz mountains was considered suitable. It had two recently completed hangars with concrete roofs 5.6 metres thick which were virtually bomb-proof. Two airstrips were available for test flights, and a workforce of 2000 persons was on hand.

The first prototype was expected to fly in the summer of 1945 and work was started on 1 April.

German Intelligence of the Manhattan Project

During the war Germany had been relatively well informed on the progress of the Manhattan Project. Most of the signals transmitted to Moscow by Klaus Fuchs' spy ring were decrypted by the SS-RSHA[109], as were those of a Canadian communist ring in Ottawa, and passed to SS atomic research groups. The information was withheld from other sections of the German project for security reasons.

The Spanish spy Alazar de Velasco[110] reported to both Germany and Japan on the American work from 1943 until mid-1944, operating from Mexico. Velasco mentioned the difficulties the Americans were having in developing an implosion fuse for their plutonium bomb design, which had already been solved by the Germans.

On 30 November 1944 *U-1230* put Erich Gimpel ashore on an American beach. On Christmas Day, a week before his capture by the FBI, Gimpel discovered from his contact that the American A-bomb would be ready by the summer of 1945. Apparently they had only two or three bombs. Gimpel transmitted this information to Berlin.

In the autumn of 1944, when he found Hitler planning the Ardennes offensive with freshly formed panzer and fighter units, his Luftwaffe ADC von Below asked him why he did not concentrate all his forces against the Russians and received the answer that he could attack them later, provided that the Americans were not in Berlin. First of all he must have space on his western border. Von Below remarked that everybody thought it preferable to allow the Americans to take the Reich so that the Russians could be held off as far as possible from the eastern frontier. Hitler did not share this view because he feared the power of the American Jews more than the Bolshevists.

It seems certain that a Doomsday Bomb test was carried out at Ohrdruf in the Harz on the night of 4 March 1945. Witness Frau Cläre Werner related[112]: "At that time I knew Hans Ritterman, who was Plenipotentiary for Reichspost and OKW Special Projects. He worked in the Arnstadt Building Department and was involved in secret Reichspost work in Thuringia. He was a good friend of the family and often came for coffee on Sundays. On 4 March 1945 Hans visited and said we should go to the tower and watch in the direction of Roehrensee village. He didn't know what the new thing would go like. About nine-thirty that evening behind Roehrensee it suddenly lit up just like hundreds of bolts of lightning. The explosion glowed red inside and yellow outside and you could read a newspaper by it. It lasted only a short time, fell dark again and then came a hurricane, after which it went quiet. Next day, like many residents of Roehrensee, Holzhausen, Muehlberg, Wechmar and Bittstedt, I had nose-bleeds, headache and pressure on my ear-drums. That afternoon about two o'clock, between 100 and 150 SS came to the mountain and asked where the bodies were and where they had to take them. They had been misdirected and a motor cyclist put them right. I watched them making for the Ohrdruf Army Training Ground."

Another witness, a former concentration camp inmate at Ohrdruf, described how he was forced to help in the cremation of several hundred charred bodies on 5 March 1945, the inference being that they had died as the result of the weapons test the previous evening.

V-4: The Doomsday Bomb Ready to Enter Service

Ashen with the pallor of the Berlin Bunker, all that kept Hitler's spirit alive in the closing months was the desperate hope that, even at the last, circumstances might yet permit him to use his weapons of frightfulness in a last throw. Accordingly, at Schloss Ferienwalde/Oder on 11 March 1945, his last visit to troops at the front, he implored General Theodor Busse and officers of the Ninth Army to stave off the Russians for as long as it might take for his new 'wonder-weapons' to be ready. He was honest in promising them that "every day and every hour are precious for the completion of the weapons of frightfulness which will bring the turn in our fortune!" Frau Werner continued, "The following night, 12 March, the second test took place about ten-fifteen. The air raid sirens went off at nine. The glow wasn't so bright as the first test and we didn't get nose-bleeds and so on. Hans spent all night on the tower with his people. He told us we mustn't ever mention about the bolts of lightning. All the people knew Hans so I suppose they were all Reichspost and Reich Research Council. None of them was in uniform and only a few wore the Party badge in the lapel."

The only rocket in Hitler's armoury able to reach London from Germany carrying a one-tonne payload was the winged A9/10. It was eighty feet long and could hit New York. The series was not yet in mass production, the project having only been resurrected in December 1944. A test launch seems to have been carried through near Ohrdruf on 16 March 1945. All four witnesses[112] gave evidence that on 16 March 1945 an "Amerika" rocket was launched successfully from "Polte II" MUNA Rudisleben (an underground munitions factory site). Witnesses (2) and (3) testified to having worked at Rudisleben on a rocket "thirty metres in length" which was launched at Rudisleben on the date in question. Witness (4) testified to having worked with a party of prisoners erecting the staging for the rocket. Cläre Werner stated: "At about nine on the night of 16 March 1945 there was an air raid warning. My friend Hans Rittermann [Plenipotentiary for Special Reichpost and OKW Projects] was visiting the tower with some friends. They had binoculars and were looking towards Ichtershausen [Polte II lay between Wachsenberg Tower and Ichtershausen]. At about eleven it got very bright, something went up into the sky with a huge tail fire, it kept going up, it was heading to the north. Hans Rittermann told us we must never speak of what we had seen, just that we had been witnesses to something unique which would be written about in every history book."

This seems to confirm the launch of an A9/10 rocket, but the war was beyond recall.

Luftwaffe Mutiny?

Senior Engineer August Cönders, who had designed the V-3 England Gun, reported in February 1945 that the new decisive weapons would not be ready for use before April 1945[113], and in the last days of March 1945 the Luftwaffe dropped leaflets across the Lower Rhine advising the population to evacuate the area, since from the beginning of April new decisive weapons were to be deployed there. A *cordon sanitaire* 50 kms wide was required. From a military point of view the period towards the end of March offered the last opportunity to shut down the Western Front by driving back the first crossings to the western side of the Rhine.[114] Rumours were rife that near Münster a number of Me 109 fighters were being converted for kamikaze operations (SO = *Selbstopfereinsätze*, self-sacrificial operations) using a special 250 kg bomb; even an Me 262 jet could not outfly the bomb's pressure wave.

There are indications that this proposed operation was in some way sabotaged by Luftwaffe personnel. On 31 March 1945 General Barber and 202 Luftwaffe servicemen including sixteen airfield commanders and eighty-five officers and pilots were executed for "refusing to obey orders".[115] It can hardly be a coincidence that the Luftwaffe War Diary for the period (19–30 March 1945) and the Wehrmacht High Command War Diary for a much longer period (1 March–20 April 1945) are missing, suggesting that there must have been a serious mutiny during the period and possibly at the instigation of Goering who in May 1945 spoke of a mysterious weapon which he had declined to use "because it might have destroyed all civilization."[116] An incident which may have been related to this situation occurred on 30 March 1945 when the second of two Me 262A-2a/U2 prototypes of the fast jet bomber version, works number 110555, became a write-off after crash landing at Schröck airfield near Marburg/Lahn and subsequently fell into American hands. This aircraft had been completed in January 1945, since when it had flown twenty-two test flights operating from Rechlin.[117] It was fitted with a bomb-aimer's position in the nose, and along both sides of this cockpit were long, feeler-like aerials,[118] almost certainly intended as a manually operated proximity fuse for the bombs.

Alsos Hot On The Trail

On 22 April 1945 Dr Edward O. Salant of the American Intelligence Mission *Alsos* addressed to all former American Air Intelligence field teams an urgent circular requesting a search for Luftwaffe 50 kg and 150 kg bombs having an aerial in the tail section.[119] Agents were to report the names of scientists, factories or laboratories linked to these bombs. The aerials were aluminium and resembled car aerials, about 40 cms long, as thick as a finger at the base where they screwed into the tail section. The bomb was 40 or 70 cms long, cylindrical and 22cms wide. There were probably brackets on the main casing. Internally were to be found radio components, metal vacuum tubes, condensers, resistors, etc. Areas of special interest were thought to be Rechlin, Celle and Stade.

On 26 April 1945 a supplementary notice widened the search to other bombs which had a 25-cm long aerial in the nose. An accompanying sketch showed a ball with small, wire-meshed covered holes at the head of the aerial. It may be recalled that during the initial experiments with the explosive in 1944, Zippermayer had had the idea that a better effect might be obtained if the powder was spread out in the form of a cloud before the explosion. A metal cylinder had been attached to the lower end of the container and hit the ground first, dispersing the powder. A quarter of a second later a small charge in the cylinder exploded and ignited the cloud. This may explain the real purpose of the 'aerial and ball' fitted to the nose of the bomb. The bombs were actually stored in Austria at a massive underground SS-weapons factory codenamed Quarz at Melk.

On 18 March 1945 the airfield commander of a fighter group at Münster, probably JG27 or JG28, received orders to accept delivery in Austria of the contents of thirty railway wagons consigned by the Office of Luftwaffe Supply. The orders were long and complicated and explained how the Me 109 fighter-bomber was to be converted to carry a new type of bomb. It was of 250 kg and would be slung under the bomb bay and kept in position by unusually long bolts which gave a clearance of 16 cms above the runway. A few days later another order arrived in which it was stated that the bomb had a destructive radius of 16 kms and would destroy the aircraft dropping it. Therefore the mission was to be flown only by unmarried volunteers.

Next came telephone orders for the airfield commander to collect two heavy tractor trucks at Linz and proceed to Amstetten railway goods yard. On this occasion he was advised that the new bomb would be suspended from a parachute when dropped, thus allowing the pilot a chance of escape. An altitude of 7000 metres was allowed.

The airfield commander's ADC, a Luftwaffe Hauptmann, was sent to Amstetten railway yard and found a train of thirty sealed wagons each bearing the words "Caution. New Explosive Type!" painted on the panelling in large white characters. A Waffen-SS Hauptsturmführer in charge of the security detachment refused to release the contents of the wagons to him, citing a *Führerbefehl* which required the release order to bear Hitler's personal signature. The Luftwaffe ADC had no document of this nature and the train remained at Amstetten until the arrival of the Americans.

The Waffen-SS and Americans Meet Up at Melk

On 12 April 1945 Grossadmiral Dönitz had spent 24 hours in Berne, Switzerland, and then returned to Berlin where he spoke to Hitler.[120] In mid-April the Soviet Army had dug in at St Pöllen, only 3 kms from Merkersdorf airfield which served Melk, from where they regularly broadcast over loudspeakers in German warning of the "the greatest treachery in world history" and inviting German troops, in alluring terms describing the unsurpassable treatment they would receive, to "come over and surrender".

Melk was being defended by the 6th SS Panzer Army with fifteen Jagdtiger tanks.

When Amstetten fell on 8 May 1945 citizens recall that the Waffen-SS were waiting quite unconcernedly in the market square to meet the American forces when they arrived. During the day when there was a Russian air raid American and SS troops sought shelter together. Later the two groups collaborated. The thirty railroad cars were taken westwards across the Enns demarcation line, while a mixed group proceeded to Melk to arrange the ceasefire. The same day the Russians moved forward and encountered American troops near Melk, where a brief exchange of fire ensued before the Americans withdrew. The US forces had examined the contents of the thirty goods trucks and satisfied themselves that the bombs were not primed with the catalyst, which was required by standing orders to be added to the bomb by the SS immediately before the fuse was set prior to take-off.

In April 1945 Otto Skorzeny's special Waffen-SS intelligence unit was ordered to provide the escort for the transport of 540 crates of documents from the Kaiser Wilhelm Institute in Berlin to the Austrian frontier. All Germany's atomic and biochemical weapons projects were included in these archives. Eventually, on 21 April 1945, the convoy reached Stechowitz, 30 miles from Prague. A rendezvous was made with the commanding general of the SS Weapons Engineering School, the crates were separated into lots and, together with other material, were interred, the entrances being dynamited. In American custody, the SS-General described how he and another SS-officer were the only survivors after concentration camp inmates and then their SS-guards had been murdered by a regular Wehrmacht execution squad. During his own interrogation the general "came clean" and spoke about a pressure bomb based on firedamp which "was absolutely devastating for everything". The SS destroyed the catalyst and formula shortly before the Americans arrived.

Did Goering "save civilization" by refusing Hitler's orders to deploy these bombs? Aside from doctrinal grounds, Hitler's objection to a full nuclear blast was that it might go on to ignite the hydrogen atoms in the atmosphere. Presumably it was thought this bomb presented the same sort of threat. The orders for its use flowed down through Luftwaffe channels. The SS refused to release the bombs because there was no order signed personally by Hitler. If it became known that Hitler had forbidden the bombs to be used and Goering was disobeying him, one can see how that might have given rise to a Luftwaffe officers' mutiny. Unfortunately Hitler's Luftwaffe ADC, von Below, is silent on the matter in his memoirs and so we shall never know.

CHAPTER 11

The First and Last Voyage of the German Submarine *U-234*

HIDEO TOMONAGA, a Samurai, held the rank of captain in the Imperial Japanese Navy and was credited with the invention of an automatic depth-keeping device for submarines. On 27 April 1943, southeast of Madagascar, he transferred from the Japanese submarine *I-29* under Captain Yoichi to Korvettenkapitän Musenberg's U-boat *U-180*. He brought with him a few items of luggage – three one-man torpedoes, a 3-cm gas-pressure self-loading cannon and, in a large number of smaller cases, a quantity of gold ingots destined for the Japanese Embassy in Berlin and said to be payment for German technology. There was in fact so much gold, probably several tonnes of it, that the U-boat chief engineer found it useful to help trim the submarine. In June 1943 *U-180* arrived safely at the French Biscay base of Bordeaux, and Captain Tomonaga went off to do whatever it was that he had come for.[121] He would reappear in the story twenty months later on the U-boat quay at Kiel.

The Preparation and Loading of *U-234*

The seven U-boats of Type XB were the largest in the Kriegsmarine, displacing 2,700 tonnes full load submerged. They had been designed as minelayers, and for this purpose were equipped with thirty mineshafts capable of carrying sixty-six mines, but in general were used as ocean replenishment boats, the so-called *Milchkühe*. 294 feet long and 30 feet in the beam, the class had diesel-electric propulsion providing a maximum

113

surfaced speed of 17 knots and 7 knots submerged. The most economic cruising speed was 10 knots which gave them a range of 21,000 miles and made them ideal for long-distance cargo missions to Japan, which could be reached from Germany without refuelling.

U-234 had been damaged by bomb hits in 1942 and May 1943 while under construction and was not launched until 23 December 1943. The boat was commissioned by Kapitänleutnant Johann Heinrich Fehler on 3 March 1944 and spent the next five months either in the builders' yard or working-up in the Baltic. Once the training period had been completed successfully, she put into Germania Werft at Kiel on 30 August 1944 for a major refit and conversion from a minelayer into a transport submarine. The important changes were the installation of a snorkel, an air intake mast enabling submerged travel under diesel propulsion and the removal of the twenty-four lateral mineshafts to create cargo stowage compartments. The outer keel plates were removed and the keel duct remodelled to receive a cargo of mercury and optical glass.

U-234 emerged from the yards on 22 December 1944 for trials. The commander had meanwhile been summoned to OKM in Berlin to be informed that *U-234* was to take important war material and twenty-seven passengers to Tokyo. Fehler argued that this number was unreasonable. They would take the place of eighteen crew members and endanger the mission. After some negotiation a compromise was struck in which twelve passengers would travel, one acting as No 1 watch-keeping officer. These would replace eight crew members. It appears from American declassified papers that a special commission, *Marinesonderzweigstelle Heimat* under Korvettenkapitän Becker, decided in December 1944 what cargo was to be carried. The OKM Liaison officer for Japan, Kapitän zur See Souchon, discussed the cargo with Japanese Military Attaché Kigoishi.

In January 1945 the final preparations were begun for the voyage to Tokyo. A Hohentwiel radar was installed which gave the boat the price-less advantage of detecting an approaching aircraft before the latter could get a fix on the submarine, but it could heat up severely if left working too long. Dr Schlicke, a former Director of the Telecommunications Testing Station at Kiel Arsenal, a passenger who had shipped aboard early, arranged in Berlin a two-for-one swap to eliminate the radar-overheating problem.

The cargo was loaded under conditions of the strictest secrecy. Over 100 tonnes of mercury in 50-lb iron bottles went into the keel ducts.

Elsewhere engineering and weapons blueprints, cameras, lenses, fuses, barrels and bales, secret documents in sealed containers, even an Me 262 jet aircraft in its component parts were stowed in the holds amidships.[122] Some of the six forward upright tubes through the foredeck were packed with anti-tank and small flak rockets, and *Panzerfäuste*.

The most important witness to all this activity was Oberfunkmeister Wolfgang Hirschfeld, the senior radio operator of *U-234*. A good observer of detail, who kept an illicit diary later published as a book,[123] he described how from a perch on the conning tower he saw an SS-lorry draw up on the quayside alongside the U-boat at Kiel one February morning in 1945 and unload the most important and secret item of cargo, a large number of small and immensely heavy metal cases of uniform size which looked about nine inches along each each side. He saw a military officer whom he later knew to be Japanese Military Attaché Kigoishi looking on.

After a few moments he noticed something which struck him as distinctly odd, for among the small knot of German crewmen working on the foredeck there were two Japanese officers who appeared to be supervising the loading. They were seated on a crate, occupied in painting a description in black characters including the formula 'U-235' on the brown paper wrapping gummed around each of the small, heavy containers. They were so numerous that he couldn't count them, but certainly there seemed to him to be well over fifty little cases.[124]

These two Japanese, who were to travel aboard *U-234* on the voyage to Tokyo, were Air Force Colonel Genzo Shosi, an aeronautical engineer, and Hideo Tomonaga, who had arrived in France aboard *U-180* nearly two years before. Once finished, each case would be carried individually to the German officer supervising the loading, third watchkeeping officer Leutnant zur See Carl-Ernst Pfaff, assisted by a bosun, Peter Schölch, for stowage in one of the six vertical loading tubes in the foredeck. They were pressure-resistant steel loading containers about 25 feet in length and six feet in diameter resembling a large cigar tube, designed to fit into each of the six vertical mineshafts set in a line down the centre line of the foredeck. These were held in place by the original mine-retention mechanism and could have been jettisoned at any time by the pulling of a lever by the commander.

Hirschfeld asked Tomonaga what the cases contained and was told, "It is the cargo from *U-235*. That boat is no longer going to Japan." When he enquired at the 5th Flotilla Office, they told him that *U-235* was Type VII training boat never intended for operations beyond the Baltic, and so he knew that Tomonaga had lied. He spoke to the commander privately a little later and was told, "For God's sake, Oberfunkmeister, I must swear you to total secrecy and ask you not to raise the matter again with the Japanese. I will explain everything to you in Tokyo."[125] Only five persons aboard *U-234* knew that the small cases contained uranium: Fehler the captain, Ernst the chief engineer, Pfaff the third watchkeeper and the two Japanese.

The commander of the 5th U-Flotilla arranged a reception for Tomonaga and Shosi, and in a ceremony aboard the hulk of the liner *St Louis* Ambassador Oshima placed Tomonaga's 300-year-old Samurai sword into Fehler's care for the voyage. The other passengers boarding in Germany were:

Kapitänleutnant Richard Bulla, first watchkeeper, Staff Officer to Luftwaffe Attaché.
Oberst Fritz Sandrath (Luftwaffe), chief of Bremen flak defences.
Oberst Erich Menzel (Luftwaffe), technical aide to Air Attaché, communications.
KKpt Heinrich Hellendorn (Navy), naval flak gunnery.
Dr (Ing) Heinz Schlicke, radar, D/F and infra-red scientist.
Oberstlt Kai Nieschling (Luftwaffe), squadron judge.
FKpt Gerhard Falck, buildings and naval architecture.
August Bringewald, senior Messerschmitt engineer, Me 262, Me 163 and rocketry.
Franz Ruf, Messerschmitt procurement specialist.

The last passenger was to board in Norway. Nieschling, the Judge, was travelling to Japan to investigate allegations against Embassy personnel implicated in the Sorge spy scandal and to keep an eye on other passengers during the voyage. Tomonaga, Shosi, Nieschling and Falck slept in the deck below the NCO's quarters, while all remaining passengers would sleep where they could.

Early on 26 March 1945, in convoy with three other U-boats and under heavy escort, *U-234* sailed for Horten in Norway and arrived there next day after surviving an air attack off Frederikshavn. There now followed a period of idleness while Fehler awaited orders to sail. During exercises at Christiansand *U-234* was rammed and damaged. Repairs had to be effected with shipboard tools in a quiet backwater. The last of the passengers, General Ulrich Kessler, the new Luftwaffe attaché to Tokyo, came aboard. Hirschfeld went every morning to the signals station to collect messages for the boat and on 15 April he took possession of a signal which read:

"*U-234*. Only sail on the orders of the highest level. Führer HQ."

A short while afterwards he was summoned to fetch an urgent signal which stated:

"*U-234*. Sail only on my order. Sail at once on your own initiative. Dönitz."

It is interesting to conjecture whether the visit of Grossadmiral Dönitz to Berne, Switzerland, on 12 April 1945 was connected with diplomatic moves following the death of US President Roosvelt that day. In order to provide a leader for Germany should the Reich be divided into two halves, north and south, on 15 April Hitler issued a decree vesting leadership in Dönitz and Kesselring respectively, and the order to *U-234* to sail was probably the first important decision in Dönitz' new role.

On the afternoon of 16 April, *U-234* sailed after a brief farewell address from the Regional Commander of U-boats North (FdU) Kapitän zur See Rösing. According to Hirschfeld, Fehler had decided to take the Cape Horn route into the south Pacific because of enemy air and sea superiority in the Indian Ocean. Use of the snorkel was abandoned at the entrance to the Iceland-Faroes Channel because of a heavy swell and on 30 April the North Atlantic was reached sailing surfaced.

On the evening of 4 May 1945 Hirschfeld copied down the order of U-boat Command that all German submarines were to observe a ceasefire with effect from 0800 hrs German time the next morning. All attack U-boats were to return to Norway. In accordance with his secret orders, Fehler could ignore this instruction since he was not commanding an attack U-boat. Once the last long-wave transmitter *Goliath* shut down, naval telegraphists had to rely on short-wave senders, but when instructed to tune in to the Distel wavelength, Hirschfeld found that he had been supplied with a table of false frequencies.

On 6 May an American news broadcast was heard reporting the official declaration of Japanese Foreign Minister Togo that Japan considered herself free from all contracts and treaties concluded with the German Reich and would fight on alone; on the evening of 8 May Reuters issued a communiqué to the effect that Japan had severed relations with

117

Germany and that, as a consequence, German citizens in Japan were being interned. Taking the two reports together, Fehler took the view that the purpose of his voyage was frustrated and that he should accept the capitulation.

His immediate problem was the two Japanese officers. He assumed they would try to prevent the cargo from falling into the hands of Japan's enemies, and Fehler, after informing them of the political developments, placed them under arrest. Tomonaga and Shosi expressed understanding for his dilemma and wished him an honourable solution. In asking him to reconsider, Shosi gave his personal undertaking that the crew of *U-234* would not be interned on completion of the voyage but would receive especially favourable treatment. Fehler had no confidence in the Japanese Government, however, and, having heard out the plea of the Japanese officers, shook his head with a smile.[126]

Hirschfeld discovered that, a short while after, Tomonaga and Shosi had made their way through the boat taking their leave of the crew, Tomonaga distributing among them the watches he had bought in Switzerland.

That same day, Kapitän zur See Rösing, FdU North, signalled Fehler in the Japan cypher:

"*U-234.* Continue your voyage or return to Bergen. FdU."

When shown the signal log, Fehler shook his head and said that he was definitely not going back.

Fehler considered that the Allied directive requiring all U-boats at sea to wear a black flag at the periscope head designated them as pirates and he decided to think about the legal position. This suited him because his surrender port based on his current position was Halifax, Nova Scotia, and he was not keen to surrender to the Canadians.

The boat continued to head south while long debates between officers and passengers were held on the question of heading for Argentina or the South Seas, but on 13 May Fehler signalled Halifax for surrender instructions. The Canadian station responded immediately by requesting the position of *U-234*, and once this had been supplied a course was given to steer for Nova Scotia. Fehler had not the least intention of going there and *U-234* now headed at full speed to the south-west in order to cross into the American sea area. At about 2300 hrs, when a Canadian patrol aircraft determined that *U-234* was not on the correct course, Halifax sent out more orders to the submarine by radio.

Towards midnight Judge Nieschling reported that Tomonaga and Shosi were lying in adjacent bunks, their arms linked, breathing stertorously and could not be woken. An empty bottle which had contained Luminal sleeping tablets was found on the deck plating nearby. A suicide note addressed to the commander was found during a search of their belongings requesting Fehler "should he find us here alive to leave us alone, please, and let us die". They had taken their action so as to avoid captivity. In closing they requested that their bodies should not be allowed to fall into the hands of the Americans, and that their diplomatic bag should be weighted and sunk, as it held secret papers useful to the enemy. There was a will confirming the assignment of certain property to members of the crew, and for the captain a sum of money in Swiss francs to be used to inform their relatives that they were dead, but not dishonoured.

Fehler merely said that he would do as they had asked. The game of cat-and-mouse with the Canadians continued over the next day until the signals of the latter were suppressed by American jamming. Because he thought he would get a better deal from the Americans, Fehler had made up his mind to surrender to them, and the Americans were so determined to get their hands on *U-234* that they sent their destroyer USS *Sutton* into the Canadian zone in direct contravention of Allied protocol. The American military authorities were in possession of a passenger manifest for *U-234* which they had obtained on occupying the Kiel naval base. The fact that there were two Japanese officers aboard *U-234* probably accounted for their unusual interest in the submarine: the first question by the American prize officer on boarding *U-234* on 17 May 1945 was not "Where is the uranium?" but "Where are the Japs?"

In fact, not long after the stern lookouts reported the approach of the American destroyer, Fehler sent for the U-boat's medical officer and said, "Tonight we must get the Japanese overboard. If the Americans get to them, they will do everything they can to bring them round. See to it that they die peacefully." Dr Walter descended to the lower deck without comment and a few hours later reported the death of Tomonaga and Shosi. Each corpse was sewn into a weighted hammock while the diplomatic pouch and the Samurai sword were bound to the body of Tomonaga after which the bodies were committed to the deep with full military honours.

On 19 May 1945 USS *Sutton* and *U-234* dropped anchor outside the naval port of Portsmouth, New Hampshire, and, after all had disembarked, the ten specialist passengers were driven off to a secret destination, the remainder to Boston Jail. Later a few members of the *U-234* crew, including Hirschfeld, were quartered in an old naval vessel and assigned to a submarine school in the yards where they were occasionally called upon to demonstrate shipboard equipment, although their principal task was to keep the U-boats in running order.

The Partial Unloading of *U-234*

During May much of the weapons material, the Me 262 jet and containers of documents had been unshipped and taken off to the Brooklyn Navy Yard. On 24 July 1945 Hirschfeld was standing on the conning tower of *U-234* with Captain Hatten, a US Navy Intelligence Officer, watching the six steel loading tubes being lifted by crane from the forward mineshafts and deposited on the quayside. The bosun, Schölch, was put in charge of the unloading because the Americans feared that the containers might be booby-trapped. Hirschfeld saw four men approach the steel tubes carrying small hand appliances and when he asked Captain Hatten for an explanation he was told, "They are scientists. They are testing for the uranium with Geiger counters."

Apparently the scientists discovered that all six steel tubes were contaminated to such an extent with radiation that they could not determine in which of the tubes the ten cases of uranium oxide listed in the loading manifest had been stowed. Schölch knew, but did not inform the Americans of this. Eventually Lt Pfaff was brought from Fort Mead camp and unloaded the ten cases of uranium oxide in exchange for some sort of inducement. Shortly afterwards he was repatriated and then returned to the United States as an immigrant, as did Schölch. Neither has ever spoken about the uranium shipments, although recently Pfaff is reported to have said that he discussed the *U-234* cargo with the US atom physicist Robert Oppenheimer in the Portsmouth Navy Yard. Shortly afterwards, the war with Japan ended and Hirschfeld spent the ensuing months at Fort Edward camp in Massachusetts until his release in April 1946.

Only one man who sailed on the first and last voyage of *U234* failed to make it home. Fregattenkapitän Gerhard Falck knew everything about the uranium consignment and probably he knew too much for his own good.[127] The German justice authorities dealing with the repatriation of Wehrmacht prisoners has no record of his return[128] and the US Government has so far been unable to account for his whereabouts in their custody after May 1945. He was a legitimate prisoner of war, having been captured while travelling as a passenger on an enemy warship at the time of it surrender. From there he was taken to Fort Hunt outside Washington DC and the declassified portion of his interrogation report indicates that he was cooperative.

In international law the Unites States as captor has a duty to account for all prisoners taken under Article 118 of the Geneva Convention Relative to the Treatment of Prisoners of War of 27 July 1929, to which the Unites States is a signatory, and to date in this case they have declined to do so. If the suspicion exists that Falck met his death unlawfully in their hands, it is not unjustified in the circumstances. The mysterious disappearance of Gerhard Falck is the first of the many secrets pertaining to the cargo aboard the German submarine *U-234*.

CHAPTER 12

"In the Interests of National Defense or Foreign Policy . . ."

IT IS CURIOUS that, after more than fifty-five years, despite the rules respecting automatic declassification of documents, much of the archive material relating to the cargo of the German submarine *U-234* still has not been made public. In 1985 American journalist Robert K. Wilcox wrote: "Inquiries to government agencies have produced nothing. It is as if the incident never occurred, as if *U-234*, its important passengers and cargo, never arrived".[129] British rocket engineer Philip Henshall wrote in 1995: "Despite requests made to the US naval authorities, the reply has always been that matters relating to nuclear affairs are still subject to official secrecy".[130]

Anybody who thinks this is legal should examine American law itself.[131] In the United States, a request to a Government agency must be answered within ten days, and if denied a reason given. The courts have ruled that the Freedom of Information Act is to be broadly construed in favour of disclosure, and its exemptions are to be "narrowly construed".

Where a matter is to be "kept secret in the interests of national defense or foreign policy" pursuant to an Executive Order, then the section relating to disclosure does not apply. If this exemption is being used secretly after 55 years, there must have been something extraordinary indeed about the heavy little cases of uranium on board the German submarine *U-234*. There is no blanket exemption by which nuclear matters generally are still subject to secrecy, and many formerly Top Secret documents in the matter have been declassified.

The Japanese Interest in Nuclear Materials

The interest of the Japanese Government in an atom bomb had waned in 1942 once it was realized that the separation of the U^{235} isotope for the purpose of making the bomb would require an enormous labour force, stupendous investment, one-tenth of Japan's annual electricity requirement and half the nation's copper output for a year. Professor Yoshio Nishina was the senior atomic scientist and headed the Army project. In 1943, when a link was established with Germany, Nishina asked for a cover story so that the Germans would not be suspicious of a request for uranium. The need for uranium as a catalyst was the excuse apparently adopted.[132] It is firmly established that Japan did subsequently request uranium from Germany for experimental purposes in 1943[133], and probably received a few tons. Japan had several hundred tons of uranium ore and had been prospecting successfully in Korea and Burma for more. Unless all this has a double meaning, one infers that Japanese physicists had worked unsuccessfully on an atom bomb project since 1941 and had not progressed beyond the early laboratory stage. The German naval historian Professor Jürgen Rohwer has confirmed from the first Magic decrypts for 1943 and 1944/45 that Japan requested from Germany a "quantity of uranium oxide" in connection with their atomic research into the fissile isotopes including plutonium.[134]

Accounting for the *U-234* Cargo: the Primary Documents

The initial US Navy Unloading Manifest of *U-234* was a translation carried out by the Office of Naval Intelligence and issued on 23 May 1945. The only item of uranium mentioned was ten cases of uranium oxide. Revised manifests, such as that of 16 June 1945, omit the uranium oxide. No mention was made of any uranium material in the long memorandum to C-in-C Atlantic Fleet of 6 June 1945 describing the *U-234* voyage and cargo arrangements in close detail.

The first manifest showed "*10 cases Uranium Oxide, 560 kilos*" consigned to the Japanese Army. As the item is part of the overall weight of the cargo, 560 kilos means the combined weight of containers and contents.

The next primary document is the copy of a secret cable #262151 dated 27 May 1945 from Commander Naval Operations to Portsmouth Navy Yard on the subject of "*Mine Tubes, Unloading Of*". Distribution of the memorandum was to the commandant and various duty and orderly officers. It reads:

"Interrogation Lt Pfaff second watch officer U-234 discloses he was in charge of cargo and personally supervised loading all mine tubes. Pfaff prepared manifest list and knows kind-documents and cargo in each tube. Pfaff stated long containers should be unpacked in horizontal position and short containers in vertical position. Uranium oxide loaded in gold lined cylinders and as long as cylinders not opened can be handled like crude TNT. These containers should not be opened as substance will become sensitive and dangerous. Pfaff is available and willing to aid unloading if RNEDT desires. Advise. CTM."

The third item is US Navy Secret Telephone Transcript 292045 between Commander Naval Operations, Brooklyn Navy Yard, Major Francis J. Smith, and Major Traynor at Portsmouth, NH Naval Yard. This recorded that on 30 May 1945, Lt-Cdr Karl B. Reese, Lt (j.g.) Edward P. McDermott (USNR) and Major John E. Vance, Corps of Engineers, US Army, arrived at Portsmouth Navy Yard in connection with the cargo of *U-234*. Large quantities were unloaded and taken by ship to Brooklyn. The following telephone conversation ensued on 14 June 1945 between Major Smith and Major Traynor:

Smith: "I have just got a shipment in of captured material and there were 39 drums and 70 wooden barrels, and all of that is liquid. What I need is a test to see what the concentration is and a set of recommendations as to disposal. I have just talked to Vance and they are taking it [i.e. the cargo] off the ship and putting it in the 73rd Street Warehouse. In addition to that I have about 80 cases of U powder in cases. Vance is handling all of that now. Can you do the testing and how quickly can it be done? All we know is that it ranges from 10% to 85% and we want to know which and what."

Traynor: "Can you give me what was in those cases?"
Smith: "U powder. Vance will take care of the testing of that."
Traynor: "The other stuff is something else?"
Smith: "The other is water."

The use of the letter "U" as an abbreviation for uranium was widespread throughout the Manhattan Project. The Corps of Engineers to which Major Vance was attached was the parent organization of the Manhattan Project and Major Vance was part of the latter project.

The fourth document originates from the Manhattan Project Foreign Intelligence files and confirms that the remaining cargo was unloaded on 24 July 1945. This included the ten cases of uranium oxide assayed as 77% pure Yellow Cake. The document confirms that the bulk of the *U-234* cargo was held in the custody of Major Francis Smith at the Brooklyn Navy Yard.[135]

Interpreting the Primary Documents

In the first manifest are listed ten bales of drums containing "confidential material" and fifty bales of barrels containing benzyl cellulose, which latter can be used for biological shielding purposes or as a coolant in a liquid reactor. The thirty-nine drums are said by Major Smith to contain "water" for which he needs a test done "to see what the concentration is": he knows that it ranges from 10% to 85%. If this is heavy water, the percentage describes the degree to which a consignment of water had been depleted of its hydrogen molecules.

It will be observed from the primary documents that uranium oxide was unloaded from *U-234* on 24 July 1945, while eighty cases of uranium powder had already been unloaded and shipped to Brooklyn by 14 June 1945. *Therefore aboard* U-234 *were two different uranium consignments and one of them never appeared at any time in the manifests translated by the Americans.*

We now observe that what seem to be discrepancies in the secondary, eyewitness evidence of Wolfgang Hirschfeld actually confirm the existence of two distinct shipments aboard *U-234*. The Unloading Manifest states "10 cases Uranium Oxide" but on the quayside at Kiel Hirschfeld said he saw "at least fifty of the little cases."[136] Obviously, what he saw the Japanese loading at Kiel was not the ten cases of uranium oxide, but the eighty little cases of uranium powder. The little cases he saw were cubic in shape about nine inches along the sides, whereas the uranium oxide described by Pfaff, and unloaded by him on 24 July 1945, was stowed in gold-lined cylinders, the dimensions of which are not known. Hirschfeld did not witness the actual unloading by Pfaff.

As to the eighty little cases of uranium powder, besides the fact that it was shipped in what seemed to be lead radioisotope shipping containers and that Major Vance of the Manhattan Project was going to test it, the American authorities have not been forthcoming.

The Ten Cases of Uranium Oxide

It will be recalled that the Magic decrypts for 1943 and 1944/45 show Japan requesting from Germany "a quantity of uranium oxide" in connection with their atomic research into the fissile isotopes including plutonium.

What is "uranium oxide"? Generally speaking, after the ore is mined, the crude concentrate know as Yellow Cake is recovered by leaching followed by solvent extraction and roasting. The material assays at between 60%–90% uranium oxide. It is poisonous, but not radioactive.

The German Army seized over 1000 tonnes of uranium oxide at Oolen in Belgium in May 1940. It was stored in wooden barrels each containing about 500 kilos. Where a barrel was damaged, the uranium oxide was repacked in a stout paper bag secured at the neck by a knotted wire. To consign this sort of material in gold-lined cylinders makes no sense unless it is radioactive in some way and handlers need biological shielding from the effects.

Experiments can be performed on uranium oxide in sub-critical reactors, and it had been Professor Harteck's idea in 1940 to use about 30 tonnes of uranium oxide to build a rudimentary low temperature nuclear reactor, and in either case some level of biological shielding would be required if the spent material was being shipped.

Gold-lined containers would be used where it was necessary to absorb fission fragments, emissions of gamma radiation or neutron radiation, or a combination of all three. Alpha and beta radiation is easily stopped by a 7mm thickness of aluminium or perspex.

What sense can be made of the fact that the ten cases of uranium oxide were stowed in a secure steel tube upright through the hull casing of the submarine and yet still leaked so much radioactivity that the forward part of the boat gave uniform Geiger counter readings over its entire surface? Men lived for months in close proximity to this radioactive contamination, yet none complained of radiation sickness. How was this to be explained?

Lt Colonel Richard Thurston, a former member of the Manhattan Project radiological team, supplied the answer[137]: the radiation could not have been gamma radiation. What occurred to him was that all the reported conditions could only be met if the substance detected was radon gas, which is notoriously difficult to contain. It would seep through the containers and steel tubes and adhere to exposed surfaces but not be particularly dangerous to humans.

Radon gas would imply the presence within the containers of radium in some form. A radium-beryllium source within a small sphere of heavy water at the centre of uranium oxide in a gold-lined cylinder would amount to a sub-reactor in miniature and meet the request of the Japanese for "a quantity of uranium oxide" in connection with their atomic research into the fissile isotopes including plutonium.

Pfaff's warning that the material must be handled like crude TNT indicates that the same precautions apply to the material as for the most unstable explosive. This is because the substance within the small cylinders becomes sensitive and dangerous on exposure to air. If these gold-lined cylinders were miniature sub-reactors, then the following dangers would present themselves when the cylinders were opened:

(1) Plutonium particles from the irradiated uranium oxide would rise into the atmosphere. The inhalation or ingestion of 1mg of plutonium will result in the lingering death of the victim within weeks and even a microgram results in a later high susceptibility to pulmonary cancer.

(2) Dangerous neutron radiation would be emitted from the reaction of the radium-beryllium source as would gamma and corpuscular radiation from the products of fission decay in the uranium powder.

This was why it was so dangerous to open the cylinders. The use of a gold lining in addition to the lead shielding is the clearest possible indication that a reaction process was continuing in the cylinders, and Professor Nishina of the Imperial Japanese Army nuclear project would have received, on the arrival of *U-234* in Tokyo, ten cases of uranium oxide containing precisely what had been requested in the Magic signals.

The cylinders though dangerous were basically nothing more than an elementary research material for the laboratory and would not have led the Americans to panic and suspect that Japan was on the verge of developing an atom bomb.

The Eighty Small Heavy Cases

To the exclusion of everything else aboard *U-234*, these eighty small containers in the custody of Major Vance, the tests performed on them by the Manhattan Project, and their ultimate disposal, are the obvious basis for further research.

They were removed from their loading tube at the end of May. Aboard the submarine there was no mystery as to where they had been stowed for probably half the crew had worked on the loading that day in February and the contents excited interest by their unusual weight. Portentous omens have been read into the meaning of the symbol "U-235" painted by Tomonaga on the wrapping of each of the small containers, but probably it served merely to identify the consignment as being uranium. I have no idea what the correct chemical formula is for natural uranium enriched with plutonium isotopes, and I doubt if Tomonaga would have known either: if on the other hand the cases actually had contained the isotope, it is unlikely in the extreme that the fact would have been advertised to all and sundry on the quayside: the Japanese, past masters of deception, even disguised their initial interest in uranium as being a sort of "catalyst".

The New Hampshire evening paper *Portsmouth Herald* announced in the week following the capture of *U-234* that the submarine had been "headed for Japan for the purpose of aiding Japan's air war with rocket and jet planes and other German V-type bombs". This is the first reference from a source well-connected to the US Navy to a "V-type bomb" and a "jet plane", neither of which feature on the Unloading Manifest. And in June the same newspaper claimed that there had been sufficient uranium aboard *U-234* to produce an explosion to eradicate all of Portsmouth and its surrounding suburbs from the face of the earth. Newspaper reports must, of course, not be awarded too much credence as historical documents, but they are nevertheless useful pointers. The *Portsmouth Herald* knew about a "jet plane" aboard *U-234* which is claimed by the German crew to have been shipped, but as to which the official record on the American side is silent. And to what extent before the first Trinity test in July 1945 was the effect of fantastic explosives openly discussed, and where did the idea come from that such a substance was aboard the German submarine?

Lt-Col John Lansdale, chief of atomic security and intelligence for the Manhattan Project, admitted that he handled the disposal of the small cases aboard *U-234*.[138] He recalled that the American military authorities reacted with panic when they discovered the cargo aboard the U-boat. Lansdale went on to say that the German material was sent to Oak Ridge where the isotopes were separated and put into the pot of material used to make America's first atom bombs.

Obviously Lansdale did not mean U^{235} isotopes here since they are the final result of the separation process. The only fissile isotopes which can be separated from irradiated uranium are the range of plutonium isotopes from fissioned material bred in a working reactor or sub-reactor assembly. This would have made them panic, particularly if they knew how a small-scale German atom bomb was constructed. All that was needed for detonation would be an effective implosion fuse.

Natural uranium powder in its natural state is highly pyrophorous and ignites spontaneously on contact with air, but this would not require it to be packed in eighty small radioisotope containers. It is, however, the manner in which plutonium-enriched uranium powder would need to be transported.

The thickness of lead required to reduce the initial intensity of gamma radiation by a factor of ten is 1.8 inches. The thickness of the walls, lid and base of the lead containers described by Hirschfeld would have provided an interior volume for each container sufficient for about 19 kilos of uranium metal powder, multiply by eighty = 1520 kilos: divide by 750 kilos = enough for two small-scale atom bombs.

The Implosion Fuses

A final twist to the *U-234* story has been suggested.[139] The German small-yield device could not have been properly detonated without an effective implosion fuse. For eighteen months the scientists at Los Alamos had failed to develop such a fuse. In October 1944 Robert Oppenheimer created a three-man committee to look into the problem. Luis Alvarez was on this team and became one of the heroes of the American A-bomb story when he solved it in the final days before the Trinity test at Alamogordo in July 1945.

The need was for a fusing system that could fire multiple detonators simultaneously. Harlow Russ, who worked on the plutonium bomb team, stated in his book *Project Alberta* that improvements were made to the detonator at the last moment. A new type of implosion fuse suddenly becoming available to the Manhattan Project gave a result four times better than expected at the Trinity A-test.

But did the real impetus for this success come from Luis Alvarez or German technology? Germany could not have detonated small-scale atom bombs without the most superior implosion fuse. According to the CIOS-BIOS/FIAT 20 report published by the US authorities in October

1946, by May 1945 Germany already had every kind of fuse known to the Americans – "and then some". Professor Heinz Schlicke, one of the passengers aboard *U-234*, was an expert in fuse technology. Infra-red proximity fuses were discovered to be aboard *U-234* on 24 May 1945, apparently as a result of the interrogation of Dr Schlicke in which he mentioned that he had fuses which worked on the principles that govern light. A memorandum by Jack H. Alberti dated 24 May 1945 states:

> "Dr Schlicke knows about the infra-red proximity fuses which are contained in some of these packages. Dr Schlicke knows how to handle them and is willing to do so."

Schlicke and two others were then flown to Portsmouth NH to retrieve the fuses. It is not suggested that these were the fuses used to explode the American plutonium bomb, but rather confirms that Schlicke knew more about fuses than the Manhattan Project did. From a transcript of a lecture given by Dr Schlicke to the Navy Department in July 1945, there seems to have been a close cooperation for some reason between Dr Schlicke and Luis Alvarez. And it is in the fact that the technological side of the Manhattan Project failed them that the real weakness of the American project is exposed.

CHAPTER 13

The Manhattan Project

THE MANHATTAN PROJECT was founded in order that the United States should have a nuclear capability in the event that Hitler developed the atom bomb. By the end of hostilities in Europe in May 1945 the United States did not have a bomb *which worked*, and, as that was the Project's raison d'être, it obviously failed. The American failure was in technology, for they were unable to devise an efficient implosion fuse.

How the Implosion Bomb Works

As any physicist will explain, the only economical way to detonate a Pu^{239} or plutonium bomb is by the implosion method. The bomb core is made as a sub-critical sphere surrounded by a layer of non-fissile U^{238}. A uniform layer of high explosive surrounds the tamper. When the thirty-two fuses are triggered simultaneously, the explosive detonates, creating a massive uniform pressure of millions of pounds per square inch which compresses the core to a supercritical density, causing the implosion. The implosion method is essential for plutonium-type bombs because the radioisotope Pu^{240}, being more fissile than Pu^{239}, would otherwise cause a premature detonation of the material known as a 'fizzle'. The least speed required for assembly of the critical mass by implosion is in the region of 3500 feet/sec.

The U^{235} bomb is more fissile than the plutonium device and the speed of assembly of the critical mass can be as low as 1000 feet/sec. For this reason an implosion fuse is not necessary for this type of bomb, but the amount of uranium material required is vastly greater.

In order to conceal the failure of the Manhattan Project, General Groves and his associates wanted people to continue to believe that ideally a plutonium bomb is detonated by an implosion fuse, while ideally the U^{235} bomb is detonated by a 'gun-type' device. The 'gun-type' detonator is, of course, what they say was used to detonate the so-called 'Thin Man' device used to devastate Hiroshima and which works in principle in the following manner: since one cannot assemble a critical mass without there being a reaction from it, two sub-critical lumps of highly enriched U^{235} are kept apart until detonation when they are fired together within a howitzer barrel with a breech at each end. The supercritical mass assembles at a reasonably fast speed in sub-atomic terms and so achieves the explosion.

The Development of the Manhattan Project without an Implosion Fuse

Since the Americans had no effective implosion fuse to hand before the end of May 1945, no question ever arose of detonating a plutonium bomb in the preceding period. The U^{235} bomb was the only possibility. Although the actual information regarding the Hiroshima bomb is probably still classified half a century later, it is known that the critical mass in the most favourable configuration as calculated by Richard Feyman was 50 kilos of U^{235}. Robert Oppenheimer put it at double that. This is an awful lot of U^{235} to expend in one bomb. Of course, nobody in his right mind would dream of putting half a field gun into a bomb to set it off if he had an implosion fuse. To separate 50 to 100 kilos of U^{235} is fantastically expensive and wasteful of resources and takes nearly three years to amass with (at today's money) an investment of about 200,000 million dollars. Depending on the factor by which the uranium material is compressed, the U^{235} rationally needed for an implosion bomb would have been, at the most, just over ten kilos.

Explaining the Delays in Producing the U^{235} Bomb

Early in 1944, the head of the Manhattan Project, General Groves, had indicated that he would have "several" U^{235} bombs ready, but it would be the end of 1945 before they were available for use. What this means is that if the United States had had an implosion fuse in early 1944, three or four bombs would have been available for use against Germany. He expected to have the material for three or four devices for implosion, but if no implosion fuse were forthcoming, then it would be fifteen months or so before there was enough material to set off one 'gun-type' bomb. This explains how it was possible for Groves to dictate to the Secretary for War, Stimson, on 23 April 1945 that the target was, and was always expected to be, Japan. Groves was not the maker of State policy; it was simply the fact that his scientists could not produce the goods within the time scale which determined the policy.

Since the autumn of 1943 the Los Alamos experts had been working without success on how to compress a sphere the size of an orange uniformly over its surface area using 32 detonators fired within the same three-thousandth of a second. They had not progressed beyond a thermo-electric fuse taking 0.5 micro-seconds, which was too slow. In the hope of finding a solution, in October 1944 Robert Oppenheimer set up a three-man committee headed by physicist Luis Alvarez.

The technical portfolio being taken to Japan by *U-234* passenger Dr Heinz Schlicke was a substantial one. He was an expert in explosives, detonators and fuses, in very high technology radar and radio systems, in the field of high frequency light waves, guided missile development and the V-2 rocket. Before leaving Germany he had met with numerous scientists to receive instruction in their technologies for later dissemination in Japan where he would serve as a scientific advisory liaison officer. A nuclear physicist with whom he had consulted was Professor Gerlach, Reich Plenipotentiary for Nuclear Science.

The fusing system to fire multiple detonators simultaneously was developed in the seven weeks between Schlicke arriving and the beginning of July. The solution was probably some kind of fuse in which a high-tension electrical impulse vaporized a wire to activate all 32 charges in 0.04–0.08 microseconds. The type of impulses involved, e.g. Thyratrons and Krytons, are produced in special high-tension and high-efficiency vacuum tubes notably in the field of HF radar in which Dr Heinz Schlicke was a specialist.

Three days after the Trinity test on 16 July 1945 Dr Schlicke delivered a lecture to the Navy Department on the subject of detonator fuses and afterwards shared the platform with Luis Alvarez for a question and answer session from the scientists present.

The likelihood exists that the Hiroshima device was detonated by an implosion fuse. The first mock-up version of the U^{235} bomb was so large that it would not have fitted into the bomb-bay of a B-29[140], but the B-29 carrying the Hiroshima bomb had room in the bomb bay for several to fit in easily.

The Oak Ridge records show a large increase in enriched uranium stocks occurring in the third week of June 1945, at about the time when the implosion fuse suddenly became available. As this could be used to detonate a U^{235} bomb with far less material, one assumes that the bomb was split down and the surplus returned to store, thus radically increasing the amount available. This, and the smallness of the bomb, increases the probability that the Hiroshima device was imploded. The sudden increase in U^{235} stock has led people to speculate that it must have been of German origin, leading to claims that "the bombs dropped on Japan came from German arsenals", but that was not, and logically cannot have been, the case.

Did the *U-234* Cargo Influence US Policy?

The weight of evidence available suggests that the decision to use the atomic bomb against Japan occurred as the result of some hitherto unexplained factor occurring between 16 and 30 May, 1945, which dictated the chief aim of American strategic atomic policy to be the military defeat of Japan at the earliest possible opportunity.

As at 16 May, no executive decision had been taken to use the bomb, and Secretary for War Stimson advised President Truman that the rule of sparing the civilian population "should be applied, as far as possible, to the use of any new weapons".[141]

On Saturday 19 May 1945 the German submarine *U-234* berthed at Portsmouth New Hampshire: her specialist passengers were interrogated during the week beginning 24 May: Major Vance of the Manhattan Project arrived on 30 May to inspect the cargo and take away the heavy water and eighty little cases of "uranium powder".

At a meeting of the Interior Committee on the morning of 31 May 1945:

> "Mr Byrnes recommended and the Committee agreed that the Secretary for War should be advised that, while recognizing that the final selection of the target was a military decision, the present view of the Committee was that the bomb should be used against Japan as soon as possible, that it be used on a war plant surrounded by workers' houses, that it be used without prior warning."

Arthur H. Compton of the scientific panel noted of that morning's decision that "it seemed to be a foregone conclusion that the bomb would be used"[142], and when the meeting reconvened that afternoon the agenda had been amended so that consideration could be given to the question of the effect of the atom bomb on the Japanese and on their will to fight.

When President Truman learned of the decision on 1 June he admitted to Byrnes that he had been giving the matter serious thought for some days and that, after considering other plans, he had reluctantly come to the conclusion that there was no alternative. Although he did not give the order on 1 June, it appears that he had made the decision by then.

The political activity during the last two weeks in May 1945 was such that Stimson appears to have been a man overtaken by events. Somewhere in that period he ceased to treasure jealously the United States' reputation for fair play and humanity. He never explained why satisfactorily. In retrospect he stated:

> "My chief purpose was to end the war in victory with the least possible cost in the lives of the men in the armies which I helped to raise."[143]

It had ceased to be his rule to "spare the civilian population, as far as possible, to the new weapons" and worse, with his words, he justified the perpetration of any atrocity against civilians in order to save military lives. If, and only if, the possibility existed that Japan might have been gifted a number of small-scale atom bombs by Germany would the American Government have had an arguable right to order the deployment of their atomic arsenal. It is one of the great ironies of war that Korvettenkapitän Heinrich Fehler disobeyed his last order and surrendered his submarine to the United States in the hope of obtaining better treatment for his crew in captivity and presented Washington with the justification for the terrible action against Japan which was to follow, and with a weapon under whose shadow the world has existed ever since.

CHAPTER 14

Gravity II

G ERMANY BETWEEN THE two World Wars was a fertile ground for research into UFOs and alternative technologies. UFO sightings go back of course to the beginnings of recorded history. Research shows that celestial lights and flying saucer shapes have been reported since the days of the Ancient Greeks. In the more recent epoch of the last two hundred years or so, marine insurers at Lloyds of London have taken note of occurrences reported in the logs of registered vessels, the majority of which were written by the most serious minded and perhaps God-fearing ships' masters and officers. The reports go on, backward in time to the first records of true oceanic navigation, proving that there never was "a time in 1947 when flying saucer sightings really began", (an expression much favoured by those striving to prove that all UFO sightings are of terrestrial US origin), but only that there was a great spate of reported sightings from that year.

The oriental influence behind Nazism has already been remarked upon and will be raised again in the final chapter, and one of the areas to which the SS directed their attentions was the Aryan scientific treatises of pre-Hindu India. These Aryans of antiquity, far in advance of the rest of humanity in terms of scientific development, devised machines called *Vimanas* which "flew the skies like aircraft, utilizing a form of energy obtained directly from the atmosphere" and whose description resembles 'flying saucers'.

There are some authenticated Sanskrit texts which, being technological, are called *Manusa* and are said by the writers to explain how certain machines were constructed for aerial flight. The *Yantra Sarvasa* deals with machinery, for example. *Rukma Vimana*[144] elucidates their construction, describing metal alloys, weights and heat-resistant metals.

According to the *Samarangana Suradhara*, the craft could fly "to great distances" and were "propelled by air". The text devotes over 200 stanzas to building plans. As to propulsion, "four strong mercury containers must be built into the interior structure". When these are heated, "the vimana develops thunder-power through the mercury, and at once it becomes like a pearl in the sky."[145] The vimanas were equally at home in the air, on water or submerged, confirming that the vimana could also be a submersible if so desired. Among the non-technical works known as *Daiva*, there would appear to be suggestions, if not evidence, that such vimanas could be put to the most gruesome and devastating use in wartime. One might be suspicious that it was for this very purpose that the Third Reich built vimanas, and not for the peaceful exploration of space, which was the supposedly secret reason why Wernher von Braun put so much effort into the V-2. There is alleged to exist a terrible sidereal force known to the Aryan rishis or wise men in the treatise *Ashtar Vidya* and to the mediaeval hermeticists as the 'sidereal light' or Milk of the Celestial Virgin and other such terms. It was the *Vril* of the coming races of mankind described in Bulwer-Lytton's occult novel *The Coming Race* published in 1871, which influenced Hitler. The force is not doubted by the rishis, since it is mentioned in all their works. It is a vibratory force which, when aimed at an army from an *Agni Rath*, or, for want of a better term, gun, fixed to a vimana or balloon according to the instructions in *Ashtar Vidya*, reduced to ashes 100,000 men and elephants as easily as it would a dead rat. The force is allegorized in *Vishnu Purana*, the *Ramayana* and other Hindu volumes. The *Vril* would be the weapon par excellence and throughout the war a precise knowledge of its manufacture must have been earnestly sought by the Waffen-SS.

By a curious coincidence, in the edition of the periodical *Science* of 3 January 1969, Schubert, Gerald and Whitehead reported that when a heat source was revolved slowly below a dish of mercury, the mercury began to revolve in the contrary direction and then gathered speed until it was circulating faster than the flame. This is the projection of energy by an exceedingly simple process, and poses two interesting questions: where does the mercury obtain its surplus energy if not from the atmosphere itself, and was this in some way connected with Aryan vimana flight?

Odd Goings-on at Führer-HQ Waldenburg

Near the town of Waldenburg in Lower Silesia was a coal mine turned by the SS in 1944 into a laboratory for V-weapons research.[146] The entire site, Führer HQ Riese, was started in the spring of 1944 and consisted of six underground systems with a 30-square kilometre area plus tunnels housing the proposed Führer HQ below Schloss Fürstenstein 25 kilometres away. Each system was a design of mostly concreted cross-tunnels on one or several levels. The most secure was Säuferhofen, whose entrances were protected by steel doors and machine-gun emplacements.

The research, which replicated a larger project at Ohrdruf in the Harz, took place between November 1944 and May 1945. It was code-named *Laternenträger* (Torch bearer) and *Chronos*. Professor Walther Gerlach, Plenipotentiary for Nuclear Science, coordinated the programme with Dr Ernst Grawitz, Chief of SS Medical Services.

The experiments were conducted within a 20-cm thick ceramic cover in the shape of a bell. The studies were aimed at analyzing the effects of contra-rotating at very high speeds two cylinders containing about 250 kgs of mercury or a mercury amalgamate around a hard and heavy metal core.

Another experiment codenamed *Leichtmetall* (light metal) used thorium and beryllium peroxides. Thorium oxide is one of the most heat-resistant metals known and beryllium has a very high melting point. By 1944 Germany had cornered all available European stocks of thorium, but, on enquiring the reason, the US *Alsos* Mission was unable to establish a satisfactory answer.

The research room was 30 metres square with ceramic-tiled walls, the floor covered with rubber mats which were burned after three experiments. The entire contents of the room were destroyed after each ten experiments. After each test the room would be doused with brine for up to 45 minutes.

Each test lasted from 45 seconds to one minute when the apparatus emitted a strange, pale blue light. Some members of the research team suffered health problems from exposure to this light. Despite the precautions employed, many personnel complained of insomnia, memory loss, imbalance, muscle spasms and a permanent unpleasant metallic taste in the mouth. The first scientific team in May-June 1944 had been disbanded after the death of five of its seven members. While the test was proceeding, all personnel stood back 200 metres from the epicentre and wore thick rubber protective suits and helmets with large red glass visors.

During the tests electrical equipment up to 150 metres from the bell would short-circuit or break down.

The research involved tests on small animals, animal substances, plants such as mosses, ferns, ivies and fungi and possibly on humans as well. It was found that, during the spinning experiments, samples exposed inside the bell were completely destroyed by an alien crystalline matter which could not be described precisely, being unknown to science. The substance formed within the host and destroyed its tissues. Liquids such as blood gelled and separated. In plants, chlorophyll disappeared after 4–5 hours, followed by decay within 14 hours. However, there was no smell of decomposition and the plants transformed into matter of the consistency of axle grease. Efforts were made to reduce the damage inflicted by the unknown substance and by 25 March 1945 this had been cut to no more than 3%.

The menial work was carried out by prisoners from the Gross-Rosen concentration camp. These people, and some lower-level German scientific workers, sixty-two in all, were murdered near Pattag at the beginning of May 1945 when the project closed down, indicating its high level of secrecy.

The interruption of electrical current is symptomatic of most close-contact UFO reports. It is an electro-magnetic effect and occurred at Waldenburg, where one assumes it was directly related to spinning containers of mercury at high speed in order to achieve some effect in the various indescribable materials being experimented upon. It was suggested in the Polish bulletin that there was reason to suspect that the subject was connected with the Waffen-SS Haunebu flying saucer research project under the SS-E-IV and SS-U-13 research teams, but nothing is known about the work of either.[147]

The Motorstoppmittel

The valley of Jonastal lies in the heart of Germany, south-west of Weimar in the Harz Mountains, at the centre of a ring of the towns of Erfurt, Waltershausen, Crawinkel and Stadtilm. Since Imperial times there had been a Military Training Area at Ohrdruf on a plateau in Jonastal. Organization Todt began work building a vast underground city in the limestone in 1937. The entrances were disguised as 'weekend chalets'. The actual size of the development is difficult to estimate since the entrances to the lower galleries were sealed off by the SS with explosives and, after exploring what remained accessible, the Americans closed down the rest.

A number of surface structures – five giant halls which can be seen in immediate post-war Allied aerial photos – were demolished in the DDR period and covered over below an unbelievably thick layer of industrial rubbish to make a hill. Exploration below ground is strictly prohibited. With a Land Rover in dry weather it takes several hours to tour the perimeter of the area. The Feldherrn hill and Musketierberg are central elevations offering a good view over a plateau of grass and scrub extending for several kilometres in all directions. The terrain is dangerous and remains littered with shrapnel, unexploded bombs and shells.

In 1944 the SS took over at Ohrdruf, which had been established as a V-weapon centre some time previously, and soon strange things began to happen. Ohrdruf was the largest underground factory city of the Third Reich and the most impregnable place on earth. The mapped tunnel system is 1.5 miles in length, although that is definitely only the tip of the iceberg.

Below ground there are thought to be four facilities consisting of many long galleries on as many as four levels designated *Jasmin*, *Wolfsturm*, *Siegfried* and *Olga*. Huge ventilation shafts are still to be found at the surface. It is known that there are sufficient generators below ground to supply current to a city the size of Berlin. At least one underground power source there has been running without any maintenance since 1945. The German writer Dieter Meinig[148] reported that when the Bundeswehr reclaimed the territory on the reunification of Germany in 1989 they discovered a large thick electric cable which emerged from the ground directly above facility *Olga*. On examination it was found to be of wartime manufacture and carrying a high voltage current. The cable was cut to see if a consumer complained, but nobody did. This deep underground facility was sealed by the SS from the inside as well as at the surface. It has never been investigated and is probably the origin of the strange glow in the night sky occasionally reported even nowadays, leading one to assume that the power plant could not be shut down and is continuing to produce energy over 55 years later. After the war the US air force photographed the region from the air and saw the underground construction as being shaped like the spokes of a huge Celtic cross. A senior American officer who saw below ground wrote of it:

"The underground installations were amazing. They were literally subterranean towns. There were four in and around Ohrdruf: one near the horror camp, one under the Schloss, and two west of the town. Others were reported in nearby villages. None were natural caves or mines. All were man-made military installations. The horror camp had provided the labour. An interesting feature of the construction was the absence of any spoil. It had been carefully scattered in hills miles away. The only communication shelter which is known is a two floor deep shelter with the code Amt 10. Over fifty feet underground the installation consisted of two and three galleries several miles in length and extending like the spokes of a wheel. The entire hull structure was of massive reinforced concrete. Purpose of the installations was to house the High Command after it was bombed out of Berlin. The place also had panelled and carpeted offices, scores of large work- and store rooms, tiled bathrooms and tubs and showers, flush toilets, electrically equipped kitchens, decorated dining rooms and mess halls, giant refrigerators, extensive sleeping quarters, recreation rooms, separate bars for officers and enlisted personnel, a cinema and air-conditioning and sewage systems."[149]

According to witnesses, from 1943 onwards Ohrdruf was a testing ground for new weapons systems above ground and new panzer weapons, guns and remote control systems are well remembered, as is the *Motorstoppmittel*, which could bring down aircraft by means of a strong electro-magnetic field. While the machine was thought to be operating at Ohrdruf automobile and panzer engines for miles around would cut out and refuse to function. The Allies do not appear to have photographed or bombed the area during the war, which suggests that the area was deliberately avoided by their aircraft.

The *Motorstoppmittel* was reported in 1944 by a member of the Technical Intelligence Division of the US Strategic Air Force:

"We were getting reports from a number of overlapping sources: planes returning to England from bombing missions over the continent kept experiencing engine trouble. The engines would suddenly become rough, cutting in and out. As the stories accumulated, scattered spy and POW reports reinforced the suspicion that a secret ground installation was responsible for our engine trouble.

"There was considerable discussion among Intelligence people as to what should be done. The general feeling – that some new German device was causing the electrical problems – presented one major difficulty: the amount of electricity required to short out a B-29 engine was calculated as greater than all the known electrical energy output of Europe!

"A special plane was fitted out with monitoring equipment. A volunteer was found to fly the plane. He flew his mission and when he returned to base, he behaved like a madman. He was angry and hysterical and raved about 'How we could have subjected him to such things'. When we tried to debrief him he cursed and screamed. He was so wild that nobody could find out just what had happened to him. He was finally sedated and put to bed.

"But the strangest thing of all was that when he woke up next day, he acted as if nothing unusual had happened. He had completely forgotten the previous day's insanity. He had no memory of his anger or hysteria. He was feeling fine, ready to return to duty. Of course, the plane's instruments showed nothing."

An interesting account of what it was like to experience this from ground level is provided by Frau Cläre Werner[150] who was a watchtower lookout on the Wachsenburg, close to the Ohrdruf military testing centre. She often observed a strange lightning effect across the territory lasting several minutes which lit up the whole horizon at night and so bright that she could read a newspaper by it. Frau Werner and two other witnesses reported that, after these phenomena, they would suffer a feeling of being completely drained and exhausted for the next three days. Scientists explain the exhaustion as a form of shock caused by waves of energy from a gravitational field.

This development probably resulted from the observation that spinning experiments with mercury caused electrical equipment and motors to short-circuit and malfunction. By stepping up the output of the device the gravitational field expanded over a far greater area. Possibly the manufacture of the gelatinous organic-metallic serum was carried out on a larger scale at Ohrdruf for the flying saucer programme.

Most of those who had worked at Ohrdruf under the SS, whether concentration camp inmates from the Buchenwald satellite camp S-III nearby, local civilian workers or lower ranking German technical staff, disappeared on or before the arrival of American forces under General Patton on or about 11 April 1945. As many as 3,000 local people remain unaccounted for. Elite SS units murdered even Wehrmacht personnel who had seen the Ohrdruf technologies and therefore knew too much[151]. In addition there are substantial rumours that large groups of SS men and their families were seen entering the tunnel system during the fighting for Jonastal just before the lower galleries were sealed while the mysterious electro-magnetic source was left operating. Whatever its purpose, the last Führer HQ at the centre of such a defence would have been impregnable so far as mechanical means of attack were concerned.

The German work at Ohrdruf may have been aimed at investigating other space-time continua. This was said to have been the purpose of the alleged Philadelphia Experiment in 1943. Scientists such as Dr Joseph Weber of the University of Maryland have confirmed that good reasons exist to suspect some form of gravitic anomaly disposed around the Earth in a particular pattern. This might be an ordinary gravitational field beyond our spectrum acting in a manner equivalent to electro-magnetism. The thinking is that there could be ten areas of the world, five in each hemisphere, where this form of gravitic anomaly operates, and in these regions it does seem that the number of disappearances of ships, people and aircraft is disproportional to the occurrence of losses else-where. The most famous of these is an oblong area with one corner at Fort Lauderdale on the Florida coast, the so-called 'Bermuda Triangle'. In order to be clear on the concept, I have cited three post-war cases. Although the basic anomaly seems to be chronometric, i.e aircraft arriving at a geographical location at a calculated speed beyond their modest capabilities, the actual cause may have been the operation of Gravity II – a second gravitic force first postulated by the geophysicist Dr John Carstoiu in his NAS thesis *The Two Gravitational Waves Propagation*.

These theories may well explain, for example, two USAF cases over the Pacific in the 1950s and the US Navy tragedy involving the mysterious loss of five Avenger aircraft on a training flight from Fort Lauderdale on 5 December 1945.

Ivan T. Sanderson investigated in his book *Invisible Residents* (Universal Tandem, 1974 at pp. 152–162) two reports by experienced military aviators involving an inexplicable time anomaly while aloft. The reports were then analyzed by Captain R.J. Durrant, an airline pilot.

J. F. O'D was a B-26 group navigator who briefed three squadrons daily on navigational routes operating while serving in Korea in late 1955. Returning from a training mission heading almost due south between Seoul and Pusan at 7000 feet, he calculated at three check points over a twenty-five minute period a ground speed for his aircraft of 550 knots. This would imply a tail wind of 265 knots for an aircraft of that type on a routine flight. There were no side-effects such as unusual turbulence reported. Meteorologists were of the opinion that such a wind blowing south at 7000 feet would be impossible. Captain Durrant stated that the only explanation available to fit the reported facts was that the aircraft must have unknowingly entered a mass moving at a speed greater that the spin of the Earth. A selective force pushing or pulling the aircraft would have shown up on the airspeed indicator.

In the second case Lt Col Frank P. Hoskins USAF stated that in the spring of 1966 he was AF advisor to 106th Air Transport Group NY Air Guard based at NASNY. On the day in question he was a basic navigator aboard an Air Guard C-97 from Kwajalein to Guam. Guam is an area notorious for unexplained aircraft disappearances. It was a 6-hour flight at 12,000 feet with a forecast side wind of 10 knots. His Loran and celestial fixes over part of the course resulted in the calculation of a speed of 340 knots, indicating a following wind of 110 knots. On landing, the weather debriefing officer admitted that he was aware of such inexplicable phenomena which occurred for a few hours eight to ten times a year.

The possibility of this assist being the jet stream was ruled out by low altitude and wrong direction, and Captain Durrant also calculated that Lt Col Hopkins had actually underestimated the strength of the assist, which was nearer to 200 knots. A wind of such velocity would have affected the land surface below. The only explanation is that this old C-97 aircraft ran into a local gravity field anomaly. To put it more simply, in both cases the two aircraft got to their destination impossibly fast. The only possible known cause, a wind of super-hurricane force, was not recorded, and if it had occurred would have had a devastating effect at ground level. Thus for a brief period the aircraft slipped into an unknown strata which happily was moving in the same direction of travel.

The third case is more complicated, since none of the aircrew survived. The verdict of the Navy Department enquiry into the loss of five Avenger aircraft and their crews on 5 December 1945 adjudged the flight leader, Lt Charles C. Taylor, culpable for the tragedy: "The flight leader's false assurance of identifying as the Florida Keys islands he sighted plagued his future decisions and confused his reasoning. He was directing his flight to fly east even though he was undoubtedly east of Florida."

On 9 November 1946 the Board of Correction of Naval Records upheld an appeal lodged by Lt Taylor's mother on a technical point and substituted an amended cause of loss attributable to "reason or reasons unknown". Unlike other so-called Bermuda Triangle mysteries, the unique factor about the loss of Flight 19 is that radio contact was maintained with the straying aircraft during the critical period for no less than three and a quarter hours, yet in all that time the shore stations were never able to obtain a radar or DF fix on them. The depositions to the board of enquiry when plotted on a chart enable us to satisfactorily resolve this mystery. A significant red herring has been the interpretation of a single word given in evidence by an instructor colleague of Lt Taylor.

The factual information which follows is from information supplied by the Department of the Navy's Naval Historical Centre, Washington, and logs compiled by the researcher Gian Quasar who has taken a special interest in the case.

On the afternoon of 5 December 1945 five TBM Avenger bombers were readied at Fort Lauderdale Naval Air Station, Florida for an authorized advanced overwater navigational training flight. Four of the aircraft had a pilot, gunner and radio operator; the fifth was a crewman short. All five pilots were qualified as basic flight instructors with up to 350 to 400 hours' flying time, of which at least 55 hours had been on TBM aircraft. The aircraft had a cruise speed of about 145 knots and a range of just over 1130 miles, which meant that the type could remain up for at least seven hours of normal flight, more if well throttled back.

All five aircraft were fitted with two compasses and carried a radio operator who worked the transmitter/receiver. A ZBX homing receiver to obtain a bearing on base and an IFF transponder for use in emergency enabling ground stations to identify aircraft were also fitted. The aircraft had been carefully serviced beforehand and carried inflatable life rafts. Each man wore a life-jacket and had a parachute. The flight leader was 28-year-old bachelor Lt Charles Carroll Taylor USNR, a 6-year Navy veteran and a senior qualified flight instructor who had over 2500 flying hours' experience, including ten months on combat missions in the Pacific. He had been appointed a flight instructor in Miami in January 1945. Two of his pilots, Edward J. Powers, USMC, and George W. Stivers Jr, USMC, were Captains and thus outranked Taylor.

On the fatal afternoon Taylor was late for duty and on his arrival at 1.15 he informed the duty officer, "I just do not want to take this flight out". Whether this was due to some premonition of impending disaster is not known, but Taylor was told he had to take it since there was nobody else.

Scattered rain showers were forecast for the sea area east of Florida that afternoon. Cloud was broken with a ceiling of 2500 feet, visibility six to eight miles, otherwise unlimited ceiling with visibility ten to twelve miles. Wind was south-westerly, 20 knots gusting to 31 knots at times, sea moderate to rough, air temperature 67 degrees Fahrenheit.

Starting from Fort Lauderdale naval air base the schedule was to fly east 91 degrees true over the sea for 56 miles and practice-bomb a concrete hulk on a rocky outcrop known as the Chicken and Hen Shoals, an exercise lasting about fifteen minutes. Flight 19 would then continue east towards the Bahamas on the same heading for another 67 miles and, using Great Stirrup Cay as a visual fix, turn left at the 123-mile point to a course NNW 346 degrees true for 73 miles. Crossing Great Sale Cay which is 60 miles long at right angles to the path of approach and could not be missed, a second visual fix was to be taken just beyond it before completing the third leg of the triangle home. The total distance to be flown was 316 miles, take-off 2.10, ETA 4.25, time 135 minutes, the average ground speed being about 147 knots, the cruise speed for the Avenger. Sundown was at 5.29. Flight 18 flew the identical course taking off twenty-five minutes earlier and arriving at base at 4.00.

Lt Taylor's Flight 19 took off at ten past two but there was a delay in forming up. A fishing vessel watched the bombing practice over the Hen Shoals at about 2.45 and then saw the aircraft fly off eastwards. Their actual bearing was 120 degrees to compensate for the strong south-westerly wind. At about 3.45, a half-hour after having turned left at Great Stirrup Cay, the five aircraft should have completed the second leg. Powers was leading, Taylor bringing up the rear.

The Flight 19 Anomaly

3.45 Taylor: (repeated several times) "Powers, what does your compass read?"

(The aircraft were transmitting on the 4805 kilocycles band which was weak over more than 125 miles and, though none of Powers' messages were picked up and logged at base, some were noted by Lt Cox, a colleague flight instructor circling Fort Lauderdale.)

Powers: "I don't know where we are. We must have got lost after that last turn."

As we shall see, Powers' apparent error of landfall was so great that it could only be accounted for by a cross-wind of super-hurricane force. This led Taylor to surmise that everybody's compass must be faulty, an

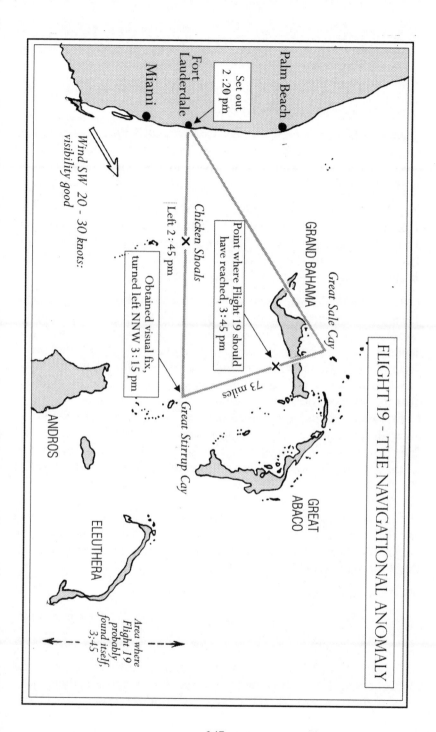

FLIGHT 19 - THE NAVIGATIONAL ANOMALY

Palm Beach

Fort Lauderdale

Set out 2:20 pm

Miami

Wind SW 20 - 30 knots: visibility good

Chicken Shoals
Left 2:45 pm

GRAND BAHAMA

Great Sale Cay

Point where Flight 19 should have reached, 3:45 pm

Obtained visual fix, turned left NNW 3:15 pm

73 miles

Great Stirrup Cay

ANDROS

GREAT ABACO

ELEUTHERA

Area where Flight 19 probably found itself, 3:45

assumption which would imply a local problem involving the Earth's magnetic field.

Taylor: "Does anyone have any suggestions? I think we must be over the [word in evidence written as 'Keys']."

After hearing this conversation, Cox requested Fort Lauderdale to notify the Air-Sea Rescue Task Unit 4, Port Everglades, to stand by.

Lt Cox had been asking Taylor persistently for half an hour what the problem was.

4.21 Taylor: "Both my compasses are out and I'm trying to find Fort Lauderdale. I'm over land, but it's broken. I'm sure I'm in the [Keys], but I don't know how far down." This statement was included in the deposition of Lt Cox and one word in it has been responsible for all the misunderstanding about what happened on this flight.

According to the board of enquiry, by the term 'Keys' Lt Taylor must have meant the chain of Florida Keys islands running a short distance west from the tip of the Florida peninsula. Taylor knew them well, and from the air the aviator can see the whole chain and the Florida mainland. Since Lt Taylor was over the Bahamas he obviously did not mean the Florida Keys, but something else, and Lt Cox also pointed out that the interpretation made no sense.

Lt Taylor was flying a navigational exercise eastwards from Florida towards the Bahamas. The Bahamas comprise 700 low-lying islands and cays that stretch over 100,000 square miles of the Atlantic Ocean seaward of the Atlantic Coast of Florida to Hispaniola. It is obvious that what Lt Taylor said to Cox was: "I'm sure I'm in the Cays, but I don't know how far down."

If he was in the Bahama cays but didn't know exactly where, we can see the dilemma, for he was supposed to be over the most northern few large cays which he knew well and which are isolated by at least 100 miles from the main chain.

Cox: "What is your altitude?"

Taylor: "I know where I am now. I'm at 2300 feet. We have just passed over a small island. We have no other land in sight. Can you have Miami or someone turn on their radar and pick us up? We don't seem to be getting far. We were out on a navigation hop, and on the second leg I thought they were going wrong. I took over and was flying them back to the right position. But I'm sure that neither one of my compasses is working." This confirms that Taylor did not mean the Florida Keys. He knew he had been on the second leg of the navigation hop, i.e. the 73-mile stretch between Great Stirrup and Great Sale Cays; he thought his trainees had gone wrong, so he took over to get them right.

But here is another strange expression Taylor uses: "*We don't seem to be getting far*". This seems to imply that he couldn't make progress physically through the air: he was attempting to fly head-on to the anomaly and was more or less hove-to, prevented from returning to the second leg of his navigational hop by an apparent force equal to his airspeed. In response to a question, Taylor said that he had not switched on his IFF transponder, and did not reply when Cox suggested he use his ZBX homing receiver. This was standard procedure and it is incomprehensible that an instructor would not have taken this step at once. In the event of disorientation he was supposed to have changed radio frequency to the 3000-kilocycles emergency band, climbed for altitude and attempted to obtain a bearing on the base homing transmitter. If over water in the Atlantic, he was supposed to fly west. But he did none of these things. All he did was fly around and talk. Already we are gaining the impression of a swiftly developing mental problem symptomatic of exposure to an electro-magnetic gravity field: a wilful lassitude and inability to see the obvious solutions to a simple problem.

4.25 Captain Stiver to Fort Lauderdale Tower: "We are not sure where we are. We think we must be 225 miles east of base." The estimate of 225 miles east of base indicates that the flight had been deposed from the northern leg of the triangle in an easterly direction by 100 miles in thirty minutes. This implied a 200-knot crosswind which naturally would not have escaped attention. A discussion of their estimated position and compasses now ensued between all five pilots of the flight. The only remaining explanation was that Powers had led the flight in the opposite direction SE at a speed of 200 knots because of compass failure. This could only account for an error of navigation of this magnitude if all compasses had malfunctioned and Powers had forgotten that he was supposed to be flying a left-handed triangle. But even then it would have brought the sun abeam to starboard and everybody would have noticed. Thus it was utterly inexplicable.

After some static interference, Stiver to base: "It looks like we are entering white water." What this latter sentence is intended to convey is not obvious, but numerous veteran pilots, shipmasters and coast guard officers have mentioned being seized by a strange vapour and their equipment going haywire while in the area known as the Bermuda Triangle. Actually that may have been at the point where Flight 19 emerged from the anomaly, for a few minutes later Lt Taylor began to steer a number of strange headings. As we saw earlier in the incident over Ohrdruf, passage through an electro-magnetic anomaly can cause temporary insanity. And that is what now seems to have befallen the pilots of Flight 19.

Lt Taylor's Mad 100 Minutes

4.45 Taylor to Flight: "We are heading NNE for 45 minutes, then we will fly north to make sure we are not over the Gulf of Mexico."

5.07 Taylor to Flight: "All planes in this flight join up in close formation. Let's turn and fly east. We are going too damn far north instead of east. If there is anything we wouldn't see it. To all planes in this flight change course to 090 degrees (due east) for ten minutes."

5.15 Taylor to Port Everglades: "We are now flying 270 degrees (due west) until we hit the beach or run out of gas." *Taylor to Flight*: "All planes close up tight. Will have to ditch unless landfall. When the first plane drops to ten gallons, we all go down together." (It will be remembered that the aircraft had enough fuel for at least seven hours, therefore it was another four hours before they had to consider ditching.)

Port Everglades to Taylor: "Can you change to 3000 kilocycles emergency channel?"

Taylor: "I cannot change frequencies. I must keep my planes together."

Just before 6.00 Lt Taylor described a large island he had just seen through a break in the clouds. Baker identified it as Andros Island, the largest in the Bahamas, and gave Taylor a course to steer that would get him to Fort Lauderdale. Taylor steered a westerly heading as instructed and the signal volume increased as he approached Florida.

6.04 Taylor to Flight: "I am pretty sure we are over the Gulf of Mexico. We didn't go far enough east. I suggest we fly due east until we run out of gas. There is a better chance of being picked up closer to shore."

Because of Taylor's use of the word "suggest" the board of enquiry stated in Opinion 34 "that at some undetermined time prior to 6:05 pm, Edward J Powers, Captain USMC, assumed the lead of Flight 19." Nevertheless Taylor was still quite certain that east was best:

Taylor to Powers: "We may just as well turn around to go east again."

From now on, reception of the transmissions from the mad hatters of Flight 19 began to deteriorate. The last message was heard at 7.04. Powers was mentally in no better state than Taylor or he would have got back on the westerly heading for Fort Lauderdale which Taylor had abandoned. It seems possible from the reconstructed records that he was heading west, but the strengthening crosswind from the SW would have pushed them 50 miles further north every hour. It was a dark, moonless night with cloud and rain. The flight was never once picked up on radar, which suggests that the aircraft themselves had undergone some structural change while in the anomaly, making them invisible to radar. According to researcher Gian Quasar, Air Training Command informed Banana River at 8.50 pm on 5 December 1945 that five aircraft, never subsequently identified, were spotted visually bearing 245 degrees 32 miles from Brunswick, Georgia, heading 150 degrees SSW. He theorized that a landing was attempted in the Okefenokee Swamps. It need hardly be added that such a proceeding in this sparsely populated region of wet forest and alligator-infested swamp on a dark night would have been utter madness.

When we speak of another 'dimension' as the possible origin of UFOs, we really have no understanding of what this word may imply. It may be that Dr Carstoiu is right, that there are two gravity fields and one is the domain of UFOs, the Underworld of mythology, so to speak. There can be no doubt that the SS experimented into the matter, and in the concluding chapters a look at the evidence of their developments provides us with a very disturbing picture.

CHAPTER 15

The "Foo-Fighter"

THERE ARE NO natural flying discoidal objects in Einstein's time-space continuum. So far as we know from declassified documents, for a great investment of time and money modern engineers could design a flying disc for subsonic speeds with a range of about 7,000 miles, but it would lack the advantages of modern aircraft. It is apparently a concept simply not worthwhile developing.

In Hitler's Germany aeronautical designer Rudolf Schriever began design work on an unmanned flying disc on 15 July 1941. The model was completed on 2 June 1942 and made its maiden flight the following day, astonishing observers with its excellent flying qualities. It was remote-controlled and propelled by a hydrogen peroxide engine. Apparently it could take off and land vertically, but nothing further is known.

Towards the end of 1942 the Waffen-SS laboratory at Wiener Neustadt began trials with a strange 'anti-aircraft weapon'. This project, details of which remain a top secret in Allied archives, was known as *Feuerkugel* and also *Kugelblitz* (ball of fire/ball-lightning) by the Germans. The extremely scanty information which can be gleaned about this mysterious development links it to Rudolf Schriever's unmanned flying saucer design.

The only known official US report[152] about the Kugelblitz states that it was an experimental anti-aircraft rocket designed by Richard Haass and developed by the Verwertungsgesellschaft Salzburg. The object sought its target automatically and was expected to enter service in January 1945. This is all they will let us know and it is a pretty terse description for an obsolete flak weapon.

A British report[153] reviewed various documents prepared by the SS and work centres of the Henschel and Zeppelin aircraft companies, the latter towards the end of the war installed in underground factories in the Black Forest. These documents refer specifically to the propulsion unit built for the Kugelblitz by Professors Kamm and Ernst at the Kreislaufbetrieb Motor D.W. in 1943 for FFKF Stuttgart Untertürkheim. The British investigators described the principle of the motor as a recycled oxygen system. It was later abandoned in favour of the Walter turbine using hydrogen peroxide, although the documents discuss the feasibility of using both systems in a composite unit.

Therefore the sum total of knowledge about the system available from Allied archive sources is that the missile was a target seeker propelled by a Walter turbine. The remaining information usually available regarding the configuration, length, diameter, warhead, speed of climb, operational altitude and so on remain highly classified.

Renato Vesco[154] had not seen a Kugelblitz but he had pieced together sufficient information to know that it was stabilized gyroscopically, had a missile guidance system developed by the Flugfunkforschungsanstalt of the Reichspost at Oberpfaffenhofen and a homing system. It was unmanned and rose vertically at a very fast speed. It was rumoured that it might have obtained its effect by discharging and instantaneously igniting a blue plasma "based on the firedamp gas found in coal-mines", and most sources said it had no offensive capability at all, which would be a strange thing for a flak rocket. It had first been tried out successfully against Allied bombers over Lake Garda. Vesco said it was known as *die fliegende Schildkröte* – the flying turtle – to German sources, who seem unanimous that its shape resembled a turtle-shell, but that was only when it was not in motion, for in flight by day it resembled "a luminous disc spinning round its own axis" and "looked like a burning balloon" by night.

The word 'flying saucer' did not come into use until the term was coined by headline writers in the United States after the war and so the description "turtle-shell" gives us a certain image. On Christmas Eve 1944, over the Rhine Valley, RAF crew Flight-Lts Gibbin and Cleary were surprised by a flaming red ball that "suddenly turned into a sort of airplane whose upper half was built like a wing". The remainder is censored. Now we begin to suspect a sinister reason for the reticence of Allied Governments to provide information about the Kugelblitz, for what sort of weapon is a fiery ball which not only has no firm shape but changes its configuration in motion?

Vesco did not seem very clear on what was the difference between the Flying Turtle and the Feuerkugel "ball of fire", and from his attempt to

153

describe how the former worked it is evident that one became the other in flight. Clearly he must have suspected that something extraordinary happened once the Flying Turtle was in the air and ascending, but, being a scientist whose book set out to prove that there is a terrestrial explanation for all UFOs, couldn't quite go so far as to say so. By some mechanism which nobody appears able to explain, the unmanned, remote-controlled Kugelblitz changed its shape from turtle to sphere, developed a "bright halo" supposedly by ionization of the atmosphere, became invulnerable and acquired the unusual ability to hover motionless. The Flying Turtle was alleged to have within its protective shell a number of Klystron tubes, the purpose of which must have been for them to home in on enemy aircraft radar. Klystron is nowadays also used in microwave ovens to generate an intense and concentrated local microwave field for cooking purposes and, applied to a suitable surface at a particular frequency, it could excite the surrounding air sufficiently to generate the 'halo'-like plasma, so at least the effect is possible.

A classified enquiry was set up by Lt-General Massey in 1943 in Britain to investigate reports by Allied pilots of harassment from 'balls of fire' during operations over Europe. It is believed that the objects were filmed for British Intelligence in high definition on several occasions, although no photos have ever been released. In 1946 a team of British investigators, assisted by Dr Ernst Westermann, a director of Speyer at Saarbrücken, was appointed to report on the German 'Foo-fighters', as they were nicknamed, but nothing was ever published. A typical report was submitted by B. C. Lumsden, the pilot of a Hurricane interceptor, who had left England early one evening in December 1942:

"At about 2000 hrs over the mouth of the Somme I saw two steadily climbing orange lights, moving less slowly than tracer flak. I did a full turn and saw the lights astern and to port, but they now appeared larger and brighter. At 7000 feet they stopped climbing and stayed level. I did some more full turns but the objects hung behind me. I nose-dived to 4000 feet and the lights kept the same relative position in pursuit. Finally they descended about 1000 feet below me until I levelled out, at which point they climbed again and resumed pursuit. The two lights seemed to maintain an even distance from each other and varied only slightly in relative height from time to time. One always remained a bit lower than the other. Once my speed reached 260 mph I was gradually able to outdistance them."

It seemed to be the purpose of these mysterious objects to fly in parallel formation with the reporting aircraft and hover at wingtips. USAF pilot Wendell C. Stevens remembers:

> "They were a greyish-green or red-orange colour. They would approach to within about five metres from the aircraft and stay there. They could not be shaken off nor shot down."

Initially pilots were reluctant to submit reports for fear of ridicule or grounding for psychiatric reasons, but eventually there were hundreds of sightings, and it would seem that between November 1944 and January 1945 every pilot in the American 415th Night Fighter Squadron had seen the phenomenon at least once.

Lts David McFalls and Edward Baker, veterans of the squadron, stated that at 1800 hrs on 22 December 1944 at an altitude of 10,000 feet over Hagenau in the Lorraine area they observed two large orange glows ascending towards them:

> "Upon reaching our altitude the objects levelled off and stayed on our tail. I went into a steep dive and the glows followed in sharp precision. I banked as sharply as I dared and the objects followed. For two minutes the lights stalked me through several intricate maneouvres, peeled off under perfect control, then blinked out."

In a heavily censored Associated Press release of 13 December 1944, which was nine days before the Hagenau sighting, Allied pilots reported seeing over the Reich "mysterious silvery balls" which just "floated in the air" singly and in clusters. B-17 pilot Charles Ogden, who had seen them over Germany, described them as "crystal balls, about the size of a basketball" which would approach to within 300 feet of the bomber formation and then "seem to become magnetized and fly alongside". After a while they would "peel off like a plane and leave". Although seen mostly at night, some airmen reported them during daylight hours. Another 415th Squadron pilot said,

"... the lights would tail the aircraft for a few moments before streaking away. They never showed up on radar but experienced crews discounted explanations such as reflections, St Elmo's fire and flares, all of which were easily recognizable."

The most striking effect of closeness to these objects was electro-magnetic and they do not seem to have been detectable on radar. One gained the impression that they might be being handled remotely, as was reported over the Rhine Valley one evening in December 1944 when Lt Henry Gibbin and his radar observer Lt Walter Cleary sighted:

"... a huge red light 1000 feet above us (we were at 1000 feet ourselves). The object was moving at about 200 mph. At the same time other crews reported a glowing red object which shot up vertically, turned over and plunged into a steep dive. It seemed under intelligent control."

It was suspected that the aerobatic fireballs were a German anti-aircraft weapon to foul ignitions and interfere with radar, but if so they appeared ineffective and in any case captured German pilots also reported being harassed by them. As the fireballs did not seem to do anything very hostile except manouevre close to an aircraft, it was assumed that they represented the experimental stage of a new weapon.

After they peeled away and plunged into a steep dive, what did they do next? On 25 March 1945 elements of the Sixth Armoured Division dug in south of Darmstadt overlooking the autobahn saw:

"... six or seven bright yellow-orange circular objects approach the autobahn from the west at an altitude of about 150 feet. They were not travelling in formation but moving in the same general direction. Each had its own distinct erratic movement as if individually controlled. They were three to four feet in diameter and so bright that they illuminated trees around them. They descended slowly at about 10 mph until entering deep into the forest, where they disappeared."

These balls of fire were also reported from the Pacific during and after the war. Author Leonard Stringfield, while piloting a 5th Air Force C-46 near Iwo Jima on 28 August 1945, described how the aircraft developed serious engine trouble when approached by:

"three unidentifiable blobs of brilliant white light, each about the size of a dime held about arm's length. The blobs were travelling in a straight line through drifts of cloud, seemingly parallel to the C-46 and equal to its speed."

From 1942 onwards German naval forces had large U-boat and transport bases on the coasts of Malaya, Indonesia and Singapore as well as mainland Japan, which could explain the origin of various wartime sightings in the region.

How Did the Feuerkugel Work?

In the normal course of events the British authorities were due to release the Kugelblitz/Feuerkugel papers in 1975. The failure to declassify reports about strange enemy weapons developments at the thirty-year mark is obviously a bad sign. The so-called 'foo-fighter' was a small German aerial machine which appeared to do nothing except change its shape in flight, after which it was invisible to radar and could not be shot down. This is a characteristic of UFOs, and as the existence of UFOs is denied by Governments in London and Washington, logically it should be perfectly harmless to release the papers.

To illustrate the similarity between UFO and Flying Turtle reports, I have selected just four examples from the hundreds of thousands of UFO reports made postwar.

(1) On the night of 12 June 1964 the police chief of Elmore, Ohio, while on patrol noticed a brilliant light, with an aura around it which extended for a quarter mile in all directions, hovering at about 2000 feet to the side of State Route 5. It was impossible to make out a distinct outline for the object, only that it was a "fuzzy ball of light with a large aura". Together with three other officers, he kept watch. The object made towards them and as it approached it grew in brightness and size, changing from a nondescript glow into the firm form of a flying 'V' and passing overhead at 500 feet. While the object was quiescent and hovering it had an indistinct glowing spherical form; when it left it transformed into a wedge shape. The hypothesis in this case is that the object re-entered this dimension in order to make its departure at speed.

157

(2) RAF Pilot Robert Pilkington stated that while flying a Vampire-5 fighter for 601 Squadron out of North Weald, Essex, on exercise in 1952 he was vectored to intercept a multi-coloured large sausage-like object at 30,000 feet. Upon his approach it changed from a sausage into a flying saucer and left at high speed – "that is to say the human eye assumed it changed shape," he added. The hypothesis in this case is that the object re-entered this dimension for a hasty departure.

(3) While en route to the Iwo Jima campaign, the US battleship *New York* (Rear Admiral Kemp C. Christian) and her destroyer escorts sighted overhead a silver sphere "about the size of a house."[156] After some discussion on the bridge the officers agreed it must be a gigantic Japanese balloon. The optical rangefinders calculated the distance as 1700 yards and the 3-inch anti-aircraft battery opened fire. Shortly afterwards the destroyer escort also began a cannonade with their 5-inch main armament. It was found impossible to hit the strange object and eventually the group abandoned the attempt and continued with their voyage. Later the US Navy offered the usual explanation that all these warships had been firing at Venus. This is pure nonsense. Naval rangefinders are either stereoscopic or work on mathematical calculations from target triangulation. In this case it was established by measurement that the object was occupying a definite geographical location in this dimension about three miles up and the guns were ranged on it. If by some mischance the battleship's gunnery officers had mistaken Venus, which is several hundred million miles away, for a balloon the size of a house hovering overhead, they would have been advised immediately of the fact by their data control centres. The nature of the problem being encountered by the gunnery officers, whether the projectiles were being ricocheted when they hit the target or were deflected by some sort of force field protecting it, was not mentioned by the crewmen reporting the incident. This balloon seems to have been hovering in the adjacent dimension where it would be invulnerable.

(4) The SS *Naviero* was an ex-Liberty freighter of the Argentine Shipping Lines. She had a cargo of explosives and gunpowder, and for that reason a very good watch was being kept. Her officers and crew were summoned on deck on the morning of 20 July 1967 off the coast of Brazil to see a powerfully glowing object in the sea not more than 15 metres away. It was cigar-shaped, 100 feet in length and had no external control surfaces or protruding parts. It made no noise and left no wake in the water. After a while it suddenly dived and headed off rapidly at very high speed. This sausage-like submersible had a measureable geographical location, was even visible optically in two media, air and water, but was not tangible enough to leave a wake.

In two of the above cases the presence of the UFO in question varied between being physical and paraphysical at different times: the other two were paraphysical throughout the encounter. It may now be becoming clearer why London and Washington will not even hypothesize the existence of UFOs for discussion. Late in 1942, at the stage of the conflict when the German leadership had accepted that the planned objectives of the war were no longer unattainable, the Waffen-SS began trying out aerial machines which acted just like the four mysterious vehicles quoted above. Who in London would want to talk about the implications of that?

The Kugelblitz/Feuerkugel was an experimental stage of the German flying disc project. What must have been learned by chasing and homing-in on Allied aircraft across another dimension over Reich and Axis Pacific airspace during 1943 and 1944 was to be put into practice aboard the real thing at a later time. Meanwhile German aeronautical engineers had worked around the clock on the project for which the Foo Fighters were the preliminary stage and next came the search for the perfect aerodynamic shape.

Germany was the world pioneer in helicopter development and in 1942 the Flettner 282 *Kolibri* became the first helicopter anywhere to enter operational military service. It was the most advanced orthodox helicopter development of the war. The German supersonic helicopter had a system in which the fuel was piped to combustion chambers at the rotor bladetips where it exploded, whirling the blades around at a fantastic speed.[158]

Germany thus led the world in helicopter knowledge and design.

Within thirty months from July 1942 German aeronautical engineers designed and built several giant circular aircraft which were basically sophisticated autogyros and first flew in early 1945.

The 1919 Treaty of Versailles had so drastically restricted German aircraft production that glider flying became important for pilot training and research. The Horten brothers transformed the living room of their parents' house into a workshop and in 1933 test-flew their first glider, Ho I, at Bonn-Hagelar. All three brothers were Luftwaffe officers and Nazi Party members. During the Battle of Britain their Ho II and Ho III designs formed part of a special glider unit for Operation Sea Lion. In 1942 at the request of the Luftwaffe they built a stronger and larger version of the Ho V to take a Schmitt-Argus pulse-jet. The variant was designated Ho VII. At about the same time as Schriever's autogyro blueprint, they were designing a strange crescent-shaped glider, the Ho VI Parabola. Everything regarding this development was destroyed in a mysterious fire at Hellegenberg that year and we hear no more about it until 1947, when the USAF were most anxious to interview Reimar Horten, who by then had escaped to Argentina and was unfortunately incommunicado.

CHAPTER 16

German Flying
Crescents and Discs

THE FLYING DISC Project in Hitler's Germany was one of three most secret research programmes and was classified *Geheime Reichssache*, the highest possible top secret. Nowhere, in any academic history of the Second World War, nor in any memoir of a military or political leader of any of the nations involved, Allied or German, will the researcher find the mention of a German flying disc. It is as if the project never existed. Here is the greatest mystery of the Second World War: why a flying vehicle held in such low regard for modern commercial and military purposes should have merited not only Hitler's but, postwar, the Allies' highest secrecy rating for it. Very recently the CIA archive has released documents full of accounts by German engineers of their work on circular aircraft capable of astonishing speeds, but useful information on the craft themselves remains elusive.

Had it not been for the spate of UFO sightings by US Air Force personnel over a twelve-day period in 1947 which led the US Army and Air Force to mount a combined project to investigate the phenomenon, the existence of the documentary evidence for the German project would have remained a secret in perpetuity. The confirmatory paper was not declassified until 1969, and only then as an appendix to a fatuous report of 964 pages issued by a University of Colorado committee under the chairmanship of Dr Edward U. Condon, and under contract to the Office of Scientific and Technical Research of the US Air Force.[159] This outfit spent two years and $600,000 of US Air Force appropriation to conduct an in-depth investigation of the UFO problem. The study was a total farce and, while having nothing useful to say about UFOs, it did, unintentionally one suspects, confirm the existence of a successful Nazi flying disc programme, and so was not a complete waste of time and money.

The official report prepared on 23 September 1947 remained classified until 8 January 1969 when it was published as Appendix R to the Condon Report. The matter enquired into had begun on the night of 28 June 1947 when two pilots and two intelligence officers at Maxwell Air Force base watched an illuminated UFO perform "impossible aerobatics". On 29 June a naval rocketry expert watched a silvery disc above the White Sands Testing Grounds. On 8 July three officers at the Muroc supersecret USAF test centre in the Mojave Desert reported three silver-coloured objects heading westwards, and ten minutes later a pilot test flying the new XP-84 reported a yellowish-white spherical object resembling nothing being currently tested or flown heading west into the wind at a fantastic speed. Two hours later a crew of technicians filed a report regarding an object interfering with a seat ejection experiment at 20,000 feet. It appeared to be of white aluminium oval construction with two projections on the upper surface which might have been fins. These crossed each other at intervals suggesting slow rotation or oscillation. No obvious means of propulsion was seen. The following day an F-51 pilot at 20,000 feet about 40 miles south of Munroc sighted a flat object of light-reflecting nature with no vertical fin or wings. He attempted to pursue but it outclimbed him.[160]

This investigation concluded that UFOs are real and not visionary or fictitious. The objects reported on by USAF personnel were the shape of a disc and as large as a man-made aircraft. Reported operating characteristics such as extreme rates of climb and manoeuvrability (particularly roll) lent possibility to the idea that some of the objects were controlled either manually, automatically or remotely. They had a metallic or light-reflecting surface, showed an absence of trail except in a few instances when the object was apparently operating under high performance conditions, were circular or elliptical in shape, flat on the bottom and domed on top, maintained formations in flights varying from three to nine objects, had no associated sound except in three instances when a rumbling roar was heard, and cruised at above 300 knots.

This is the US Air Force describing UFOs in flight, quite a contrast to the usual official type of opinion released to the public. The signatory to the report, Lt Gen Nathan Twining, Commanding General, Air Material Command, stated that:

"It is possible within the present US knowledge – provided extensive detailed development is undertaken – to construct a piloted aircraft which has the general description of the objects in the sub-paragraphs above, which would be capable of an approximate range of 7000 miles at sub-sonic speeds. Any developments would be extremely expensive, time-consuming and at the considerable expense of current projects . . ."

Thus it seems that the USAF had no knowledge of domestic flying disc construction by the United States, nor was it particularly keen to get involved in it.

On the afternoon of 24 June 1947, while en route to Yakima, Washington, private pilot Kenneth Arnold saw a formation of nine bright objects flying south from Mount Baker towards Mount Rainier (about 130 miles apart). The leader was higher than the rest and they were flying diagonally in an echelon with a larger gap between the first four and the last five. Arnold assumed they were jets, but he could see no tailplanes. He calculated their speed over a 50-mile distance between two elevations as 1700 mph. They were next "in a chain in the neighbourhood of five miles long, swerving in and out of the smaller peaks, flipping from side to side in unison, dipping and presenting their lateral surfaces". Eight of the objects looked like flat discs, the other, larger than the rest, resembled a *crescent*. The following day in a newspaper interview, Arnold likened the objects' movements to "a flat rock bouncing up and down as it skipped across water". He was subsequently misquoted and later asserted, "the objects were not saucer-shaped but flew erratic, like a saucer if you skip it across water. They were not circular but reporters misunderstood the term". Dr Jacqueline Mitton of the Royal Astronomical Society, a firm disbeliever in UFOs, agreed that "Arnold's original drawings were much more a kind of boomerang shape". Arnold's description of the leader, the flying crescent, coincides very exactly with an object reported on numerous occasions by USAF pilots and scientists.

A secret *Draft of Collection Memorandum* signed by Brig-Gen G. F. Schulgen for the Air Intelligence Requirements Division on 30 October 1947 stated that the alleged flying saucer-type aircraft in which the USAF was interested approximated the shape of a disc and had been reported by many competent observers, including USAF rated officers, from widely scattered places such as the USA, Canada, Hungary, Guam and Japan, both from the ground and from the air. The object had a relatively flat bottom with extreme light reflecting ability. Its plan form approximated an oval or a disc with a dome shape on the top surface, about the size of a C-54 or Constellation aircraft. It was silent except for an occasional roar when operating under super performance conditions. It left no exhaust except occasionally a bluish Diesel-type trail which persisted in the atmosphere for about an hour. Other reports mentioned a brownish smoke trail which could be from a special catalyst for extra power. It had extreme manoeuvrability and the apparent ability to almost hover: it could disappear quickly at high speed or dematerialize, and to suddenly appear without warning as if from extremely high altitude. Several of the craft formed a tight formation quickly and evasive tactics indicated possibly manual or remote control. Under certain power conditions, the craft seemed able to cut a half-mile-wide path through cloud, but this was only seen once.

The draft continued by saying that the first sightings in the United States were reported mid-May 1947 and the last over Toronto on 14 September that year. The greatest activity over the United States was during the last week of June and first week of July. Arnold's sighting occurred on 24 June. Brig-Gen Schulgen regarded the strange object, "in view of certain observations", as "a long-range aircraft capable of a high rate of climb, high cruising speed (possibly sub-sonic at all times), highly manoeuvrable and capable of being flown in tight formation. For the purpose of evaluation and analysis of the so-called flying saucer phenomenon, the object sighted is being assumed to be a manned aircraft . . . based on the perspective thinking and actual accomplishments of the Germans".

The signatory was assuming at the time that the aircraft was built by the Soviets to German blueprints, but we know now that was not the case. The craft described had "a high rate of climb", but did not lift up vertically. It was "possibly sub-sonic at all times" but could dematerialize or appear suddenly without warning which, at sub-sonic speed, suggests it entered and left Gravity II at will. Supporting this hypothesis is the fact that the hull had "extreme light reflecting ability". Brig-Gen Schulgen was by no means convinced that this craft was extraterrestrial: "There is a possibility that the Horten brothers' perspective thinking may have inspired it – particularly the Parabola, which has a crescent plan form [see Appendix]. The Horten brothers' latest trend of perspective thinking was definitely toward aircraft configurations of low aspect ratio. The younger brother, Reimar, stated that the Parabola configuration would have the least induced drag – which is a very significant statement. . . . What is known of the whereabouts of the entire Horten family? All should be contacted and interrogated regarding any contemplated plans or perspective thinking of the Horten brothers."

These USAF sightings were of an aircraft at a much higher stage of development than anything the United States could have put into the air at the time, (or now, if it was capable of Gravity II travel). It was admitted by the US authorities in the CIOS-BIOS/FIAT 20 report that in aeronautics and all methods of jet and rocket propulsion and guidance systems, at the war's end the Germans were ahead of the US by at least ten years. By virtue of the quality of observers involved – rated USA officers, test pilots and aeronautical scientists – we can make a positive statement. Either the crescent-shaped aircraft was German-built and operating from some clandestine base. Or it came from the Beyond. One must choose, for there is no third plausible possibility.

German Flying Saucers –The Alleged Machines

The German tradition alleges that Spitzbergen was used for some of their test flights. In a video-recorded interview, Andreas Epp, an aeronautics writer and one of the five principal engineers involved in the German project during the war, stated that a flying disc under remote control from Breslau crashed and was wrecked on Spitzbergen while attempting a landing. In late August 1946 Air Force General James H. Doolittle arrived in Stockholm to investigate UFO sightings along with Swedish military intelligence but his first mission was to visit Spitzbergen, where he supervised the shipment aboard the battleship *Alabama* of the remains of "a crashed UFO". According to former crew members of the warship, the bodies of "aliens" had been found, but the craft was thought to be "a short-range reconnaissance saucer" because "no provisions were found aboard".

Since Lt General Twining's report also stated that there was:

> "lack of physical evidence in the shape of crash-recovered exhibits which would undeniably prove the existence of these unidentified flying objects"

this tends to confirm that the wreckage of the Spitzbergen flying saucer brought to the United States by sea in 1946 was of terrestrial origin and German,[161] and that the craft, though remote-controlled, had crew aboard, probably to handle the tricky landing procedure which led to their demise.

In the 25 April 1953 edition of the Hamburg quality newspaper *Welt am Sonntag*, scientific correspondent Dr Werner Keller interviewed Senior Engineer Georg Klein, former special adviser to Reich Minister Speer. Klein confirmed that prototypes had been built in Germany during the Second World War:

> "On 14 February 1945 in Prague I witnessed personally the first start of a manned RFZ (circular aircraft). This machine reached a height of 12.4 kms within three minutes and in level flight could maintain a speed of 2200 kms/hr. The flying disc has a practically perfect aerodynamic form and speeds in excess of 4000 kms/hr are feasible. These fantastic velocities require special metal alloys, for existing materials for aircraft construction would melt. We had a special alloy. The start in Prague was the culmination of research and development begun in 1941. By the end of 1944 there were three different models completed. Miethe had built a discus-type, non-rotating disc of 42 metres diameter. The designs of von Habermohl and Schriever had a broad-surfaced outer ring which revolved about a fixed spherical cabin. This ring had adjustable vanes and could take off and land vertically. On the approach of the Red Army the prototypes in Prague were destroyed."

If Engineer Klein witnessed this flight personally he would not have seen much of it, for the Luftflotte VIII War Diary entry for the day in question records that Prague had low cloud cover down to 800 metres with complete overcast, rain, snow and poor visibility. This is excellent weather if one does not wish the neighbourhood to witness the miraculous attributes of your flying saucer. Klein does not state whether it was the Miethe discus-type or the Schriever VTOL design which ascended into the low cloud at Prague. Another unmentionable is the method of propulsion. All German aeronautical engineers were contradictory or silent on these two points. The fantastic claim by Klein that the Prague flying disc could fly at 2000 kms per hour justifies the heat-resistant alloys used in the craft's construction. The reason for these machinations we will see shortly.

The German tradition states that the first proposed designs for a jet-propelled circular aircraft (RFZ) were offered to the Luftwaffe in 1938 but declined. The USAF report in 1947 considered that even a subsonic flying saucer development "would require extensive detailed development, would be extremely expensive, time-consuming and at the considerable expense of other projects". All the more astonishing then that the entire German programme, from flying model to maiden manned flight, occupied less than three years between 1942 and 1945 in wartime Germany.

Following the successful flight of Rudolf Schriever's model Flying Turtle on 3 June 1942, he teamed up at once with Professor von Habermohl to build the manned version. Three or four types were produced, fitted with hydrogen peroxide engines, but were found unsatisfactory in one way or another and the Luftwaffe supposedly rejected all of them. Prototype MIIB, for example, was a broad-surfaced outer ring with adjustable vanes revolving about a fixed spherical cabin, thus more helicopter than flying saucer. This VTOL machine was allegedly also tried with a motor designed in the Kertl Factory, Vienna, by the Austrian inventor Professor Viktor Schauberger, "the pioneer of anti-gravity", it being claimed that the motor worked on the implosive principle. Whatever the method was it has never been revealed, but rapid declutching was hinted at. The energy process is supposed to have used a small electric motor of 20,000 revs. Calculations showed that a 20-cm disc gyrating at this speed generated a tornado-like vortex sufficient to levitate a weight of 228 tonnes to an indefinite height. Nothing was ever patented, its like is not seen today and the Luftwaffe did not want it despite its fantastic vertical flight ability; therefore we look upon it with a jaundiced eye. A separate group, Richard Miethe and Giuseppe Belluzzo, had been working on the V-7 turbo-jet disc, which had a definite UFO look about it, since 1942 and co-opted Schriever, Habermohl and occasionally Andreas Epp into the development team in 1943. The design was developed to the stage of 'operational readiness'. The V-7 jet disc (also known as the V-3 Flying Disc Model III long range version) was 42 metres in diameter. The outer shell, we are told, was a light metal alloy, mainly of titanium, while the inner hull was of heat-resistant duralium. A claim was made that a helium engine was used. A way to use helium as a fuel had been devised by the Austrian physicist Dr Karl Nowak[162] and registered at the German Patent Office on 16 March 1943 under number 905-847. The patent describes a reciprocating engine using atmospheric oxygen to oxidize atmospheric nitrogen. This involved generating very high voltage sparks to produce temperatures exceeding 50,000°C within a combustion chamber. The effect was similar to lightning. Lightning burns the surrounding air leaving a vacuum which suddenly collapses in on itself producing thunder. The engine did the same, but also injected super-cold liquid helium directly into the combustion chamber. Helium is an inert gas and does not burn. Dr Nowak's idea was that the very cold liquid sprayed into the combustion chamber to cool it also caused a tremendous expansion as it heated, thus producing the motive force for the engine.

One concludes, looking at the short time-scale for this project, that it would assuredly have been a most laudable engineering feat if Nowak's helium engine could have been brought to the stage of operational use within two years of registering the patent, and fitted, moreover, inside a flying saucer, the initial designs for which had been begun only the previous year. An additional drawback would have been the embargo imposed on the sale of helium to Germany since before the war by the world's only supplier, the United States. Helium had been wanted at that stage to build safer airships than the *Hindenburg*, but the United States suspected the Germans might want it for work on developing a hydrogen-based weapon. For this reason it does not seem very likely that Germany would have had enough helium to realize helium engine development and use.

A V-7 variant on the drawing board had a V-2 rocket engine slung below the fuselage for a top speed of 4000 kms/hr in level flight, but the burn would last only a minute or so and the advantage of bothering to build this variant is not obvious. The V-2 rocket engine was the only propulsion unit which might have required the disc to be constructed of special heat-resistant alloys, and the sketch of this variant probably came into existence precisely to explain that purpose. Having disposed of the less likely prime movers, we are left with a reported engine plant consisting of five kerosene-fuelled turbines, three for lift and two for forward thrust which, though less exotic than the other ideas, satisfy the requirement for vertical and horizontal flight at fast sub-sonic velocities. From their earlier work with helicopters it was not a particularly big step in the short period of time available to the idea of an advanced autogyro, its multi-bladed propellors forming a perfect circle and linked together by an outer ring. The blades rotated independent of the central fixed cabin and, unlike orthodox autogyros, there was no torsion factor. At take-off blade rotation was accelerated and, after acquiring speed and tremendous inertia, the blade angle changed from −3° to +3° and the machine would rise up suddenly. There should have been no problem piloting the craft with five engines: authoritative sources such as Andreas Epp stated that in earlier proving flights the disc would have been remote-controlled but with crew aboard. When the blades were closed to 0° for a continuous surface, a high sub-sonic speed (0.8 Mach) would have been possible and at least 25 kilometres altitude. Rudolf Schriever, who had been a Heinkel test pilot at Eger in the Sudentenland, worked on his design in a secluded hangar at Prague. BMW's Design Bureau tested the engines. Initially He 178 turbines had been intended for propulsion but were not powerful enough for a perpendicular take-off speed of 100 metres/sec. The replacements caused vibration problems, but these had been overcome within a week. There was a ring of reactors on board, one located bottom centre of the blade disc for vertical take-off. Schriever made the claim that the *Flugkreisel*, which was first airborne in October 1944, had flown supersonic, "this being possible by virtue of its aerodynamic shape", he said. One suspects that what he really meant was that on flights from Norway to Spitzbergen, the 600-knot *Flugkreisel* achieved a ground speed in excess of Mach 1 when flying in the 175-knot west-east jet stream over Sweden at above 35,000 feet.[163]

Physically this autogyro was not capable of supersonic speed. There was no call for it to be built of heat-resistant alloys, but it obviously was. This is the big secret we are not supposed to know. Allied aircrew in very close proximity to the 'fire-balls' reported scorching of the fuselage. *Feuerkugeln*, the glowing spheres which chased aircraft, were very hot. If the same principle whereby the Flying Turtle changed into a ball of fire during its ascent applied to the German VTOL circular autogyro, that is to say that at some stage while climbing vertically it changed into a large glowing sphere, then it would need an outer and inner shell of heat-resistant alloys for when it was operating in that mode.

Festung Norway

Bases existed in Norway for the completion work on the Supreme V-Weapon. Heavy water for the German atomic research project was produced at Vemork and the former Rjukan power house is now the Norwegian Industrial Workers' Museum. In correspondence the curator, Frode Saeland, referred to construction work begun by the Germans on the 5,700-feet Gaustad mountain peak about 50 miles from Oslo which he thought might be worth investigating. The Norwegian Government in exile had concluded at the time that it was a station for forecasting air activity over southern Norway, working in parallel with a similar station on a mountain top at Skavlen near Sauda.

Extracts from Norwegian books published in 1946 and 1980 respectively[164] described the Gaustad installation as "the biggest and most expensive radio installation built by the Germans in Norway", while Skavlen was a radar base. The construction work on Gaustad peak began in early October 1944, probably in the same week the SS took over at Ohrdruf in the Harz. The mountain and surrounding district were sealed off and huge quantities of sand, cement and building materials were taken to the 5,700-foot peak by caravans of mules. A telephone line was laid from Gausta to the valley of West Fjord. Day and night German reconnaissance aircraft circled above the activity while from below machinery could be heard working at all hours. The German regional commander was once overheard to use the expression "V-centre Gaustad Mountain Top". The work progressed with such urgency that small platforms, large aerial masts and small huts could soon be made out. For the eventuality of air attack the Germans had brought in enormous flak resources on the other side of the valley. The area around the cable car terminus was an absolute confusion of gun emplacements, ammunition dumps and barracks.

The information from Frode Saeland ties in very precisely with a report by the Stockholm Special Correspondent of the English newspaper *The Daily Mail*, Ralph Hewins, who in his article appearing in the 9 December 1944 edition *Nazis Will Run V-War From Norway* spoke of reports from the Norwegian resistance that the Germans were rushing to complete new V-bases in Norway to make up for their lost sites in the west. The main bases were on the peaks of southern Norway's highest mountains, the 5,700-foot Gaustad, 50 miles west of Oslo, two 5,200-foot heights north of Bergen, and various other high points as far north as Trondheim. There was thought to be an important base on the wild, high and windswept Hardanger Plateau. Contrary to policy on the European continent where a slave labour force was used for large-scale construction work, Organization Todt was using only German labourers at Gaustad. Up to a hundred square miles of the terrain was cordoned off and patrolled by battalions of mountain troops and SS. Building materials were being brought up not only manually but by light railway and cable-car systems slung across valleys and chasms.

Mr Hevins then described the "firing positions", which consisted of huge concrete halls embedded deep in rock, each with a semi-circular roof of reinforced concrete. At firing, the launching platform was extended through the hangar entrance along a runway.

The very salient point puzzling all experts, however, was why the bases were being built on the highest and most inaccessible peaks: neither the V-1 nor V-2 required height for a successful launch. Additionally one might add that neither was manufactured in Norway. These enormous rockets and flying bombs would have had to be transported in batches from Germany to Oslo by sea – a dangerous undertaking by 1944 – then shipped overland to Gaustad and brought up the 5700-foot mountain by mule or cable-car. This enables us to rule out the V-1, V-2 and anything series-produced, remote-controlled or otherwise. Obviously, the monumental radio and radar system and the 'firing' halls were all meant for a super-secret 'aircraft' which operated from V-Centre Gaustad.

That the neutral Swedes were highly indignant at German infringements of their airspace by what they alleged were remote-controlled flying bombs is evident from the following newspaper cuttings of the time. On 14 October 1944 *Sydsvenska Dagbladet Snallposten* of Malmö under a heading *Boomerang-Bomb from the Hardanger High Plateau*? said that heavy construction work of a secret nature being carried out by the Germans on the sealed-off Hardanger Plateau north of Rjukan had reached such a stage as to lead one to suspect that it had to do with a secret weapon project and "it is not impossible that they are launch ramps for robot-bombs and that the flying bombs which crossed southern Sweden today were fired from there".

In a separate article *Robot Aircraft over Skane* the same newspaper said that "a foreign robot aircraft – probably a flying bomb" crossed over Sweden that afternoon, flying from west to east or north-east at great velocity. The aircraft was at so high an altitude that it could not be seen even using binoculars. However, it left a very long white condensation trail which could be seen clearly. The engine made a noise reminiscent of a four-engined bomber. The speed of the aircraft exceeded the velocity of the newest fighter aircraft. From all this we deduce that the aircraft was a multi-engined, possibly remote-controlled, compressed-air-launched missile resembling a boomerang which brings to mind various Horten brothers' designs, including the cresent-shaped Parabola.

The *Svenska Dagbladet* for 14 October 1944 reported another infringement of Sweden's airspace by a flying bomb the previous morning. On 28 October the London *Daily Telegraph* carried a report of an announcement of the Swedish Military Staff that a "small number of robot or rocket bombs were seen flying high over southern Sweden this afternoon". It is not clear from this article if the objects were in formation or overflew singly. On 15 January 1945 the London *Daily Express* reported an infringement of Swedish airspace by flying bombs the previous day. The objects came from the north-west and were believed to have originated from the Hardanger Plateau. On 20 January 1945 Ralph Hewins of the *Daily Mail* reported that Swedish military authorities were compiling a dossier of infringements of their airspace by German flying bombs for a diplomatic protest to Berlin. Quoting an expert writing in the Swedish journal *Expressen*, Mr Hewins reported that the new robot bomb was a hybrid of the V-1 and V-2. It could fly at very high altitude and was very fast. It could be steered better than the V-2, but did not fly as fast or as high as the V-2. It was a flying bomb of the rocket type and could be steered from the ground to a certain extent – "German experts have for long been interested in radio-steering instruments and have been carrying out research in this field". All very true, but of this advanced flying bomb, a cross of two different species of missile, no evidence exists.

In any case, none of this talk of robot flying bombs in Norway makes sense. Germany had impregnable mountain tops in the Harz, Tirol and other alpine areas. The logical place to try out a new remote-control system, no matter how sophisticated, was Peenemünde. The manufacturing centres of the V-1 were in underground factories dotted around the Reich proper. Supplying even a few dozen V-1 flying bombs by sea to Oslo, and thence by mule and cable-car, to remote mountain peaks in Norway for experimental flights in late 1944 seems ludicrous. As for teleguidance systems, as has been mentioned, serious experiments were made using the *Radieschen* homing radar and *Sauerkirsch* radio remote for the V-1 in the last few months of the war. The American peacetime project to build a pilotless bomber based on the V-1, the Martin B-61 Matador, probably with all the German preparatory design papers in front of them, still took a full five years from its inception in 1946.

Of several things we can be tolerably certain. The excavation of the emplacement on a remote mountain peak, and the stringent security measures in force, indicate a project of the highest secrecy, and the two great radio and radar masts in the vicinity suggest a remote-control system. The contents of the hangars could be concealed as easily at ground level as in the clouds: what altitude and cloud provided was secrecy for whatever emerged from the innards of the mountain and took off – either the form of the aircraft or something peculiar about its mode of ascent – which nobody alien to the project could be permitted to see.

The Germans were never going to manhandle their special aircraft even once up that huge mountain: obviously it would fly there under its own power and land on the small apron before the 'firing hall'. Accordingly, the aircraft can only have been a Fieseler Storch, a helicopter or a flying disc or crescent. Since neither a Storch nor an orthodox helicopter could fly at 40,000 feet and faster than the latest jet fighter, we are left with only one possibility, and all the claims made for it seem true. Overflying Swedish airspace on a north-easterly heading would eventually bring the flying disc or saucer across the polar seas towards – Spitzbergen.

As to whether the proposed Swedish diplomatic protest was ever made in Berlin we do not have the information. What we do know is that in the latter half of 1946 thousands of 'ghost' flying bombs described as a cross between a V-1 and V-2 appeared in the skies over Sweden. Newspaper accounts of the time described them as 'cigar-shaped' with orange flames issuing from the tail. They were generally seen at night, at low altitudes up to 1000 metres, and estimates of their speed varied "from that of a slow airplane to 500 mph". Over the period 9 to 30 July 1946, for example, the Swedish military received more than 600 reports. The matter was taken extremely seriously. It was concluded that it must be Germans working for the Russians at Peenemünde who were responsible and it was to help investigate the phenomenon with Swedish Intelligence that USAF General Doolittle arrived in the summer of 1946. As was mentioned earlier in the chapter, his immediate interest was a visit to Spitzbergen, where it was rumoured that the wreckage of a flying disc was to be found, and actually was found.

The ghostly V-1s over Sweden could sometimes be picked up on radar, were not meteors, weather balloons, Venus or any other such natural phenomena and half the Swedish population appears to have seen them. The furore died down once it was clear that these "robot flying bombs" were not doing anything aggressive, they were merely interested in overflying Sweden's airspace which of course was nothing new. Ten per cent of Sweden's land surface is under fresh water, and it was not possible to get hold of a single ghostly rocket flying bomb because "all of them fell into the lakes", although curiously nobody thought that was strange.

This is German humour, and the coincidence here is so great that if the apparitions were not UFOs we would immediately suspect that the

Germans had put on the show for a laugh at the Swedes. If, in fact, the Germans were responsible for the UFO activity, the whole thing would become clear.

The German flying saucer assertion quoted earlier in this chapter was made by Senior Engineer Klein, former special adviser to Reich Minister Speer. The curious fact that neither Speer nor Hitler's Luftwaffe ADC Nicolaus von Below, who was also Speer's direct liaison officer to Hitler, nor General Koller, last Chief of the Luftwaffe General Staff, ever once mentioned in their copious memoirs the subject of helicopters, of which the German Reich was the world pioneer and had at least sixty operational models, or flying discs, underlines the fact that even on the German side the whole subject was for some reason still taboo decades later.

We require no great stretch of the imagination to see that if a four-foot diameter remote-controlled turtle-shaped object can change into a glowing sphere visible but intangible at altitude, then the same must also be possible for a giant manned VTOL disc. The Germans might not have reached the stage of constructing interplanetary UFOs, but they did not need to go that far, any more than they needed to build supersonic flying saucers or work on anti-gravity fields for the craft. The objective was and is world conquest, and by early 1945 they had the vehicle they needed for their purpose. This was the miracle weapon for which the shrinking perimeter of the Third Reich had been defended so desperately for no obvious reason for so long.

The scheme of things should now be becoming clear. Of the dimension coincident with the space of the physical Earth nothing can be predicted except that it is probably the Underworld of myth and the domain of hierarchies of beings normally imperceptible to man who worked on this plane through Adolf Hitler. The craft built by Schriever and Reimar Horten were to be crewed by men and women of a particular level of psychological development as to permit them to enter that region and associate with the entities there. Hitler once asked the scientist Horbiger if it were possible to shift the Earth's axis. To do so would provoke a catastrophe of unimaginable magnitude and it is possible, for the great palaentologist Dr Immanuel Velikovsky proved[165] that it is something which has befallen the Earth on more than one occasion in recent pre-history. The cause was always the effect of an external magnetic field ten and often up to one hundred times stronger than terrestrial magnetism. The cause is unknown, but the facts are well attested. If the date when the external agent was to operate next against the Earth's axis were known, then the National Socialist mystics, assisted by their allies, would return afterwards to mop up when the waters receded, assuming their rightful role as Lords of the Earth since they would be the only survivors.

If many modern UFO sightings are of *Reichsdeutsche* flying saucers and some of the remainder are their allies from elsewhere beyond this planet and dimension, allies moreover who know all there is to know about magnetic fields, it is understandable that certain Governments who know what the threat is would rather that the UFO phenomena were ignored, since nothing can be done to prevent the cataclysm when the time comes.

The UFO phenomenon is a psychic phenomenon. If there is any truth in what has been suggested by this chapter, some evidence of a serious long-term project in Hitler's Germany aimed at expanding psychic consciousness in particular groups of young men and women for the specific purpose of their obtaining supernormal powers must be presented. And that is something which is investigated in the concluding chapter.

CHAPTER 17

The Vril Reich

"Hitler saw his own remarkable career as a confirmation of hidden powers. He saw himself chosen for superhuman tasks, as the prophet of man's rebirth in a new form. Humanity, he proclaimed, was in the throes of a vast metamorphosis. A process of change that had lasted literally for thousands of years was approaching its completion. *Man's solar period was coming to its end.* The coming age was revealing itself in the first great human figures of a new type. Just as, according to the imperishable prophecies of the old Nordic peoples, the world has continually to renew itself, the old order perishing with its gods, so must man now turn back, in order to attain a higher stage."

Hermann Rauschning: *Hitler Speaks: A Series of Political Conversations with Adolf Hitler on his Real Aims*, Thornton Butterworth, 1939.

THE NAZI SWASTIKA was the expression in symbol of the italicized phrase above, in which Hitler says that Man's solar period is coming to its end. The anti-clockwise direction of spin of the Nazi swastika does not signify evil but cosmic dissolution. The present solar period, particularly since the Industrial Revolution, is the nadir and final point of Man's progress. In the citation at the head of the chapter we have the very simple idea that Hitler was the prophet of man's rebirth in a new form. The German race was not yet the Master Race, Man-becoming-God, rather that was the goal for which they had to strive. It was a Herculean task, the like of which, so far as we know, no race had ever been set previously. The attempted destruction of the Jews and gypsies, whatever the rationale behind it, was only the first stage of a process culminating in the elimination of all *homo sapiens*, including the Germans themselves, mankind as we know it being replaced by the New Man, *homo mysticus germanicus*. A widespread grasp of this fact in the greater Reich would most certainly have led to the failure of the programme, or at least moderated the enthusiasm of the Germans for National Socialism, and the need to eliminate all influential elements in society likely to divine correctly the course of future developments can now be understood. Sixty years later, however, the occult fraternity at large has still not perceived correctly what was afoot.

Vril and The Order of the Green Dragon

The Rt Hon Edward Bulwer-Lytton MP (1803–1873) was a popular Victorian novelist. In 1838 he was created a baronet and thereafter indulged his fascination for the occult by becoming a Rosicrucian adept. As author, the book for which he is best remembered, at least in circles interested in the paranormal, is *The Coming Race*, published by George Routledge in 1871. It is a short novel about the *Vril-ya*, a race possessing intelligence and powers far in advance of normal humanity and living in deep tunnels from where ultimately they intend to emerge to the surface of the Earth to take control of the planet. Their ruler is a supreme magistrate called the *Tur* (a runic symbol). There is sexual equality, although the females are sinewy and both taller and superior in physical strength to the males. The race was an ancestor of the great Aryan family "from which in varied streams has flowed the dominant civilisation of the world". It looked down on the human nations "with more disdain than the citizens of New York [once] regarded the negroes". They believed in the survival of the fittest, the triumph of the strong over the weak, and the dominance of the Aryan race. The *Vril-ya* dismissed democracy, free institutions and elected government as "one of the crude and ignorant experiments which belong to the infancy of political science". Their ultimate objective was "to attain to the purity of our species and *supplant all the inferior races now existing*".

The *Vril-ya* were named after the all-permeating fluid in nature which they denominate *Vril*. They had discovered the latent powers stored in *Vril* to which can be ascribed their mastery over the elements: *Vril* could "be raised and disciplined into the mightiest agency over all forms of matter, animate and inanimate." Although no language had a word exactly synonymous with *Vril*, it seemed to be electricity comprehending in its manifold branches other forces of nature, "the unity in natural energic agencies conjectured by many philosophers." The narrator described a hollow rod of adjustable length with several keys or springs in the handle to modify the force. The exercise of *Vril* power could only

177

be acquired through heredity. A 4-year-old *Vril* female infant could accomplish effects which would be impossible for an ordinary human technician after a lifetime of trying.

The Coming Race was supposed to be simply an occult novel, although it reads like a treatise and, bearing in mind its author's affinities, was considered by many to be fiction containing a number of occult truths. For Hitler and the National Socialist Movement it crystallized into the blueprint for the world's future.

What could *Vril* be? The aviation historian and author Trevor James Constable wrote:

> "The daily etheric breathings of the Earth produce a baro-metric pressure wave twice daily, which formal science has never been able to explain. There is enough energy in these barometric waves to run the world's machines – if we can but find the transducer. The torque drive of the Earth itself is an inexhaustible, life-positive energy source of staggering magni-tude. Before long, someone will uncover that all important step (discovered by Wilhelm Reich but not disclosed by him) by which etheric force can be transduced . . . the price for this new technical epoch is a forced overhaul of our whole mode of existence. We will see the beginning of a reunion between science and religion as the cosmic energies – pervaded with life and themselves the milieu of living beings – come into tech-nical utility. Man will find the central parts of his own physical existence inseparably bound up with etheric energies, and he will be opened to a wider understanding of himself and the cosmos that produced him. *The ultimate consequence will be a new humanity.*"[166]

And how was this to be achieved? First there had to be produced by mutation the men and women who would form the new humanity capable of understanding and controlling *Vril* power. Bulwer-Lytton had stated that the power could only be acquired through heredity, indicating that the secret was transmitted through the blood. At once we begin to suspect a mystical answer involving *siddhis* or super-normal powers. The only access to the sum total of the knowledge in the Universe is through mystical enlightenment which, so it is claimed, involves changes in the blood. The progeny of enlightened mystics would themselves be enlight-ened mystics from conception.[167]

According to Rudolf Hess, the Master Magician of the Third Reich was Karl Haushofer.[168] Prior to the Great War, Haushofer was attached to the Staff Corps of the German Diplomatic Mission in Tokyo. He was a clairvoyant of mystical inclination and during his tour of duty in Japan, the language of which he spoke fluently, was initiated into a Buddhist sect known as The Green Dragon. He left the Army following the defeat of 1918 in the rank of general and graduated in political geography at Munich University shortly afterwards. The periodical *Geo-Political Review* which he founded was dedicated to propagating the idea of Aryan supremacy, a belief he had embraced while travelling in Central Asia in 1905. Karl Haushofer believed that the Earth was a living being and a cosmic organism: the world was a system of undulating waves, matter was nothing more than vibration and energy. This is Hermetic doctrine. If an initiate of an esoteric monastic order professes Hermeticism, it is a safe bet that his order is Hermetic. A disciple of Karl Haushofer was the Egyptian-born Rudolf Hess, a fanatical vegetarian and abstemient, who served as his assistant at Munich University and was the intermediary between Haushofer and Hitler. The first meeting with the latter occurred in 1924 at Landsberg Prison. Subsequently Haushofer visited Hitler every day and spent hours expounding his theories. It was the doctrine of Haushofer which eventually formed the basis for *Mein Kampf*, compiled by Hess at Hitler's dictation and published in 1925. That same year Haushofer founded an occult organization known as The Luminous Lodge of the *Vril* Society. Hitler was allegedly much impressed by Bulwer-Lytton's book, a copy of which he received in 1924 from Haushofer, who believed it contained occult truths dressed as fiction.

The German rocket scientist Willy Ley who left Germany in 1933 stated that the purpose of the *Vril* Society was to create the Aryan super-race.[169] For this purpose a large contingent of Tibetan lamas with connections to the esoteric disciplines was invited to take up domicile in Berlin. They wore a green cap and gloves and one assumes there was a connection with Haushofer's Order of the Green Dragon in Japan. As it also had initiatory centres in Turkey for its clandestine connection with Islam through Sufi, Druze and Dervish doctrines it was also transreligious. The Tibetan lamas were not particularly secretive. The senior lama gave an interview to the *Berliner Zeitung* predicting correctly on three occasions the number of deputies that the NSDAP would send to the Reichstag. The French spy Teddy Legrande wrote extensively about these Tibetan lamas in Berlin in his book published in 1933, the year of his mysterious suicide.[170] Hitler

179

often made visits to one particular Tibetan lodge in Berlin where he consulted with the senior lama.[171]

Hess informed his OSS inquisitors that the *Vril* Society was an active occult organization drawn from the upper echelons of society:

> "There are all sorts of rumours that some sort of oriental monk is often seen around Nazi Party functions. He is a dark Tibetan who looks incredibly old and wizened. His eyes glow a faint green. He wears a black long woollen cloak with cap, belt and gloves of green. Hess confirmed what most occult experts believe, that the Nazi Party operates on a deeper level still, that perhaps a group of mystic lamas somewhere in Tibet might be the puppet-masters connected with the shadowy organization known as the Green Dragon."

Haushofer, the leading member of the Luminous Lodge, remained in Berlin with the supreme lama, known only as The Man with the Green Gloves, until the capitulation, when all the Tibetans died either as a result of enemy action or by ritual suicide. It was widely reported on 25 April 1945, for example, that Russian troops in the eastern sector of Berlin found in the ruins of a three-storey building the corpses of six Tibetans dressed in German military uniform without insignia and arranged in a circle around a dead Tibetan monk wearing a pair of bright green gloves. Before Berlin fell on 2 May the bodies of several hundred, some sources say up to a thousand, more Tibetans were found in similar circumstances. Haushofer ended his own life by ritual suicide in 1946.

The Methodology of the *Vril* Society

Many may think it extraordinary to suggest that an advanced western industrial society such as Nazi Germany would have had such links with an undeveloped country in Central Asia, the majority of whose male inhabitants were monks. Tibet was xenophobic, believing that foreigners were the cause of all their misfortunes, and they were always anxious to see them depart. This was especially so in the case of the British, together with the Chinese the only influential presence in Tibet. The British were keen to start up the Tibetan economy but the Tibetans were firmly convinced that in western-style progress there lay a terrible danger. Tibet was so backward that the country had not affiliated to the International

Postal Union and the nearest post offices were in India, to where all mail was taken by yak caravan. They had not accepted metric measurement and had a phobia against the wheel, whose use was prohibited in certain territories on the grounds that it threatened the equilibrium of nature. What could not be carried by the arm of man caused death and destruction. Western medicine was held to be a flagrant violation of the life-death equilibrium. Both polygamy and polyandry were practised, together with a form of ritual prostitution of which even the most refined availed themselves. Sex was an effusion only slightly more intense than a handshake and offered to foreigners as a courtesy. Mystics used it "as a means of ascent to the sacred".

The Tibetan monasteries seem to have been the repository of scientific techniques long lost to the world. The mystery of how the pyramids were constructed, for example, continues to baffle Western scientists and historians, yet the lamas do appear to have the solution. A scientific writer on harmonic theory, Bruce Cathe[172], investigating a report on levitation which had appeared in a German magazine, described how Dr Jarl, a Swedish doctor working on behalf of the English Scientific Society in 1939, visited a certain monastery in Tibet and was offered the opportunity to observe a number of phenomena including the construction of a rock wall in front of a cave entrance about 250 metres up a sheer cliff. In a meadow below the cliff was a polished concave slab of rock on to which blocks of stone measuring 1½ metres in length and 1 metre in width and thickness were manouevred by yak oxen. Thirteen drums and six trumpets (all described in detail in the text) were set in an arc of 90° at a distance of about 63 metres from the stone slab. Together with the chanting and singing of the monks, the orchestra began to play, the noise reaching a tremendous crescendo over a period of four minutes at which point the stone block began to rock and sway and then rose in the air towards the rigging platform 250 metres above. The ascent lasted three minutes. The German magazine report continued:

"They brought new blocks continuously to the meadow and using this method the monks transported five to six blocks per hour on a parabolic flight track approximately 500 metres long and 250 metres high. Because Dr Jarl . . . had the opinion in the beginning that he was the victim of a mass psychosis he made two films of the incident. The films showed exactly the same things that he had witnessed. The English Society for which Dr Jarl was working confiscated the films and declared

181

them classified for fifty years. This action is rather hard to explain or understand."

Mr Cathe pointed out that it is not difficult to understand why the British classified the films once the given measurements had been transposed into their geometric equivalents, for then it became obvious that the monks of Tibet in 1939 were fully conversant with the laws governing the structure of matter.

"The secret is in the geometric placement of the musical instruments in relation to the stones to be levitated, and the harmonic tuning of the drums and trumpets. The sound waves being generated by the combination were directed in such a way that an anti-gravitational effect was created at the centre of focus and around the periphery, or the arc, of a third of a circle through which the stones moved. The distance from the block to the rear face of each drum could be close to 63.75 metres. My theoretical analysis, by calculator, indicates that the exact distance would be 63.7079 metres for the optimum harmonic reaction. I believe that there is not much doubt that the Tibetans had possession of the secrets relating to the geometric structure of matter and the methods of manipulating the harmonic values."

Linking the yogic practices of the *Vril* Society in Hitler's Germany to mystical Tibetan techniques, the writer Alec Maclellan[173], unfortunately without stating his source, claimed that he had examined copies "of certain strange documents which once belonged to initiates of the *Vril* Society". What he writes seems authentic, for he admits:

"if the two methods sound like mumbo-jumbo associated with mediaeval witchcraft spells, then it is also a feeling shared by the author. However, as I am not a practising mystic – nor can I claim profound knowledge of the secrets of mysticism – I would not hastily denounce the documents."

For the foregoing reason, i.e. that Mr Maclellan does not understand the documents and reports them merely as a matter of passing interest, I believe it safe to accept them as genuine. I do not propose to reproduce them here, but for those interested the paperback version of Mr

182

Maclellan's book is still in print, and anybody who has studied Tibetan mysticism will recognize their purpose at once. They are undoubtedly the "methods of concentration and the whole system of internal gymnastics by which the mind is transformed" spoken of by Dr Willy Ley in his Essay *Pseudo-Sciences under the Nazi Regime.*

A lodge of the *Vril* Society was essentially a Berlin annexe to a Tibetan monastery. The utmost determination was required of the young women and men accepted as initiates. Mystical attainment is not a matter of performing rites: the prime necessity is to be virtuous and firmly abstain from evil. The difference between realized mortals and ordinary humanity is simply that the former are aware of their underlying identity with Reality. Once the illusory ego falls away, Man becomes heir to special powers and all the knowledge of the Cosmos. Under the close supervision of a lama, who would employ additional techniques such as communication through trance states, a point made by Bulwer-Lytton in a lengthy passage, the initiate would eventually achieve the expansion of consciousness desired. Mr Maclellan's document shows the 'Mystic Way', a Tibetan meditation technique of the Kalachakra School in which the mind has to be concentrated on a mandala while endlessly intoning the Tibetan letter K. The 'Scientific Way' is that technique of meditation practised in ritual intercourse between a male initiate and a female adept.

In the chapter of his book headed *Green Dragon, White Tiger*, the Taoist John Blofeld[174] described in outline this dual cultivation or sexual yoga which is a strictly regulated discipline. The process is far from simple and requires great yogic skill. It is not a licence for sexual pleasure and is in fact dangerous for men who have difficulty in freeing themselves from the bondage of the senses. Tantric sexual exercises have powerful effects on the bio-tensile field and are capable of charging them with a great quantity of energy. These energies can be directed by the mind, producing effects of movement in matter but the object is to attain mystical understanding. The onset of cosmic consciousness triggered unexpectedly by sexual activity was vividly described thus by a 32-year-old woman:

"Every time we made love, I had an out-of-the-body trip. It was like moving through a tunnel at warp speed, moving through space, passing stars and planets until I seemed to be at the centre of the cosmos. The Universe opened up to me. All kinds of knowledge and mathematical equations were passing through me. I understood them all in a split second and forgot them just as quickly. After three months of this I had to shut down . . . or die. I couldn't possibly handle the knowledge and information passing through me."[175]

This woman's fear of death was very real and was due to the fact that people:

"are afraid to forget their own minds, fearing to fall through the void with nothing on to which they can cling."[176]

The terror is the reason why monastic training, under the close supervision of a guru or enlightened lama, is essential at all stages. Without it the condition can never be stabilized so as to use the "mathematical equations and knowledge", the sum total of knowledge in the Universe, becoming available to a human mind within the limits of the individual personality as vast dormant areas of the brain are suddenly opened.

Minds linked in the Reality merge at that level and this linkage ends the destructive competitiveness caused by the concept of separate identities. Ultimately a race of mystics would acquire a single integrated consciousness as compared to the fragmented billions of personalities of which humanity presently consists. Each person of the super-race would then function as an individual but in harmony with the Whole. The initial mystery is to understand how the personality:

". . . can be merged like a drop of quicksilver in the Whole, yet be still separate as a grain of sand in the desert"[177]

and it is purposeless to attempt to secure the answer except through meditation, for:

"it cannot be looked for or sought, comprehended by wisdom or knowledge, explained in words, contacted objectively or reached by good works."[178]

One can only know it intuitively. Humankind as a species composed of enlightened mystics linked in mind and conscience would be a truly formidable advance. All the world's problems caused by individuation simply fall away; because the only thing to do is the right thing, poverty, war, crime, hunger, fear, intolerance, in fact all misery, are gone. A few moments' reflection on the implications of access to universal knowledge should be sufficient to convince one that the super-race would

184

eventually exert direct dominance over time, space and matter, that is, it would begin to manifest 'god-like' powers. In this way, Man would begin to become God. The tremendous struggle to understand this sixth stage of evolution accounts for all metaphysics, philosophy and religion.

> "Now do you appreciate the depth of our National Socialist movement? Can there be anything greater and more all-comprehending? Those who see in National Socialism nothing more than a political movement know scarcely anything of it. It is more even than a religion: it is the will to create mankind anew."[179]

So said its founder. But did his plan die with him and with the defeat of Germany in 1945, or were the adepts of the *Vril* lodges secreted to distant subterranean fastnesses to develop and breed in readiness for the appearance of the new race at another time? And if so, does the modern UFO phenomenon represent the post-natal care stage of the new race?

Major Donald Keyhoe, Director of the National Committee on Aerial Phenomena (NICAP) stated in his 1957 book *The Flying Saucer Conspiracy* that UFOs were of tremendous importance and that a cover-up had been put in place at the highest level:

> "There is an official policy, believed in the best interests of the people, not to confirm the existence of UFOs until all the answers are known."

On 27 June 1967 the New York Post quoted UN Secretary-General U Thant as saying that:

> "next to the Vietnam War, I believe UFOs to be the most important problem facing the UN."

The morbid interest of President Ronald Reagan in UFOs is well known. In November 1985 at the World Summit Conference in Geneva, President Reagan told Soviet President Mikhail Gorbachev before the world's Press:

> "How much easier his task and mine might be in these meetings that we held if suddenly there was a threat to this world

185

from another species from another planet outside in the Universe. We'd forget all the little local differences that we have between our countries, and we would find out once and for all that we really are all human beings here on this Earth together."

Two years later, on 16 February 1987, during a speech at the Kremlin, Gorbachev referred to Reagan's remarks and said:

"I shall not dispute the hypothesis, though I think *it's early yet* to worry about such an *intrusion*."

On 26 April 1990, in a reply to question about UFOs while visiting workers in the Urals, Gorbachev observed:

"The phenomenon of UFOs is real. I know that there are scientific organizations which study the problem."

In a well-publicized speech at UN Headquarters in New York when addressing the 42nd General Assembly on 21 September 1987, President Reagan reiterated his earlier remarks with:

"Perhaps we need some outside, universal threat to make us realize this common bond. I occasionally think how quickly our differences worldwide would vanish if we were facing an alien threat from outside this world. And yet, I ask, *is not an alien force already among us?*"

President Reagan spoke here as if he were in possession of information made available to the heads of various States, including the USA and USSR, communicating from an ultraterrestrial force a threat of an intrusion and some sort of date by when it is to be realized. If we look dispassionately at *Vril*, Green Dragon, German flying saucers and Presidential fears the general drift and meaning behind events over the last sixty years or so must, I think, be growing clearer. It will be well, perhaps, at the risk of some repetition, to bring the argument together in a few sentences.

From time to time over the millennia there occurs a sudden step in human psychological evolution. Formerly, one suspects, this occurred in the form of an abrupt expansion in consciousness, or in the physical volume of the brain, such as the leap from Neanderthal to Cro-Magnon Man, and the impression has always been, despite Darwin, that the change has been engineered.

Since the beginning of the 20th century we have been in the epoch of a revolution which is now approaching its climax. The horrors perpetrated during the National Socialist years should not blind us to the possibility that it is in such an environment that higher powers, should they be involved, are best able to wreak changes of a cosmic magnitude, and particularly if they are controlling the leader. From the earliest stirrings of Nazism, the enemy to be smashed was Bolshevism, and Bolshevism was Soviet Russia. This meant overruning the hinterland of Asia, to the Himalayas where the Aryan race originated and the mountains of Tibet, to the cold deserts of Mongolia and beyond to the Yangtse. Russian historians are now telling us that even before the outbreak of war with Poland, Stalin was planning to roll across Europe by 1942.[181] History does not take account of possible paranormal foreknowledge of an enemy's aggressive intentions but the more important inference here is that the war with Soviet Russia seems to have been fore-ordained. Neither should we lightly dismiss the significance of Rudolf Hess' mission in May 1941. Hitler's defeat in the East meant that the New Race was not going to be bred at leisure in that same Asiatic hinterland from where flowed its Aryan ancestors and the whole scheme had to be hurriedly redesigned. The signs were obvious even before Barbarossa was launched in June 1941 that Hitler's forces were insufficient for the task in hand against so many enemies – as the Germans say, the shirt was too short. Thus was born the advanced aircraft project.

The development of such a machine to utilize the knowledge the SS had acquired of how to travel in Gravity II, combined with Hitler's idea of shifting the world's axis to provoke a cataclysm to drown mankind seems an alien concept. Certainly the Germans were good at building the pioneer helicopters and flying boomerangs, but to have completed the project with its alien alloys and new aeronautical technology within three years was a great achievement. Obviously the craft were built for a reason so secret that the evidence that they ever existed has been deliber-ately concealed officially ever since. The reason for building them, at such a late stage in an apparently lost cause, was assuredly not to carry passen-gers across the Atlantic at phenomenal speeds, but to ferry the founder members of the super-race into the Underworld for safety and, for an ulterior motive prejudicial to *homo sapiens*, to liaise with the entities which inhabit it.

187

The transfer of the German gold reserves and thousands of scientific technicians to South America at the end of the war, and the huge number of UFOs reported over Argentina and Chile since, has accordingly given birth to the suspicion amongst many that some modern UFO sightings are of the new generation of *Reichsdeutsche* flying saucers.

According to the Tibetan prophecies, the final battle for control of the world known to us as Armageddon will occur in a specific year which can be calculated forward from the invasion of Tibet by the Younghusband Expedition. After this final battle the new race will take over.

This is the sense, so it occurs to me, in which one must interpret Hitler's incomprehensible prediction when, having renounced use of the miracle weapon and staring defeat fully in the face in 1945, he forecast that, despite everything, *"The last battalion will be a German battalion!"*

The German Small Scale Atom Bomb

The bomb design was similar to Heisenberg's B-III experiment at Berlin-Dahlem in early 1942 which involved alternating layers of uranium powder and paraffin inside an aluminium sphere. The neutron source was a radium-beryllium preparation dropped into the centre of the apparatus by way of a chimney.

The laboratory-built device in the diagram would have given a low-yield atomic explosion when compressed uniformly at Mach 3.5 if the uranium powder had been enriched with plutonium by leaving it to breed in a sub-reactor for some months.

That seems to have been the purpose of Heisenberg's experiment at Leipzig commencing 2 June 1942. The bomb would be about two feet in diameter. The paraffin prevented the premature fission of the material caused by the energetic Pu^{240} isotopes.

Tests to prove the reaction probably using a lead-jacketed bomb were almost certainly carried out in the Baltic and in Norway during late 1944. These would have had almost negligible fallout and no significant blast. Hitler was against using the atom bomb operationally on doctrinal grounds.

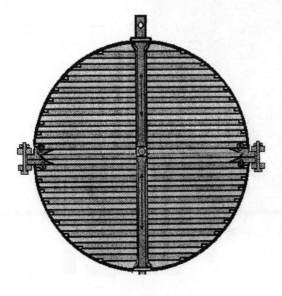

Heisenberg's bomb

The Leipzig Experiment starting on 2 June 1942 had an outer aluminium sphere 740 mms in diameter filled with 750 kgs uranium metal powder. A concentric inner sphere contained 220 litres heavy water. A radium-beryllium neutron source was introduced through a central chimney to begin the reaction.

The neutrons from the centre were slowed on passing through the heavy water before radiating into the uranium powder where they fissioned U^{235} isotopes to release more neutrons or combined with U^{238} resonances to form plutonium. Left to work for several months this is a subtle means of uranium enrichment and plutonium production. The irradiated powder, assembled in alternate layers with paraffin in a spherical casing, would then serve as a low-yield atom bomb if detonated with an effective implosion fuse.

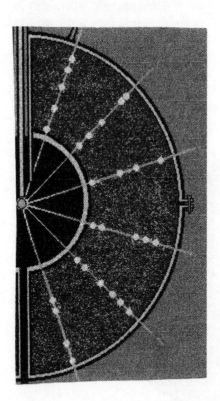

Goudsmit's Version of Heisenberg's Bomb

From his book *Alsos – The Failure in German Science* published in 1947, Professor Goudsmit provided this sketch of what he suspected was the German atom bomb. Above is a drawing from a photograph of the experimental assembly "which they believed could make a bomb" and (right) a diagram of the "experimental bomb" which consisted of layers of uranium and paraffin. Goudsmit might have been joking, but he was right. What he may have been hinting was that (1) if the plutonium-enriched U-powder is layered with paraffin in the top hemisphere and the lower hemisphere filled with iron ballast and (2) fitted as the warhead in a V-2 rocket, the speed of impact replaces the tons of HE to detonate the weapon. The paraffin disperses and the fissile material smashes into the ballast to form a non-symmetrical critical mass resulting in a small "fizzle" explosion with meltdown and fallout.

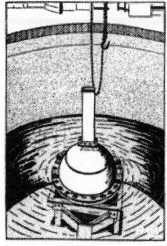

GERMANY'S "ATOM BOMB"

(Above) Drawn from a photograph of the German experimental "uranium pile," which they believed would make a bomb.

(Right) Diagram for the experimental "bomb" which consisted of layers of uranium and paraffin.

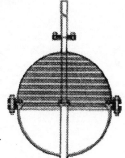

The German Flying Saucer

During the spate of UFO sightings over the US in midsummer 1947, a flying crescent was often seen. It was suspected by USAF Intelligence to be man-made and of German origin. A declassified secret report identified it as approximating the 1942 designed Ho VI Parabola, the plan form of which is shown here. Reimar Horten disappeared to Argentina at the war's end.

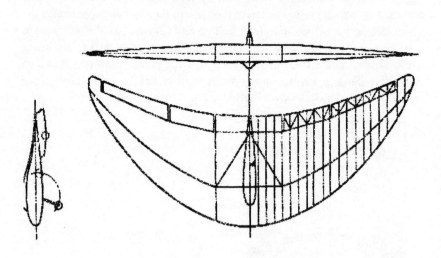

1. *Bariloche Nazi –Guia de Sitios Relacionados al Nacional Socialismo* unpublished anonymous manuscript registered in Argentina at the Registro Propiedad Intelectual, File 132840 (5.6.2001).
2. Burrowed into the chalky rock of the Kohnstein mountain, and originally designed as a chemical storage facility, Nordhausen comprised of two parallel tunnels 2½ kilometres long, 200 metres apart and wide enough for a double railway track in each, with 46 connecting chambers. A third tunnel at the level of the eighteenth chamber ran at a right angle to the main corridors. Floor area amounted to 125,000 square metres. The available space was million cubic metres. Heating was maintained at 17°C with low humidity. All corridors and chambers were equipped with strong electric lighting. .
3. Needless to say, the conditions for the prisoners at SS-Mittelwerk were barbarous. Initially the mortality rate was 15%, although admittedly this was better than the 84% rate at Auschwitz for forced labourers. When Wernher von Braun visited the tunnels in January 1944, where he saw 10,000 inmates at labour, he walked the corridors in silence and left despondent. Following the intercession of Speer in the wake of a visit in December 1944, food and living conditions improved beyond measure and the prisoners were eventually lodged in barracks outside the caves. Hitler's Luftwaffe ADC von Below stated in *At Hitler's Side*, Greenhill Books, 2001, that when he visited in January 1945 "the prisoners seemed well-treated and were in good physical condition as far as I could determine" but he was not there on the day in March 1945 when guards hanged fifty-two slave labourers in Gallery 41, tying a dozen at a time to a beam which was then pulled up by a crane while those next in line were forced to watch.
4. Nick Cook: *The Hunt for Zero Point: One Man's Journey to Discover the Biggest Secret Since the Invention of the Atom Bomb*, Century Books, 2001, wherein the author, a leading writer for Britain's most authoritative military journal, *Jane's Defence Weekly*, advances the theory that Kammler gave the Americans "Nazi anti-gravity technology" in exchange for his own security. Mr Cook invokes this line of reasoning to explain "the thousands of sightings of UFOs that

have occurred since the Second World War", i.e. there are no UFOs but American UFOs. Sightings of flying saucers and so forth are not a modern phenomenon and go back to at least the time of the Ancient Greeks. Persons claiming close contact with a UFO are invariably given a medical examination which will include a routine check for radiation. Two Government-documented contactee cases in South America are those of Villas Boas (Brazil, 15.10.1957) who was found to have genital radiation poisoning and bodily evidence of abnormal healing after claiming to have been kidnapped by the female crew of a UFO, and 71-year old Ventura Maceiras (Argentina, 30.12.1972, radiation sickness after claiming to have approached a UFO which landed near his shack: began to grow his third set of teeth in February 1973.) The documented medical evidence in the multiplicity of similar cases is overwhelming. The United States is unlikely to have been responsible for either of the quoted incidents, and fought off an action brought by Mrs Betty Cash and others claiming $20 million damages for exogenous radiation poisoning necessitating a mastectomy following an incident at Houston on the night of 29 December 1980. A US court threw out the application in August 1986 after accepting pleadings on behalf of the US Government, armed forces and NASA that they neither owned nor operated "a large oblong flaming object with a rounded top and pointed lower half".

5. Konrad Heiden: *The Führer*, first published London, 1944: reprinted H. Pordes, London 1967; Robinson Publishing reprint, 1999, page 591.
6. Hermann Rauschning: *Hitler Speaks, A Series of Political Conversations with Adolf Hitler on his Real Aims*, Thornton Butterworth, London, 1939.
7. Henry Picker: *Hitlers Tischgespräche im FHQ* Seewald Verlag, Stuttgart, 1976.
8. Erich Gröner: *Die deutschen Kriegsschiffe 1815–1945* , Band III, Bernard & Graefe, 1985.
9. Wilfred von Oven: *Finale Furioso, Mit Goebbels bis zum Ende*, Tübingen, 1974.
10. Public Record Office, PREM 3/89.
11. Günther Gellermann: *Der Krieg der nicht stattfand*, Bernard & Graefe, Koblenz, 1986.
12. Jürgen Michels: *Peenemünde und seine Erben in Ost und West*: Bernard & Graefe 1997.

13. Otto Skorzeny: *Wir kämpften, wir verloren*, Helmut Cramer, 1973.
14. OSS Report A44 316 Report 5958 7 November 1944.
15. Jüngen Michels, *op cit.*
16. Jürgen Michels, *op. cit.*
17. Rudolf Luhser: *Die deutschen Waffen und Geheimwaffen des Zweiten Weltkrieges*, Lehmanns Verlag, Munich, 1958.
18. Günther Hessler: *The U-boat War in the Atlantic 1939–1945*, HMSO.
19. Philip Henshall: *Vengeance*, Alan Sutton, Stroud, 1995.
20. *Musée Nationale d'Histoire Militaire*, Diekirch-Luxembourg.
21. Hermann Rauschning: *Hitler Speaks*, Thornton Butterworth, 1939.
22. See Dr Ernst Weisz: *Augenzeuge*, 1939, a thinly fictionalized account of Hitler's miracle cure, and William Bramley: *The Gods of Eden*.
23. Hermann Rauschning, *op. cit.*
24. The original German version of this booklet under the title *Der Bolschewismus von Moses bis Lenin: Ein Zweigespraech zwischen Adolf Hitler und mir* can be read at:
    http://www.abbc.com/berlin/moses.htm
    The English translation published by the Historical Review Press (Tr. William L. Pierce) can be read at:
    http://www.ety.com/HRP/booksonline/mosestolenin/mosesfw.htm
25. John Blofeld: *Taoism*, Mandala Books, 1986.
26. Nora Waln: *Reaching for the Stars*, Crescent Press, London 1939. A Chinese-American historian and translator, Nora Waln spent the pre-war period in Germany.
27. OSS Interrogation Archive document #12678 *Nazi Occult Organizations*.
28. Michael Talbot: *Mysticism and the New Physics*, Arkana, 1993.
29. Albert Speer: *Erinnerungen*, Polypropylaen Verlag, Ullstein, Berlin, 1969.
30. Albert Speer, *op. cit.*
31. *Die Wissenschaften*, 28.1.1939.
32. C. F. von Weizsäcker: *Atomenergie und Atomzeitalter*, Fischer, 1957.
33. *Heereswaffenamt*=Army Weapons Bureau.
34. Werner Heisenberg: *Individual Behaviour in the Face of Disaster*, essay. Where not specifically referenced, Heisenberg's reports and commentaries mentioned in the text can be found in W. Heisenberg and K. Wirtz: *Grossversuche zur Vorbereitung der Konstruktion*

eines Uranbrenners in *FIAT Review of German Science 1939–1945* republished in Series B: *Gesammelte Werke von Werner Heisenberg* (Springer Verlag, Berlin, Heidelberg and New York, 1984) and in Series A, the Original Works under the title *Atomenergiegewinnung*.

35. Robert Jungk: *Brighter Than a Thousand Suns*, Gollancz, 1982.
36. Karl Wirtz: *Im Umkreis der Physik*, KFZ Karlsruhe, 1987: Joseph J. Ermenc: *Atomic Bomb Scientists: Memoirs 1939–1945*, Greenwood Press CT, 1989.
37. Armin Herrmann: *Heisenberg*, Rohwohlt Verlag, Rheinbek, 1976.
38. *Die Möglichkeit der technischen Energiegewinnung aus der Uranspaltung*, Paper G-39, KFZ Karlsruhe. The German wartime uranium project reports are filed on microfilm at the Karlsruhe Nuclear Research Centre (KFZ), from where photocopies may be obtained. Each document of the series is listed with the prefix G. Many of Heisenberg's reports have been reproduced in the various volumes of his lifetime's work *Gesammelte Werke* (Springer Verlag, Heidelberg, 1989).
39. Margaret Gowing: *Britain and Atomic Energy 1939–1945*, UKAEA and Macmillan, 1964.
40. Leslie Groves: *Now It Can Be Told*, Harper, New York, 1962, pp 336–340.
41. C. F. von Weizsäcker: *Atomenergie und Atomzeitalter*, Fischer, Frankfurt am Main, 1957.
42. *Die Wissenschaften*, Vol. 27 pp. 402–410.
43. Joseph J. Ermenc: *Atomic Bomb Scientists 1939–1945*, Greenwood Press, CT, 1989.
44. David Irving: *The Virus House*, Wm Kimber, London, 1967.
45. Karl Wirtz: *Im Umkreis der Physik*, Karlsruhe, 1987.
46. Re Sengier see Harald Steinert: *The Atom Rush, Man's Quest for Radioactive Materials*, Thames & Hudson, London 1958: Gowing, *op. cit.*; Groves: *op. cit.*
47. Ermenc, *op. cit.*
48. Karlsruhe KFZ report G-55.
49. *Die Absorption thermischen Neutronen im Elektro-graphit*, KFZ report G-71.
50. Ermenc, *op. cit.*
51. *Über den Nachweis von Boron und Kadmium in Kohle*, G-46 and G-85, Karlsruhe KFZ.
52. *Bestimmung der Diffusionslänge thermischen Neutronen im Schwerem Wasser*, KFZ report G-23.

53. *Bestimmung der Diffusionslänge thermischen Neutronen im Präparat 38*, KFZ report G-22.
54. *Bericht über die Versuche mit Schichtenanordnungen von Präparat 38 und Paraffin*, KWI Berlin-Dahlem, 18.4.1941, KFZ report G-93.
55. *Zur Frage der Auslösung von Kernkettenreaktionen*, G-94 Karlsruhe KFZ, August 1941 and amendment G-267, August 1944.
56. Armin Herrmann, *op. cit.*
57. Weizsäcker.
58. Bohr was not anti-Bomb when it suited him and collaborated in the theoretical work on the Manhattan Project. He was indiscreet to the extent that after a meeting with Churchill arranged in 1944 by the President of the Royal Society, Sir Henry Dale, Churchill wrote that Bohr should either be locked up or at least be made aware that he was very close to committing a hanging offence. This seems to have been the only ex-officio attempt made to interest Churchill in the atom bomb. It was a term of the Roosevelt-Churchill Tube Alloys Deal of 19 September 1944 that "enquiries should be made regarding the activities of Professor Bohr and steps taken to ensure that he is responsible for no leakage of information particularly to the Russians.".
59. *Versuche mit einer Schichtenanordnung von D_2O und Präparat 38*, 28.10.1941: KFZ paper G75.
60. Ermenc, *op. cit.*
61. *Die Energiegewinnung aus der Atomkernspaltung*, document G-217 Karlsruhe KFZ, presented by Heisenberg on 5 May 1943 at a meeting assessing problems in nuclear physics in Berlin.
62. Jungk, *op. cit.*
63. Klaus Hoffmann: *Otto Hahn*, Verlag Neues Berlin, 1978, p.227.
64. *Die Neutronenvermehrung in 38-Metall durch rasche Neutronen*, Döpel and Heisenberg, document G-137 KFZ Karlsruhe.
65. *Vorläufiger Bericht über Ergebnisse an einer Schichtenkugel aus 38-Metall und Paraffin* (BIII) by F. Bopp, E. Fischer, W. Heisenberg, C.F. von Weizsäcker and K Wirtz: 6.1.1942, document G-126 at Karlsruhe.
66. *Der experimentelle Nachweis der effektiven Neutronenvermehrung in einem Kugel-Schichten System aus D_2O und Uran-Metall*: R. and K. Döpel and W. Heisenberg, G-136 Karlsruhe KFZ. This is undated but had a covering letter marked July 1942.
67. G-217 above.
68. G-136 above.

197

69. Albert Speer: *The Slave State*, Weidenfeld & Nicolson, 1981.
70. Albert Speer: *Erinnerungen, op. cit.*
71. Picker, *op. cit.*
72. Albert Speer, *Erinnerungen, op. cit.*
73. Philipp Lenard: *Erinnerungen eines Naturforschers*, Heidelberg 1943, p.202.
74. Hoffmann, *op. cit.*, p.227.
75. *Soldatenzeitung*, East Berlin, 16 March 1962: a copy of the article was reproduced in the autobiography of Manfred von Ardenne, *op. cit.*
76. Field Marshal Milch was Jewish by his mother and obtained Aryanization by having her sign a disclaimer of parenthood. He owed his spectacular career to the protection of Hermann Goering who declared of Milch: "I decide who's Jewish." Professor Rose points out that in a speech to RFR and KWG leaders on 6 July 1942, Goering reported that after a recent discussion with Hitler, he had determined that "he will make exceptions gladly if it is a question of an important research project or researcher". Another example of how it was done appears in *The Ochre Robe* by Swami Agehananda Bharati (Leopold Fischer), an Austrian who served in the Wehrmacht Indian Legion in southern France during the war and later became a Hindu wandering monk: "It seemed that there was something wrong with one of my grandmothers. Of course, in those days there were lawyers who specialized in the provision of non-kosher forbears and it was easy to buy yourself one.".
77. Manfred von Ardenne, *op. cit.*
78. Charles Gibson: *Death of a Phantom Raider*, Robert Hale, London, 1987, p.172.
79. Nicholaus von Below: *Als Hitlers Adjutant 1937-1945*, Koehlers Verlag 1980: English version *At Hitler's Side*, Greenhill Books, 2001.
80. Otto Skorzeny, *Meine Kommandounternehmen* Universitas, 1993.
81. Jungk, *op. cit.*
82. RSHA=*Reichssicherheitshauptamt*, Reich Security Headquarters.
83. Samuel Goudsmit: *Alsos – The Failure in German Science* , Sigma Books, London, 1947.
84. Franz Kurowski: *Von der bedingungslosen Kapitulation bis zur Mondorfer Erklärung* in *GFP eV Kongress Protokoll 1985, Potsdam und Jalta*, Bassum, 1985.
85. Renato Vesco: *Intercept UFO*, Pinnacle Books, 1976. Vesco

(1924–1999) held a doctorate in aeronautical engineering and aerospace development. He was a Professor at the University of Rome and in the 1930s studied aeronautics at the German Institute. When war broke out he worked for the Germans in their secret subterranean Fiat factory near Lake Garda in Italy. In the 1960s his experiences had qualified him for a post with the Italian Ministry of Defence as a technical agent investigating the UFO phenomenon, which he considered to be of terrestrial origins. He wrote several books about his wartime collaboration with his country's ally and from these emerges a picture of a strange technology which had veered in a direction far from that anticipated by Allied intelligence.

86. William Stevenson (also Stephenson): *A Man Called Intrepid*, Sphere Books, 1977, at page 414.
87. Private confidential papers pertaining to former Commanding General, SS Weapons Engineering School and made available to the author for inspection.
88. Picker, *op. cit.*
89. Skorzeny, *op. cit.* at pp150/151.
90. von Below, *op. cit.*
91. Valentin Falin: *Die zweite Front –Die Interessenkonflikt der Anti-Hitler Koalition*, Knaur 1997.
92. Thomas Powers: *Heisenberg's War*, 1996.
93. Edgar Mayer: *Die Hochtechnologie-Lüge*, Amun Verlag, 2001.
94. Harald Fäth: *1945 Thüringens Manhattan Projekt*, CTT Verlag, Suhl, 1998.
95. The V-4 Doomsday Bomb was not ready for use operationally until March 1945 and according to Schaub was under SS control. Probably the plotters had no knowledge of its existence at that stage.
96. cf. Ward Price: *I Know These Dictators*, Harrap, 1937 quoting Hitler: "I was messing in the trench with some comrades. Suddenly I had the impression that a voice was saying to me Get up and go over there. The voice was so clear and distinct that I obeyed mechanically as if it were a military order." A short while afterwards a shell landed where he had been sitting and his comrades were all killed.
97. John Blofeld: *Taoism*, Mandala, 1986, at page 101.
98. Goudsmit, *op. cit.*
99. Karl Wirtz, *op. cit.*: also see An Annotation to Werner Heisenberg, *The Collected Works*, *op. cit.*

100. Groves, *op. cit.*

101. Jacques Caval: *L'Intransigeant*, Paris Presse, 1955.

102. Powers, *op. cit.*

103. APW/U (Ninth Air Force) 96/1945, 373.2 of 19 August 1945, Pkt 47 to 53, released COMNAVEU 1946: Nat Archive RG 38, Entry 98C, box 9-13.

104. Luigi Romersa, quoted in *Defensa*, July/August 1984 reproducing an article from the 19.11.1955 edition of *L'Intransigeance* under the title *J'ai vu exploser la bombe atomique de Hitler*. The location seems to have been an artificial offshore platform near Rügen island.

105. *Encyclopaedia of Science and Technology*, Vol. 12, p.131, McGraw Hill.

106. Skorzeny, *op. cit.* Both quoting as their source Lt-Gen Putt, Kurowski (*op. cit.* at page 22, footnote 80) stated, "Only a few more weeks and, in the V-2 armed with nuclear weapons, the Germans would have had the decisive weapon." In the August/September 1984 edition of *Defensa* under the subtitle "Hitler's Secret Weapons, Something More Than Fantasy", Luigi Romersa stated: "Only a few weeks more and the Germany would have used a weapon to decide the war, a V-2 carrying an atomic bomb . . .". Even if a small atom bomb with all the HE required to detonate it had been crammed into a V-2, the payload of which was only one ton, there was still the necessity for a proximity fuse able to set off the implosion fuse in the last quarter-second before the rocket hit the ground. It is not thought that such a proximity fuse existed in that epoch. The only logical atomic explosive for the V-2 was Heisenberg's sphere which detonated on impact.

107. von Below, *op. cit.*

108. Myhra, *op. cit.*

109. Gregory Douglas: *Geheimakte Gestapo Müller*, Band II, Druffel, 1996.

110. Robert Wilcox: *Japan's Secret War*, Marlowe, 1995.

111. Gimpel's mission is described in Günther Gellermann: *Der andere Auftrag – Agenteinsätze deutscher U-boote im Zweiten Weltkrieg*, Bernard & Graefe, 1997: also see Erich Gimpel: *Spion für Deutschland*, Süddeutscher Verlag, 1956. Gimpel was sentenced to death for espionage but was reprieved three days before the date set for his execution, 15 April 1945, benefiting from the traditional amnesty granted the condemned following the death of a President.

He served ten years in Fort Leavenworth before his release.

112. Wachsenberg Document, Arnstadt Municipal Archives, Report of Committee of Enquiry to Establish Local History, DDR Department of Culture District Committee Depositions of 16 May 1962 of witnesses who in March 1945 had been (1) Wachsenburg watchtower keeper, (2) a rocket technician and (3) a fuel storage tank builder (4) an inmate of Ohrdruf concentration camp.

113. Karsten Porezag: *Geheime Kommandosache, Geschichte der V-Waffen und der geheimen Militäraktionen des Zweiten Weltkrieges an Lahn, Dill und im Westerwald*, Verlag Wetzlardruck, 1996.

114. US forces crossed the Rhine at Oppenheim on 23 March 1945 and at Wesel on the 24th. The Ruhr area was brought under threat within the next few days.

115. Vajda and Dancey: *German Aircraft Industry and Production 1933-1945*, Airlife, 1998.

116. Kurowski, *op. cit.*

117. Smith and Creek: *Me 262* Vol II, Classic Publications 1999.

118. and 119. Friedrich Georg: *Siegeswaffen I*, Amun Verlag 2000, from his personal file PH/Int./Adm No XXXI-3, "microfilm USAF/117". Herr Georg informed this author in an E-mail that the material was obtained by some form of negotiated process.

120. USS NationalArchive, Box RG 260 Entry 121, Box 136: cable 20.4.1945.

121. Jochen Brennecke: *Haie im Paradies: der deutsche U-bootkrieg in Asiens Gewässern, 1943-1945*, Heyne, Munich, 1973 at pp. 26-34. *U-180* sailed from Bordeaux for Japan in August 1943 with a cargo including mercury, radar equipment, dismantled V-weapons, blueprints and technical personnel and was mined and sunk off the mouth of the Gironde Estuary on the 22nd.

122. The US authorities have never admitted the presence of this Me 262 jet fighter aboard *U-234* and it was not included on any of their Loading Lists. The Japanese television network company NHK Tokyo, which produced a documentary in tribute to Hideo Tomonaga, showed film extracts originating from the US Archive in which *U-234* passenger August Bringewald, the Messerschmitt aeronautical engineer, was shown examining an Me 262 jet in apparently good condition at Wright Field air force base in May 1945. In the (somewhat romanticized) biographical account of his career *The Warring Seas* (A. V. Sellwood: White Horse Publishers, 1955), Fehler told the author then that there was a dismantled Me

262 jet aircraft aboard *U-234*. As commander it is not likely that he would be mistaken.

123. *Feindfahrten*, Neff Verlag, Vienna, 1983 and in various reprints. An abbreviated English language version by this author appeared under the title *Hirschfeld – The Story of a U-boat NCO 1940–1946* (Leo Cooper and USNIP, 1997, also in Orion paperback and Cassells Military).

124. Reported in Geoffrey Brooks: *Hitler's Nuclear Weapons*, Leo Cooper, 1992, after correspondence with Wolfgang Hirschfeld, 21.1.1991. Since the US Unloading Manifest shows only ten containers, I pressed him on this matter and suggested his memory was at fault. "I know what I saw," he said, "and there were definitely more than fifty of those little heavy cases." The total weight of all material aboard *U-234* was 260 tonnes.

125. Letter from Wolfgang Hirschfeld, 21.3.1998.

126. Fehler's assumption was uncharitable. On 15 May 1945, when the diplomatic missions and Party organs of the Third Reich in East Asia were finally closed down, German citizens were interned for the remainder of the conflict under the most hospitable and generous conditions.

127. The documents relating to the *U-234* affair at the US National Archive are located in Box RG38, Box 13, Documents OP-20-3-G1-A dated May 1945 (Unloading Manifests) and 373/3679/B0x 22/folder OP-16-Z, Day file 1.1.1945 which includes the Nieschling Memorandum dated 24 May 1945. Judge Nieschling was interviewed by Lt Best. Under a heading Regarding "Uranium Oxide" and other cargo aboard *U-234* the material part of the report reads: "PoW does not know anything in particular about this ore, but only heard that it was valuable and that it was to be exchanged for some other valuable ore that the Germans needed. The meaning behind the ore would, according to PoW, be known by the technician FKpt Falck. He took some secret courses before he boarded the U-boat. He was to be chief technician on all naval matter under Admiral Wennecker."

128. Letter from Staatsanwalt Wacker of the Zentral Stelle der Landesjustizverwaltungen, Ludwigsburg dated 2 September 1998.

129. Wilcox, *op. cit.*

130. Henshall, *op. cit.*

131. Opinion of Alaskan lawyer Sidney Trevethan, title 552 section (a) sub-sections (3) and (6)(A) USCA, in *The Controversial Cargo of U-234*, Revision 13, January 1999.

132. Kunihiko Kigoshi, letter of 7.8.1998 reported in *The Controversial Cargo of U-234, op. cit.*

133. Yomiuri Shimbunsha, *Showashi no Tenno* (The Emperor and Showa History), Tokyo, 1968, vol 4, pp.146-148: John W Dover, *Japan in War and Peace*, New Press, 1993, p.80.

134. Author's correspondence: letter from Professor Rohwer, 28 March 1996.

135. Charles W. Stone: the cited material was illustrated in *Lasuto U-boto Noshinjitsu*, in *Sekai Shuh* (World Affairs Weekly), Sept. 1997. The unpublished English version entitled *U-233 U234 U235* contains a facsimile of the document as attested by US attorney Sidney Trevethan in *The Controversial Cargo of U-234*. See remarks in Introduction.

136. Hirschfeld: *Feindfahrten, op. cit.*

137. Lt. Col Richard D. Thurston, USA (Ret.) was a contributor to *The Controversial Cargo of U-234*, January 1999, a forum of scientists and writers researching the *U-234* enigma.

138. English newspaper *Mail on Sunday*, 7 January 1996, and *Der Spiegel*, February 1996, article entitled *Heisse Ladung* at pp 148–9.

139. US Navy secret despatches #262151 of 27.5.1945 and #292045 of 30.5.1945 are filed at US Archive Nara II Box U-234. The transcript entitled *Telephone Conversation between Major Smith WOL and Major Traynor of 14.6.1945* is filed at US Archive SE Region, East Point, Georgia.

140. Chuck Hansen: *US Nuclear Weapons – The Secret History*, Aerofax, 1998.

141. Henry L. Stimson Diaries, Sterling Memorial Library, Yale.

142. A. H. Compton: *Atomic Quest –A Personal Narrative*, New York, 1956.

143. Henry Stimson: *The Decision to Use the Bomb*, Harper's Magazine, February 1947.

144. D. H. Childress,: *Vimana Aircraft of Ancient India and Atlantis –the Complete Vimanika Shastra Text*, Stolle, Illinois, per Axel Stoll: *Hochtechnologie im Dritten Reich*, CTT-Verlag, 2000.

145. Ivan T. Sanderson: *Invisible Residents*, Tandem, 1970.

146. E-mail correspondence with the Polish writer Igor Witkowski: information assimilated from prosecution files and depositions in the war crimes trial of former SS-Gruppenführer Jacob Sporrenberg, head of the SS Special Evacuation Commando subordinated to the Gauleiter of Lower Silesia, Karl Hanke.

147. According to a statement by an Argentinian journalist with access to confidential official papers, (see Footnote 1) the Bell and all documents pertaining thereto arrived safely at Gualeguay aerodrome in the province of Entre Rios aboard a Junkers 390 transport aircraft at the war's end. From there it was transported first to San Carlos de Bariloche, then known as "Nazi Bariloche", and onwards to a secret underground destination.

148. Dieter Meinig: *X-Akte Jonastal –die Rätsel des letzten FHQ* , article in *Wissenschaft ohne Grenzen*, Jan-Mar edition, 1997.

149. Col. R. Allen: *Lucky Forward: The History of Patton's 3rd US Army*, Vanguard, NY 1947.

150. Account of long interview in Edgar Mayer: *Die deutsche Atombombe und andere Wunderwaffen des Dritten Reiches*, Amun Verlag, 2001.

151. Harald Fäth: 1945–*Thüringens Manhattan Project*, Suhl 1998.

152. A 1946 document obtained under the Freedom of Information Act by Henry Schuren and reported in UFO Focus on 31.3.1991. The so-called weapon was not ready to enter service until March 1945 by when it was too late.

153. BIOS Final Report No 61 (Weapons/Volkenrode).

154. Vesco, *op. cit.*

155. Vesco, *op. cit.*

156. Brad Steiger: *Strangers From The Skies*, Tandem, 1966 at p.149.

157. Sanderson, *op. cit.*

158. US 1946 report CIOS-BIOS/FIAT 20 at CIOS-XXXI-5.

159. Edward U. Condon: *Scientific Study of Unidentified Flying Objects*, Bantam, NY, 1969, pp. 894–5, Report of the Official University of Colorado UFO Project, Appendix R: copy report dated 23.9.1947 AMC Opinion Concerning Flying Discs from Lt Gen. N. Twining, USA Cmmdg. To Commdg. General, Army Air Forces, Washington 25 DC, Brig Gen. George Schulgen AC/AS2.

160. See E. J. Ruppelt: *The Report on Unidentified Flying Objects*, Doubleday, NY, 1956 at page 38.

161. In early September 1943 the German Navy landed troops on Spitzbergen island, a large, wild, barren and remote windswept island in the Arctic Circle 500 miles north of North Cape. A small weather station was set up in the interior in 1944 and remained there until relieved in 1946, but an actual occupation just to install a seven-man meteorological team seems improbable. Its use as a proving ground for advanced VTOL aircraft types would have

justified taking the island from the point of view of secrecy. An account of the Norwegian discovery of German *Flugkreisel* wreckage in 1952 (which initially they thought was from a UFO since the Americans had not bothered to inform them otherwise) appears in Frank Edwards: *Flying Saucers –Serious Business* , NY, Lyle Stuart, 1966.

162. Dr Karl Nowak was also the inventor of the Molecular Bomb, which was never built. So far as can be made out, his idea was that electrons within the nucleus would have been brought to a state of very low energy at a temperature of almost absolute zero and then returned to their normal velocities instantaneously. This expansion force (10^{15} electrons) would have enabled a bomb vastly more powerful than the hydrogen bomb to have been constructed. Official quantum physics dismisses the idea as an impossibility but recently the physicist Randall Mills has stated that Nowak's concept can be proved theoretically and in practice.

163. For this description I have consulted the work of aviation historian Justo Miranda: the account of Luigi Romersa appears in *Uomini, armi e segreti della seconda guerra mondiale*, part 7, Storia Verita, 1992.

164. Per A. Boehn: *Norsk Innsats i Kampen om Atomkraften*, Trondheim, 1946, and Sigmund Fjeldbu, *Et lite sted pa verdenskartet-Rjukan 1940–1950* , Oslo 1980.

165. Immanuel Velikovsky, *Earth in Upheaval*, Dell, NY, 1955.

166. Trevor James Constable quoted in Brad Steiger, *Gods of Aquarius*, Panther Books 1980.

167. The Gnostic writer Samael Weor alleges in his manual *El Matrimonio Perfecto* that where conception occurs as the result of a spermatozoa emitted but not ejaculated into the vagina during ritual intercourse practised by a mystic pair, the child will be "a creature of an elevated order. This is the way in which the super-race will be bred".

168. OSS Interrogation Archive document #12678 *Nazi Occult Organizations.*

169. Dr Willy Ley: Essay, *Pseudo-Sciences under the Nazi Regime*, 1947.

170. Teddy Legrande: *Les sept têtes du Dragon Vert*, Eds. Berger-Levrault, 1933.

171. Reported in 168 above.

172. Bruce Cathe: *The Bridge to Infinity, Harmonic 371299*, Quark Enterprises/Brookfield Press, Auckland, NZ, 1983.

173. Alec Maclellan: *The Lost World of Agharti*, Souvenir Press, 1982 at page 178.
174. Blofeld, *op. cit.*, at pages 113–120.
175. I have kept cuttings from the book but lost the annotation. My apologies to the author.
176. From Zen Teachings of Huang Po.
177. Warner Allen *The Timeless Moment* from F. C. Happold *Mysticism*, Penguin NY, 1970.
178. Huang Po, *op. cit.*
179. Rauschning, *op. cit.*
180. USSR Special Archives number F.7/op. l/d 1223. Published Moscow, 1995 by historians at the University of Novosibirsk.

Index

209

211